T0280982

Building Applications with Azure Resource Manager (ARM)

Leverage IaC to Vastly Improve the Life Cycle of Your Applications

David Rendón

Apress®

Building Applications with Azure Resource Manager (ARM): Leverage IaC to Vastly Improve the Life Cycle of Your Applications

David Rendón
Ags, Mexico

ISBN-13 (pbk): 978-1-4842-7746-1   ISBN-13 (electronic): 978-1-4842-7747-8
https://doi.org/10.1007/978-1-4842-7747-8

Managing Director, Apress Media LLC: Welmoed Spahr
Acquisitions Editor: Joan Murray
Development Editor: Laura Berendson
Coordinating Editor: Jill Balzano

Cover designed by eStudioCalamar

Cover image designed by Freepik (www.freepik.com)

Distributed to the book trade worldwide by Springer Science+Business Media LLC, 1 New York Plaza, Suite 4600, New York, NY 10004. Phone 1-800-SPRINGER, fax (201) 348-4505, e-mail orders-ny@springer-sbm.com, or visit www.springeronline.com. Apress Media, LLC is a California LLC and the sole member (owner) is Springer Science + Business Media Finance Inc (SSBM Finance Inc). SSBM Finance Inc is a **Delaware** corporation.

For information on translations, please e-mail booktranslations@springernature.com; for reprint, paperback, or audio rights, please e-mail bookpermissions@springernature.com.

Apress titles may be purchased in bulk for academic, corporate, or promotional use. eBook versions and licenses are also available for most titles. For more information, reference our Print and eBook Bulk Sales web page at www.apress.com/bulk-sales.

Any source code or other supplementary material referenced by the author in this book is available to readers on GitHub via the book's product page, located at www.apress.com/9781484277461. For more detailed information, please visit www.apress.com/source-code.

Printed on acid-free paper

To Jaime and Juan.

Table of Contents

About the Author

David Rendón is an eight-time Microsoft MVP currently working as a solutions architect at Progress-Kemp Technologies. As an Azure expert and IT professional with more than 15 years of experience, most of his professional experience has been with Microsoft technologies. He conducts private training classes globally (India, South America, United States) that help companies migrate critical applications to the cloud and train their staff to be certified cloud architects. He is passionate about travel, action-packed tech days with peers, and getting down in the trenches of technology road maps. He regularly presents at public IT events such as Microsoft Ignite, Global Azure, and local user group events across the United States, Europe, and Latin America. He is also active on Twitter: @DaveRndn.

About the Technical Reviewer

John Folberth is an instructor, speaker, and technologist. He is a Microsoft MVP and primarily works within Azure while evangelizing DevOps best practices. He has spoken at various conferences and user groups on topics including Bicep, modern data analytics, the DevOps mindset, and multistage YAML pipelines within Azure DevOps.

John is currently a Microsoft Certified Trainer while also holding Microsoft certifications in Azure for architecture, DevOps, development, data engineering, data analyst, and security engineering. Additionally, he is certified in AWS and Terraform. He has a BA in journalism and a BSCS in computer science from Creighton University in Omaha, Nebraska. Additionally, he has a master's degree in management information systems from the University of Nebraska – Omaha.

You can read John's blog at blog.johnfolberth.com or follow him on Twitter: @j_folberth.

Acknowledgments

Writing a book is always a new adventure. Our journey on this project began in Orlando, Florida, at the Orange County Convention Center, where I met with Joan Murray of Apress. We had actually met before, but this was our first in-person meeting. I was surprised and delighted when she agreed to work on this project.

Since then, Joan and her team have helped me through all the publishing processes to ensure you enjoy reading this book as much as I enjoyed writing it. The Apress team, Joan, and I worked closely together to navigate each step and refine the chapters and examples. The experience of working with Joan and her team was nothing less than outstanding. This project would have remained a relic of wishful thinking if not for Joan Murray, Jill Balzano, and John Folberth, who encouraged me to make it a reality.

In fact, this project wouldn't have been possible without the support of many people. To enumerate the entire cast of friends, colleagues, and mentors who have contributed ideas to this book despite these challenging years would amount to writing another book.

On a personal level, I would like to thank Peter De Tender, Michael Jimenez, Andrew Redman, Omar Avilés, Juan Carlos Ruiz, Francisco Corona, and Glauter Jannuzzi for providing guidance and for the benefit of their professional advice.

My most profound debt is owed to my family for the understanding, inspiration, drive, and support that you have given me, especially to my son, André, for bringing joy into my life. I wish you all the best that this life can bring and may you always know you are treasured and loved.

—David Rendón

Introduction

"Deployment failed."

Have you ever gotten this message after attempting to deploy your resources in the cloud?

The usual next step is the developer telling you they are going to see if there's a misconfiguration in the code of the template that has to be fixed or if there's a need to go in another direction.

More system administrators/IT professionals want to understand the deployment and provisioning process of applications in the Microsoft Cloud using the infrastructure-as-code approach through Azure Resource Manager. To do this, they have to work with developers and get a better understanding of how to effectively collaborate with people, processes, and technologies to deliver business value.

Speed and Agility: The Two Core Cloud-Native Principles

Two main principles are true for cloud-native systems: Speed and Agility. The IT team of the organization might have an idea of what they want and what they need to change in an application to make it work fully in the cloud, while customers might be looking for something else and certainly want to have the best user experience. So what happens?

For the past decade, and especially since the pandemic, the transition to the cloud has been vital for organizations to lower costs while improving business continuity.

Cloud systems differ from those running in a datacenter on-premises, and they require applications to embrace a set of principles, including speed and agility. In fact, as per the Cloud Native Computing Foundation:

> *"Cloud-native technologies empower organizations to build and run scalable applications in modern, dynamic environments such as public, private, and hybrid clouds. Containers, service meshes, microservices, immutable infrastructure, and declarative APIs exemplify this approach."*

As a system administrator, what strategy would you follow to design a cloud-native app? What set of patterns would you leverage to deploy and scale a reliable cloud-native system while considering speed and agility as core principles?

System administrators initially think about how to solve the need to be scalable in the cloud since that is the principle that they have been taught to incorporate and that they have had success in delivering in the datacenter. In other words, they feel comfortable creating cloud-native applications that are scalable. However, scalability should be tied to how agile we can make resources available to stakeholders.

You need to look for ways to better provision the cloud environments where your systems will run and rapidly deploy new features and updates to your application.

Early in the design process of your cloud-native system, a focus on both of these core principles—speed and agility—substantiates your proposal's value for the teams across your organization, including operations and development.

So, how can you adopt practices that can help you reduce the time to make the infrastructure resources available for your cloud-native systems? More importantly, how can you keep consistency across testing and versioning of those environments?

Welcome to *Building Applications with Azure Resource Manager (ARM)*, where you'll learn to leverage the infrastructure-as-code approach to vastly improve the life cycle of your applications, lowering the cost and time to deploy and increase in agility for your organization.

## CHAPTER 1

Why Infrastructure as Code?

In this chapter, we will cover how organizations have deployed applications in their datacenters and the evolution of the software-defined datacenter approach. We'll also cover why it's now more important than ever to master the skills of infrastructure as code (IaC), as well as the current state of IaC.

More succinctly, we will cover the following:

- Evolution of software-defined everything

- Overview of IaC

- Current state of IaC

Given the evolution of cloud computing and IaC and the impact both have had across multiple industries, we first need to understand where they are derived from.

Evolution of Software-Defined Everything

A decade ago, organizations used to own hardware assets and enable virtualization to provision multiple virtual machines on top of their physical hardware and multiple types of application servers. One of the main reasons organizations adopted virtualization was to reduce server provisioning time.

1

© David Rendón 2022
D. Rendón, *Building Applications with Azure Resource Manager (ARM)*,
https://doi.org/10.1007/978-1-4842-7747-8_1

With virtualization, the software-defined datacenter (SDDC) approach became a key form factor to help organizations deliver systems in a simple way that offered the flexibility and mobility that their workloads needed. Instead of taking months to order a physical server, bring it into the datacenter, install it, configure it, and deploy the required applications on it, system engineers started leveraging the SDDC approach, which was a game-changer, because they were able to reduce deployments of systems down to hours or minutes.

The SDDC approach has some challenges in that there are still many components associated with deploying applications that have to be put in place before going live. While virtualization helped organizations to reduce the time to production, most organizations still had to set up their networking, firewall rules, and security or regulatory compliance, in addition to configuring a bunch of other components before delivering the application.

Often, when thinking about adopting an SDDC approach, organizations struggled to see the big picture. SDDC involves not only virtualization or networking or storage; there are other components within SDDC that have to be considered such as high availability, redundancy, fault tolerance, and security and compliance. These are in addition to the management and monitoring capabilities in place to accomplish a more complete SDDC approach.

The benefits of SDDC are really about leveraging the intelligence in software to minimize the need for additional resources and people to manage the infrastructure. You want to have self-service, metered, and autoprovisioning capabilities to improve efficiency and be more effective in your IT organization.

SDDC simplified the allocation of resources to create an architecture for private and hybrid clouds that significantly improved IT efficiency and performance. This helped organizations meet business expectations in a timely manner, but there was a lack of visibility into the applications and data combined with a rapid growth in the number of applications and amount of data to be managed.

SDDC extended the virtualization concepts we all know, such as abstraction, pooling, and automation, to all datacenter resources and services. System engineers were able to manage storage, networking, and security components by creating the same kind of software-driven abstraction layer that transformed computing. This led to the "software-defined everything" trend.

With the software-defined networking (SDN) boom, logical networks were decoupled from the physical network topology, allowing multiple, independent, and isolated logical networks to be created, provisioned, and managed while utilizing the underlying physical network as a simple backbone. The combination of server virtualization and logical network devices in addition to security policies could be assembled into any topology.

In addition, organizations adopted software-defined storage (SDS), where the physical storage layer was decoupled from the virtual workloads, meaning the storage resources were abstracted to enable pooling, replication, and on-demand distribution. This way, the storage layer is more flexible, efficient, and scalable.

SDS has some benefits such as across-the-board reductions in the cost and complexity of the storage infrastructure. SDS also defines consistent policies across all resources in the heterogeneous storage pool, making consumption as simple as specifying the capacity, performance, and availability requirements for each application or virtual machine.

With the recent improvements on object-based storage and core design principles, such as scale-out capability, secure multitenancy, and superior performance for both small and large objects, SDS solutions evolved into a distributed system following the principle of cloud applications, where every function in the system is built as an independent layer.

Additional features like storage replication or snapshots are delivered in software; these virtual-based data services are provisioned and managed on a per-virtual machine basis.

In the past, datacenters were typically built around silos of operating system servers and storage and networking technologies that were managed separately, and this really constrained the ability of IT to respond to changing business demands quickly.

The SDDC approach removed those limitations by refactoring every single layer so the datacenter infrastructure is now a software service running across pools of industry-standard hardware. Compute and memory resources are abstracted from the physical layer through virtualization and pooled into a compute resource that provides scalability and resiliency.

Storage resources are virtualized into a software service that can be fully automated and intelligently deployed as needed and that is consumed from anywhere and fully secured.

IT organizations coming from the virtualization approach that adopted SDDC are transitioning and have started the process of building a private cloud and have the ability to access public cloud resources to get the services they need on demand at a cost factor that better fits their business needs.

Once the datacenter infrastructure is defined "as a software" through services you can control, automate, and manage through software, the infrastructure becomes a "programmable" infrastructure that can be configured dynamically based on the IT organization's predefined policies ensuring maximum availability, throughput, agility, and efficiency.

The transition process from a traditional datacenter to a software-based datacenter provides three significant benefits.

- *Economics*: The cost for running an application goes down dramatically versus an OpEx approach.

- *Automation*: It is possible to achieve a certain level of automation and operational efficiency that didn't exist in the past.

- *Flexibility*: Due to the nature of the software-defined elements, any IT organization can now flexibly allocate and configure all the components needed so that they can respond to the business needs.

This software-based datacenter definition evolved to a point where system engineers were able to automate the provisioning of new systems on their virtualized platforms and achieve some level of automation through scripting.

However, system engineers would mainly rely on the initial hardware the organization acquired, and therefore, they faced scalability limitations and technical difficulties to achieve high availability of applications.

The advent of cloud computing along with the adoption of hybrid or multicloud environments led cloud providers to develop certain frameworks and control planes to facilitate the provisioning of on-demand resources through a more "programmable" approach utilizing different programming languages, frameworks, and APIs.

IT organizations can now provision and maintain their deployments across hybrid environments and maintain this level of flexibility and scalability on-demand using infrastructure as code.

Overview of Infrastructure as Code

With the advent of most recent cloud technologies that allowed IT organizations to become more agile to improve their time to market, IaC was the natural response from the different cloud providers to diminish the pain of planning, provisioning, delivering, and monitoring applications and maintaining a consistent layer in a hybrid or multicloud environment.

During the last few years, IaC has been strongly related to the DevOps ecosystem and in general the multicloud world and is generally used to describe the configuration of solutions, products, and services helping to improve application life cycle management.

IaC evolved to become a way to manage the infrastructure and applications running in private and public clouds, with the main intention that the configuration of a given environment could be reproduced in a consistent manner across different deployments. IaC is now the new paradigm that will allow you define the resources you want to deploy in your environment, manage the life cycle of the resources that describe your infrastructure, and have more control over versioning.

Infrastructure as code redefines the way you plan, deploy, and maintain your business applications, as you will be able to provide the definition of the resources that are part of your application.

If you look up the meaning of IaC, you will find a lot of proposed definitions. To keep it simple and concise, I will take the definition from Sam Guckenheimer, shown here:

> *"Infrastructure as Code (IaC) is the management of infrastructure (networks, virtual machines, load balancers, and connection topology) in a descriptive model, using the same versioning as DevOps team uses for source code."*

Moreover, IaC is a key approach that enables best practices in a DevOps culture and reduces the need to perform a manual replication of the same application across different deployments. Therefore, automation becomes a critical part of the workflow to allow DevOps teams to ensure they can provide an exact copy of the desired infrastructure and desired state configuration across multiple deployments.

This way IaC will ensure DevOps teams can deliver the environments needed at scale with the same level of consistency every time. IT organizations can benefit from IaC in three ways.

- Increased efficiency
- Reduced operation costs
- Improved time to market

Increased Efficiency

IaC allows organizations to define the resources the application needs to run and to deploy these resources in a consistent way multiple times, enabling DevOps teams to spin up an entire environment as many times as needed with the confidence that the resources will behave the same way every single time.

This enables DevOps best practices when it comes to versioning and testing and minimizes the risk of human errors.

Reduced Operation Costs

The automation of the deployment process has impacted how application environments are provisioned and managed.

When an IT organization achieves this level of automation, the outcome is a standardized way to provision environments and allows the engineering team to focus on more valuable tasks while avoiding the cost of additional resources and saving computing costs.

Improved Time to Market

IaC also includes the definition of the desired configuration of the resources that are supposed to be part of the environment, which reduces dramatically the time needed to move from testing environments to a production environment.

The final goal of IaC through Azure Resource Manager is to empower organizations to deliver solutions in a consistent manner through a cloud-native language.

Current State of IaC

These days it's increasingly crucial to automate your infrastructure in a hybrid or multicloud approach, as applications can be deployed multiple times to staging and then perform the cutover to production.

A huge benefit of leveraging cloud computing is that every single organization can adopt best practices to provision or deprovision resources in response to the load and ensure business continuity.

IaC is now a key form factor to maintain environments, and whether you're a developer, you're a systems engineer, or you're in the DevOps space, there are skills that you have to develop and master to ensure a proper collaboration across the organization and leverage IaC principles the best way.

Cloud providers like Microsoft Azure deliver a consistent management layer to give you the flexibility and an easy way to manage the resources that are part of your environment through IaC.

In fact, Microsoft Azure through Azure Resource Manager provides you with the capabilities needed to manage the life cycle of your environment, including the creation, update, and management of resources that are part of the environment.

Have you noticed how some of the applications you use often are updated on a daily or monthly basis? Consider Microsoft Windows 10 and Microsoft Windows Server updates, where you can now decide when and how to get the latest updates.

We are now used to this approach of getting updates so often that you probably sometimes don't even notice when an application that you have on your phone is updated.

The approach for releasing new updates for a given application has changed from the legacy software development process, where developers basically wrote code and then sent a new version to test to the QA engineer. If the testing environment was successful, this new version would then be forwarded to the ops team to prepare the environment and perform the configuration needed to release this new version of the application.

This approach impacted different teams across the process to release the new version of the application, going from a bug fix to a major security implication. While most companies have moved from the waterfall model, there's a need to fully understand how IaC can improve the process from development to testing in a consistent manner.

Systems engineers have to better understand modern methodologies to deliver new software and to manage environments, including the infrastructure and resources needed to keep the application up and running whether the system is running on-premises or in the cloud.

Therefore, there's a need to improve the collaboration and communication across the development and operations teams to provide more value to customers. This comes down to effectively understanding the processes, people, and technology utilized by the development and operations teams, most commonly referred as DevOps.

In fact, IaC is one of the main pillars of DevOps; its adoption can help engineers manage the entire application life cycle and create processes to improve productivity. Some benefits of leveraging IaC include the following:

- *Version control*: The use of versioning is a fundamental practice, as it helps developers to better work together by tracking versions and changes made to the code so that it is easier to review and recover if needed. Version control can also help configure pipelines for continuous integration and continuous delivery to automate the required steps to deploy a new version of the application into a production environment.

- *Scalability*: Teams can easily scale their environment as IaC can help automate deployment processes while reducing the risk of human errors. The environments can be provisioned through automated pipelines to ensure consistency and removes the risk of misconfigurations.

- *Configuration management and reusability*: Operating large environments can become a challenge; by leveraging IaC, the desired configuration of a system can be defined beforehand and can reduce the complexity by being included in templates. The process can be automated to deploy the same environment across multiple regions or to reuse the same templates for multiple deployments with different configuration parameters.

In this chapter, you learned about the evolution from a traditional virtualization approach to the software-defined datacenter and the benefits that SDDC brings to organizations. Then we moved on to an overview of infrastructure as code and how system engineers transitioning to a DevOps approach need to adapt to a new methodology in order to maintain reliable systems. In the next chapter, we will do a deep dive into Azure Resource Manager.

Summary

This chapter reviewed how organizations have deployed applications in their datacenters, the overview and evolution of the Infrastructure-as-Code, and the core benefits for your organization when adopting the Infrastructure-as-Code approach.

CHAPTER 2

Azure Resource Manager

A few years ago, the former Windows Azure used a classic deployment model through Azure Service Management (ASM) to provision and maintain your resources in Microsoft's public cloud offering.

At that time, organizing and securing applications in the cloud at scale was a huge pain for everyone who wanted to get the most of the former Windows Azure. If an organization had just a couple of small applications like web services that had to be migrated and managed in the cloud, that would probably be an easy task to do in the early days of Azure.

But given the rapid pace of Azure and the new services and third-party solutions and integrations available, plus the increased complexity to maintain different applications across multiple Azure regions and subscriptions, Microsoft Azure had to provide a new way to maintain consistency and flexibility while maintaining highly scalable scenarios.

Microsoft invested in providing a new approach to better manage the resources that were deployed in Azure. The outcome of that investment was a new way that simplified the deployment, organization, security, and management of applications in the cloud, called Azure Resource Manager.

Azure Resource Manager provides a consistent management layer for your resources living in Azure. It provides a single API endpoint for multiple clients to communicate with all the different services or components that exist in Azure.

The uniqueness of Azure Resource Manager is that it involves a technology that was developed for the public cloud, but it also spans across the Azure Stack Hub offering. So, Azure Resource Manager now provides a management layer for applications that live in the public cloud or in a private datacenter.

© David Rendón 2022
D. Rendón, *Building Applications with Azure Resource Manager (ARM)*,
https://doi.org/10.1007/978-1-4842-7747-8_2

Azure Resource Manager is now the way to create, update, and manage your resources in the Microsoft Cloud. This means that Azure will provide you with the right tools for the right job when it comes to managing your environments in the Microsoft Cloud offering. These tools include the APIs, SDKs, and IDEs that will enable you to better manage your environments. See Figure 2-1.

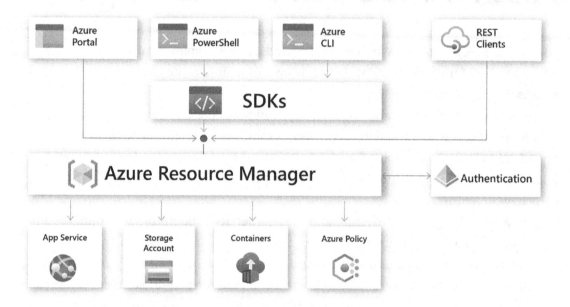

Figure 2-1. *Azure Resource Manager*

Azure Resource Manager communicates via different provider contracts called *resource providers*; therefore, you will find a broad set of resource provider contracts. Examples of resource providers include resources that you might be already working with, such as networks, SQL, compute, web, etc.

Azure Resource Manager Life Cycle

Azure Resource Manager helps you provision and manage the life cycle of resources in a simple declarative way through four main phases: authoring, validation, deployment, and management. See Figure 2-2.

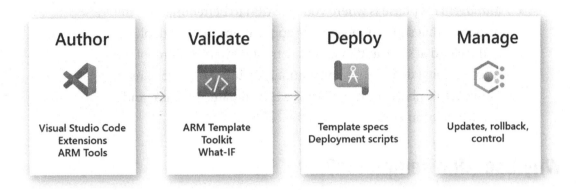

Figure 2-2. *Azure Resource Manager life cycle*

- *Author*: This phase is where you describe your environment through a simplified authoring experience with the new Visual Studio Code extension for Azure Resource Manager (ARM) templates and the most recent ARM language, called Bicep.

- *Validate*: This phase is where you assess the impact on the resources and adopt best practices when it comes to template testing, policy awareness, and updates to existing resources in your environment. For example, the Azure Resource Manager Template Toolkit (arm-ttk) will help you perform predeployment impact assessment and drift detection in addition to static analysis and testing.

- *Deploy*: This phase is where you use ARM to speed up the deployment process of your apps to the cloud and more specific to the staging area and orchestrated deployments. This phase involves the definition of modules, environment setup, and deeper continuous integration and continuous deployment (CI/CD) integrations. You can think of this phase as the template specifications and deployment scripts that will help you complete the "last mile" of your deployments and perform easy staging and sharing of templates and artifacts.

- *Manage*: This phase is where you use ARM to better organize the resources that support the various applications that are deployed in the cloud at scale and maintain consistency and control of the resources that define your applications, focusing on ease of use. Think of this phase as the ability to easily update, roll back, and delete environments.

Why Use ARM Templates?

First, let's understand what an ARM template is. This is according to Microsoft:

"Azure Resource Manager templates (ARM templates) allow you to specify your project's infrastructure in a declarative and reusable way. The templates can be versioned and saved in the same source control as your development project."

This way you can define the resources that make up part of your environment in a file that will be reusable and will include the configuration of Azure resources in source control (infrastructure as code).

ARM templates will allow you to repeat the deployment process numerous times and maintain consistency across all your deployments.

As mentioned earlier, one of the great benefits of using IaC is the automation capabilities that will help you speed up your deployments but also reduce risk of human error. These capabilities also employ continuous integration techniques utilizing DevOps principles and practices.

Benefits of Using ARM

If you're getting started with Azure Resource Manager, then you will find ARM templates very helpful. First, Azure Resource Manager is template-driven, which means that it provides a way to deploy your apps to the cloud as many times as needed in a declarative and idempotent or repeatable manner.

This characteristic of the ARM templates will allow you to perform a first deployment of your app for testing purposes and redeploy that template as needed to ensure that the state of your application matches your intent. This allows you to define the resources you want to provision on Azure in the template, and you will be able to reuse the template as needed.

Also, ARM templates are natively multiservice, so you will be able to deploy any service or component that exists on Azure via Azure Resource Manager; you will also find that ARM templates span regions, so you can deploy any resource in any region as long as the region supports the resource you're trying to deploy.

Deployments can be extensible through third parties to build resource providers and connect to Azure Resource Manager so that you can provision those services.

Before reviewing the anatomy of an Azure Resource Manager template, we have to ensure we understand some core concepts of Azure. *Resource groups* are like folders on your file system. A resource group is your container for multiple resources. Resources can exist on only one and just one resource group; however, resource groups can span regions and services. A resource group can be utilized to group resources that share the same life cycle, permissions, and policies.

Now, to organize the resource groups with the services that you need to deploy, there are primarily two mechanisms.

The first of them is the *imperative way*, for instance, when you use PowerShell or the Azure portal to provision a new service, and you use a command to create the service you need on Azure.

Listing 2-1 shows the PowerShell to provision a new resource group.

Listing 2-1. PowerShell Code, Imperative Way

```
# Create variables to store the location and resource group names.
$location = "local"
$ResourceGroupName = "myResourceGroup"

New-AzResourceGroup `
  -Name $ResourceGroupName `
  -Location $location
```

The second option is in a declarative mode, where you describe the goal state of your application through a JSON file format. You define the inputs and the resources that you want to provision, and then Azure Resource Manager will provision those resources.

We will explore these two deployment models when we build our ARM templates later in the book.

Deployments

A *deployment* is basically an entity that tracks template execution, so you can create, manage, and update deployments through the API. It is important to highlight some characteristics about deployment.

- Deployments are always created within a resource group.

- Deployments doesn't span multiple resource groups.

- It is possible to nest deployments so you can have large, complex applications that are modeled in a flexible manner.

Anatomy of an ARM Template

ARM templates are the native infrastructure solution for managing your Azure resources declaratively. Essentially, you describe in a JSON file the resources and the properties of the resources that you want to deploy.

Then Azure takes care of the validation of your ARM template to ensure that the resource will be created successfully with the configuration you previously defined on your template. See Figure 2-3.

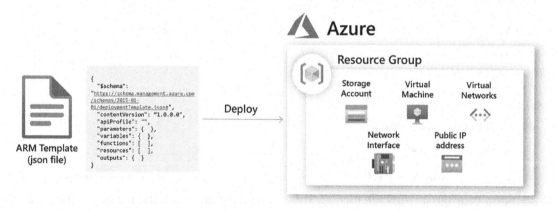

Figure 2-3. Azure Resource Manager template deployment process

Overall, an ARM template comprises some core elements. Some of the elements are strictly required, while others are optional. Each element might have its own properties, as shown in Listing 2-2.

Listing 2-2. Core Elements of an ARM Template

```
{
  "$schema": "https://schema.management.azure.com/schemas/2015-01-01/
  deploymentTemplate.json#",
  "contentVersion": "",
  "apiProfile": "",
  "parameters": {  },
  "variables": {  },
  "functions": [  ],
  "resources": [  ],
  "outputs": {  }
}
```

The following table highlights whether a core element of the ARM template is strictly required:

Element Name	Required
$schema	Yes
contentVersion	Yes
apiProfile	No
Parameters	No
Variables	No
Functions	No
Resources	Yes
Outputs	No

Azure Resource Manager Template Core Elements

Let's see a high-level overview of each core element in an ARM template. We will deep dive into each one of them in the next chapters. See Figure 2-4.

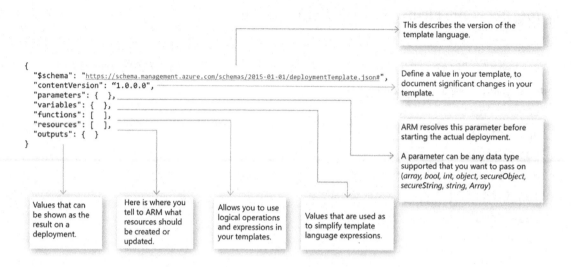

Figure 2-4. *Azure Resource Manager template core elements*

- schema: This describes the version of the template language. The version number used depends on the scope of the deployment and the JSON editor; in this case, we are using Visual Studio Code.

Note   ARM schemas are regularly updated. The Microsoft recommendation is to utilize a major release unless your deployment depends on a minor version update. You can check the releases here: `https://github.com/Azure/azure-resource-manager-schemas/tree/master/schemas`.

- contentVersion: This helps you to define a value in your template to document significant changes in your template. For instance, it could be 1.0.0.0 and on a most recent update could be 1.0.0.1.

- apiProfile: Although this is not a required field, this defines the API version that serves as a collection of API versions for resource types. Note that if you specify an API profile version but there is not a specification for the API version for the resource type, Resource Manager will then use the API version for that resource type that is defined in the profile.

- `parameters`: These are string values, and when you deploy your ARM template, ARM resolves this parameter before starting the actual deployment.

- `variables`: These are values to simplify template language expressions can be set statically or compute dynamically based on the parameters provided to you by the user.

- `functions`: This allows you to use logical operations and expressions in your templates.

- `resources`: This is where you tell ARM what resources should be created or updated.

- `outputs`: These are values that can be shown as the result of a deployment.

Now that we have reviewed the core elements of an Azure Resource Manager template, including why you should leverage ARM templates, let's move on to the topic of how to prepare our environment so that you can start building your own ARM templates.

Summary

This chapter introduced the core concepts about Azure Resource Manager, including how you can leverage Azure Resource Manager along with ARM templates to deploy resources in Azure and the core benefits of this approach. We also the anatomy and the core components of an ARM template.

CHAPTER 3

Preparing Your Environment

Several tools are available for you to write and maintain your Azure Resource Manager (ARM) templates. In this chapter, we will review some of the tools that will be utilized throughout the following chapters.

Azure Resource Manager utilizes a JavaScript Object Notation (JSON) file that defines the infrastructure and configuration for your resources; this means you can determine the pieces of code that will build your environment in Azure.

If you want to take advantage of the ARM templates, you will need an editor; it can be any tool that can provide support for JSON files such as Visual Studio Code as it is a lightweight, multiplatform, open source editor.

That said, you could easily use any editor to define your Azure Resource Manager template, but we will leverage some of the Visual Studio Code extensions to speed up the process of writing and testing ARM templates.

Building and maintaining your infrastructure at scale is a task that can become overwhelming if you have no control over versioning. By leveraging ARM templates, you can define the infrastructure that needs to be deployed and control the versions of those templates to keep track of potential changes in your environment.

It is important to define the process you will follow to provision and manage the life cycle of resources in a simple declarative way, as mentioned in the previous chapter, by emphasizing these phases: authoring, validation, deployment, and management.

Now that we have briefly covered the ARM templates' life cycle, let's go install the tools you can leverage for each of the phases.

© David Rendón 2022
D. Rendón, *Building Applications with Azure Resource Manager (ARM)*,
https://doi.org/10.1007/978-1-4842-7747-8_3

Installing ARM Extensions

Once you have Visual Studio Code installed in your local machine, which you can download from `https://code.visualstudio.com/download`, you can leverage some extensions to speed up the creation of the ARM templates.

These are two essential extensions:

- Azure Resource Manager Template Tools extension

- The ARM template viewer extension

Azure Resource Manager Tools Extension

The Azure Resource Manager Tools extension includes comprehensive language support for your templates; it will also help you simplify how you create templates. It includes resource snippets, in-line help, and IntelliSense, among other features.

You can install the Azure Resource Manager Tools extension from within Visual Studio Code. Open Visual Studio Code, go to Extensions, and search for *ARM*. You should see the Azure Resource Manager Tools extension listed. Go ahead and install it, as shown in Figure 3-1.

Figure 3-1. *ARM Tools extension*

The next extension that you will enable on Visual Studio Code is the ARM Template Viewer extension.

ARM Template Viewer Extension

The ARM Template Viewer extension will allow you to visualize the resources described in your ARM template using the official Azure icons and see the relationship between the resources.

The extension allows you to manipulate the icons as needed in the canvas, and you can click specific resources to show a pop-up and expand on the details of that particular resource. The best part is that the ARM Template Viewer extension is now a native part of the Azure portal, so it is useful when authoring ARM templates.

To enable this extension, open Visual Studio Code, click the extension icon, and search for *ARM template viewer*, as shown in Figure 3-2. Figure 3-3 shows the description of the extension.

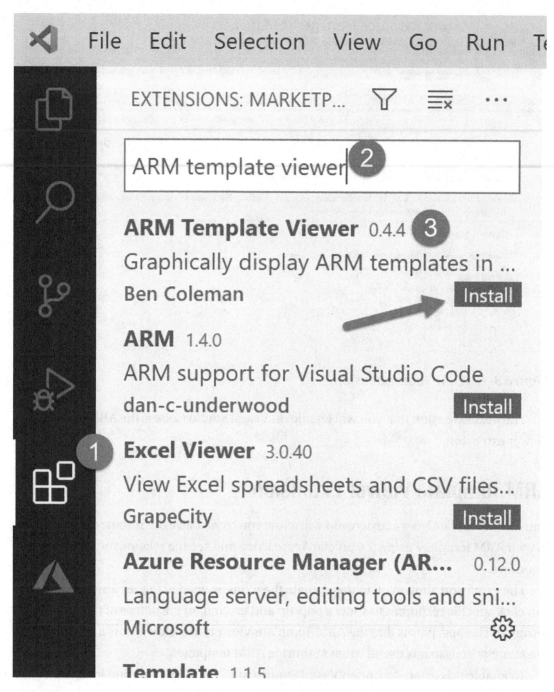

Figure 3-2. *ARM template viewer extension*

Figure 3-3. *ARM Template Viewer extension description*

Now we will configure Azure PowerShell.

Configuring Azure PowerShell

Azure PowerShell includes a comprehensive set of cmdlets to manage Azure resources directly from PowerShell.

First, launch a PowerShell console; you can use Windows Terminal with PowerShell. Then verify the PowerShell version with the cmdlet shown here (see Figure 3-4):

```
$PSVersionTable.PSVersion
```

```
PS C:\> $PSVersionTable.PSVersion

Major    Minor    Build    Revision
-----    -----    -----    --------
5        1        19041    1
```

Figure 3-4. *Checking the PowerShell version*

As per Microsoft, PowerShell 7.x and later is the recommended version of PowerShell for Azure PowerShell on all platforms.

You can grab the latest bits from PowerShell from here:

`https://github.com/PowerShell/PowerShell/releases`

Scroll down to Assets, where you will find the PowerShell package. For this particular environment, we're running a Windows 10 machine and downloading the `.msi` package. Once downloaded, open the setup wizard, as shown in Figure 3-5, and start the installation, as shown in Figure 3-6. Follow the wizard steps; Figure 3-7 shows the complete process.

Figure 3-5. *PowerShell install setup wizard*

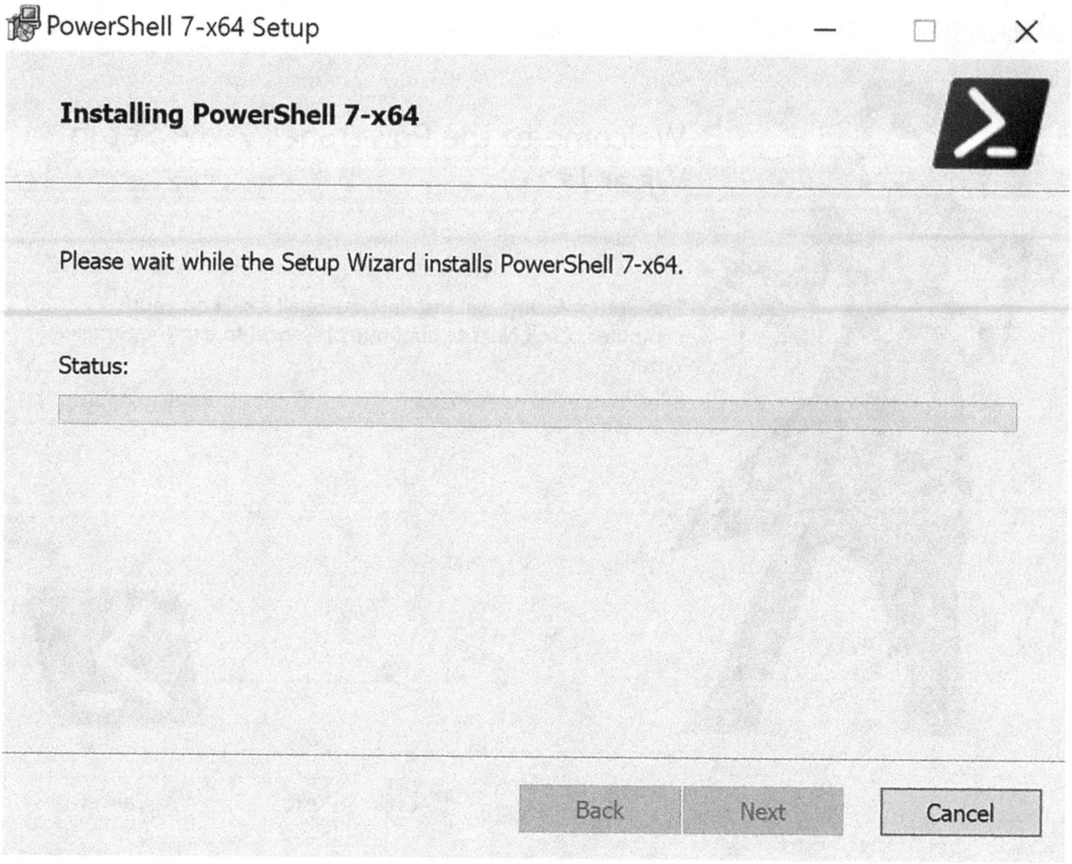

Figure 3-6. *PowerShell installation progress*

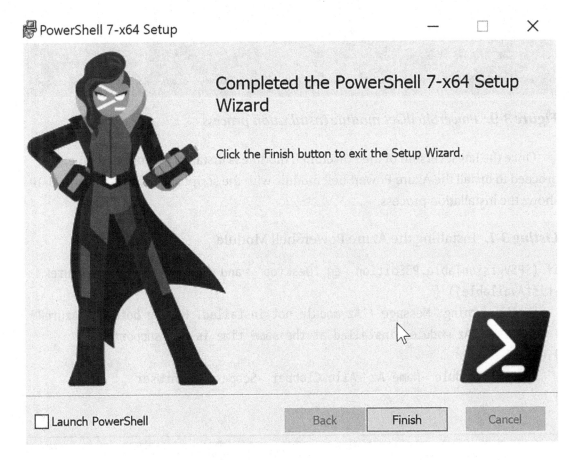

Figure 3-7. *PowerShell completed setup*

Now make sure to install the latest version of PowerShellGet using the following cmdlet, as shown in Figure 3-8:

```
Install-Module -Name PowerShellGet -Force
```

```
PS C:\> Install-Module -Name PowerShellGet -Force
```

Figure 3-8. *Installing the PowerShellGet module*

Figure 3-9 shows the installation process.

```
Windows PowerShell
Copyright (C) Microsoft Corporation. All rights reserved.

Installing package 'PowerShellGet'
    Unzipping
    [ooooooooooooooooooooooooooooooooooooooooooooooooooooooooooooooooooooooooooooooooooooooooooooooooooo
```

Figure 3-9. *PowerShellGet module installation process*

Once the latest version of the PowerShell module is installed on your machine, let's proceed to install the Azure PowerShell module with the script in Listing 3-1. Figure 3-10 shows the installation process.

Listing 3-1. Installing the Azure PowerShell Module

```
if ($PSVersionTable.PSEdition -eq 'Desktop' -and (Get-Module -Name AzureRM
-ListAvailable)) {
    Write-Warning -Message ('Az module not installed. Having both the AzureRM
    and ' + 'Az modules installed at the same time is not supported.')
} else {
    Install-Module -Name Az -AllowClobber -Scope CurrentUser
}
```

```
PS C:\Users\dave> if ($PSVersionTable.PSEdition -eq 'Desktop' -and (Get-Module -Name AzureRM -ListAvailable)) {
>>      Write-Warning -Message ('Az module not installed. Having both the AzureRM and ' +
>>          'Az modules installed at the same time is not supported.')
>> } else {
>>      Install-Module -Name Az -AllowClobber -Scope CurrentUser
>> }
```

Figure 3-10. *Azure PowerShell module installation*

You will see a confirmation message; type Y, as shown in Figure 3-11.

```
Untrusted repository
You are installing the modules from an untrusted repository. If you trust this repository, change its
InstallationPolicy value by running the Set-PSRepository cmdlet. Are you sure you want to install the modules from
'PSGallery'?
[Y] Yes  [A] Yes to All  [N] No  [L] No to All  [S] Suspend  [?] Help (default is "N"):
```

Figure 3-11. *Untrusted repository*

Shortly after you should see the progress on the Azure PowerShell module installation, as shown in Figure 3-12.

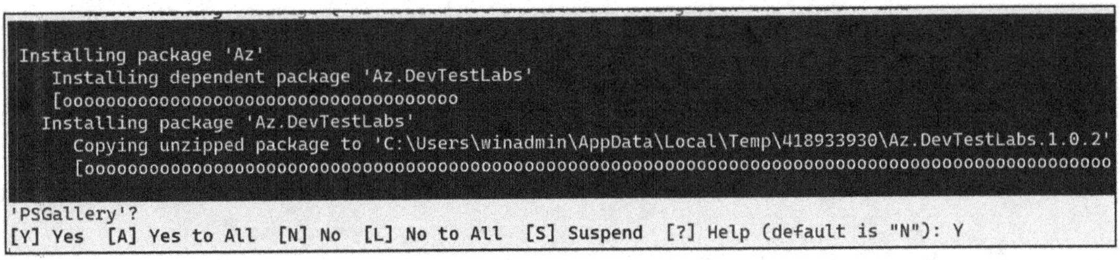

```
Installing package 'Az'
    Installing dependent package 'Az.DevTestLabs'
    [oooooooooooooooooooooooooooooooooooo
Installing package 'Az.DevTestLabs'
    Copying unzipped package to 'C:\Users\winadmin\AppData\Local\Temp\418933930\Az.DevTestLabs.1.0.2'
    [oooooooooooooooooooooooooooooooooooooooooooooooooooooooooooooooooooooooooooooooooooooooooooooo
'PSGallery'?
[Y] Yes  [A] Yes to All  [N] No  [L] No to All  [S] Suspend  [?] Help (default is "N"): Y
```

Figure 3-12. *Installing Azure PowerShell module*

Once the installation is complete, you can start working with Azure PowerShell.

Ensure you have an active Azure subscription; you can register for a free Azure account at the following link: https://azure.microsoft.com/en-us/free/.

Let's sign in to our Azure account using the following cmdlet:

Connect-AzAccount

This cmdlet will prompt you to open a browser to authenticate your device, as shown in Figure 3-13.

```
PS C:\Users\dave> Connect-AzAccount
WARNING: To sign in, use a web browser to open the page https://microsoft.com/devicelogin and enter the code ALW8ACBVX t
o authenticate.
```

Figure 3-13. *Connect-AzAccount*

You will be redirected to https://microsoft.com/devicelogin to log in and access to your Azure account, as shown in Figure 3-14.

 Microsoft

Enter code

Enter the code displayed on your app or device.

ALW8ACBVX|

Figure 3-14. *Device login page*

After this process, you should see a notification that you are signed in, as shown in Figure 3-15.

 Microsoft

Microsoft Azure PowerShell

You have signed in to the Microsoft Azure
PowerShell application on your device. You may now
close this window.

Figure 3-15. *Azure PowerShell notification*

Back in the PowerShell console, you should see your Azure subscription listed, as
shown in Figure 3-16.

Account	SubscriptionName	TenantId	Environment
dave			AzureCloud

Figure 3-16. *Azure subscription*

Now that you have installed Azure PowerShell, let's proceed to install the Azure
command-line interface (CLI).

Installing Azure CLI

The next tool to install is Azure CLI. You can download it from here:

`https://docs.microsoft.com/en-us/cli/azure/install-azure-cli`

Once you download the installation package, run it as an administrator to start the Azure CLI setup wizard, as shown in Figure 3-17.

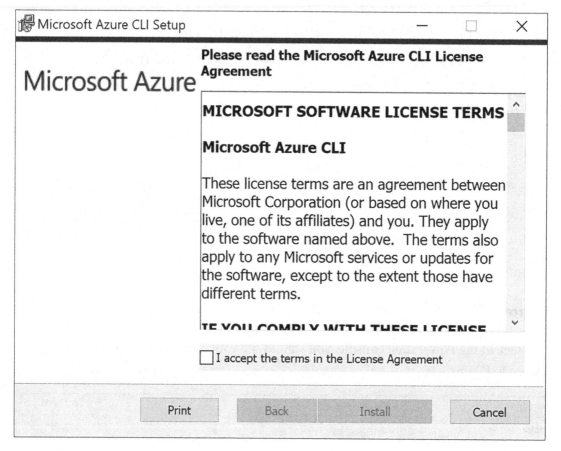

Figure 3-17. *Azure CLI setup*

Accept the license agreement and click Install, as shown in Figure 3-18.

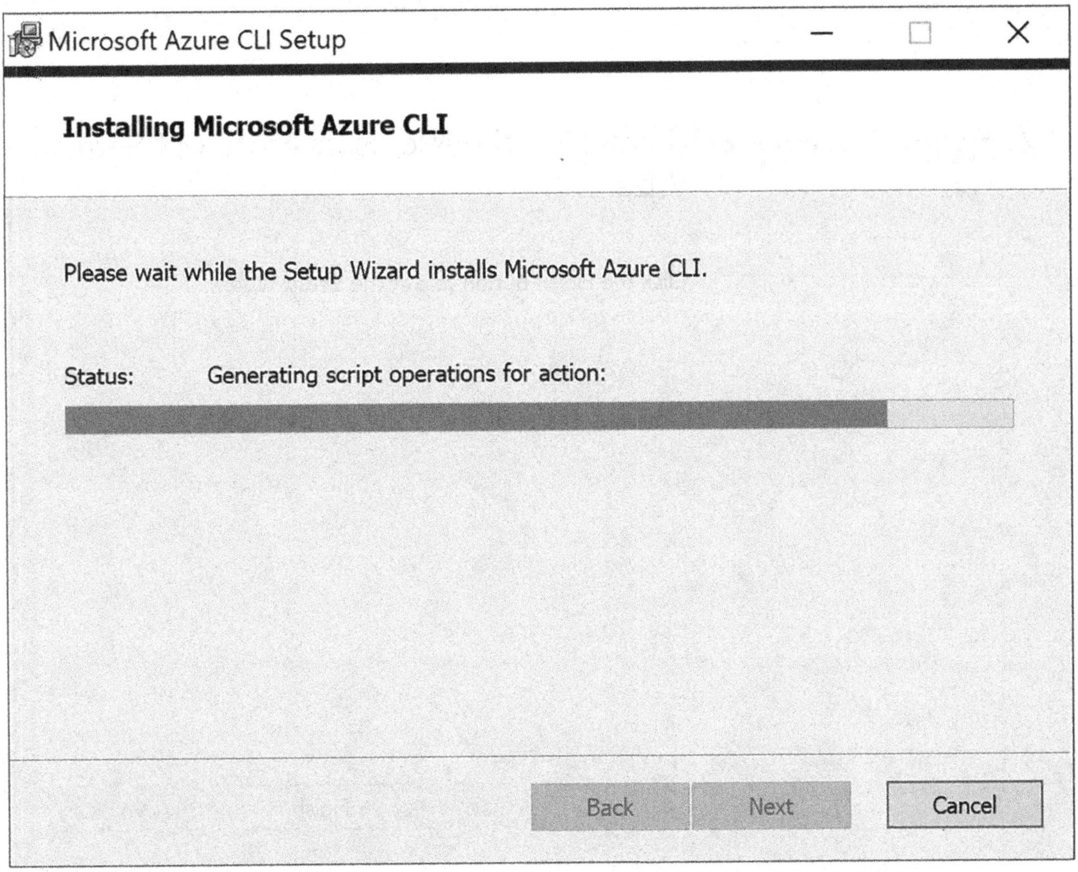

Figure 3-18. *Installing Microsoft Azure CLI*

After a few minutes the installation will be complete, as shown in Figure 3-19.

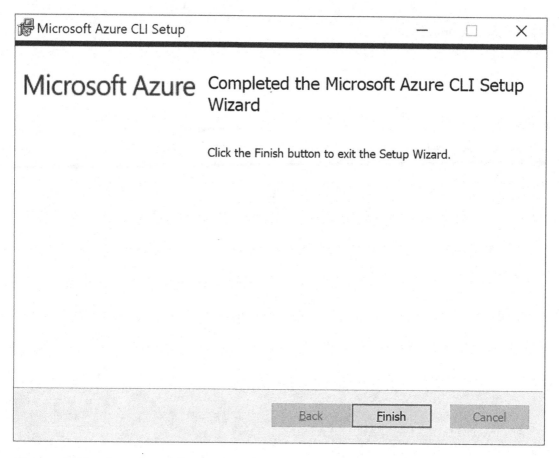

Figure 3-19. *Completed the Microsoft Azure CLI setup wizard*

At this point, we have gone through the installation of the basic tooling to work with Azure, including the installation of Visual Studio Code, the installation and configuration process of the Azure Resource Manager extensions for Visual Studio Code, and the installation of Azure PowerShell and Azure CLI.

In the next chapter, you will learn how you can start authoring your Azure Resource Manager templates.

Summary

This chapter provided you with the tools available to author your Azure Resource Manager templates. We reviewed the installation process of some of the tools that we will leverage in the following chapters to work with ARM templates.

CHAPTER 4

Building Your First Azure Resource Manager Template

This chapter will cover how to build your first Azure Resource Manager (ARM) template that will create a storage account in Azure. We will go over the core elements of an ARM template to better understand what the Azure Resource Manager capabilities are and how you can leverage ARM templates based on your organization's needs.

Topics covered in this chapter include the following:

- Working with Visual Studio Code and the ARM extension

- Azure Resource Manager snippets

- Your first look at an ARM template

- Your first ARM template deployment

In Chapter 3, we reviewed the tools needed to author your ARM templates, so now we will go over the creation of an ARM template. We will start from scratch to create your own ARM template, and then we will proceed to our first deployment of the ARM template.

The first thing to do when working with ARM templates is to define the *schema*, which contains the definition of the properties that will be part of your ARM template.

To help you speed up the writing process of an ARM template, you can utilize Visual Studio Code and create a new file, as shown in Figure 4-1.

© David Rendón 2022
D. Rendón, *Building Applications with Azure Resource Manager (ARM)*,
https://doi.org/10.1007/978-1-4842-7747-8_4

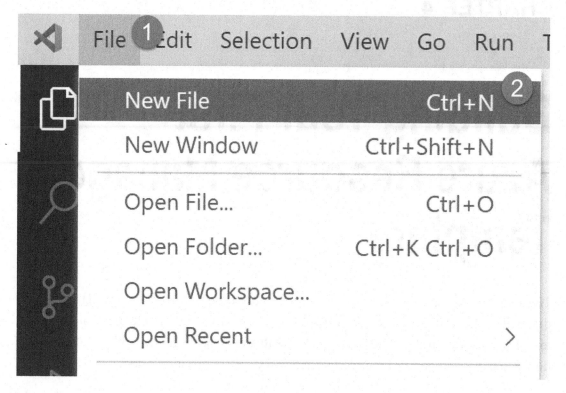

Figure 4-1. *Creating a new file in Visual Studio Code*

Save the file as `azuredeploy.json`. You will note that Visual Studio Code has identified that this file is an ARM template through the ARM extension for Visual Studio Code; in addition, by leveraging the ARM extension, you will be able to validate your ARM template definition.

To speed up the writing process, type `arm!`. You will see that Visual Studio Code (VS Code) provides you with a list of snippets. Let's select the first option, which is the Azure Resource Manager template snippet, as shown in Figure 4-2.

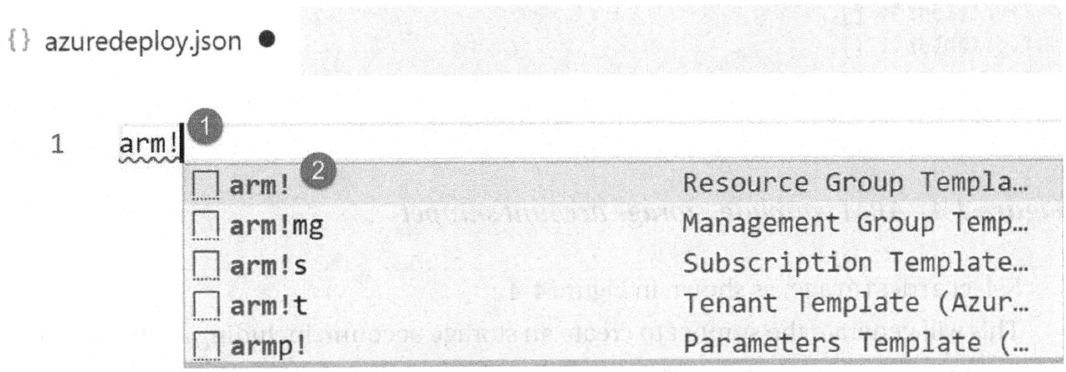

{} azuredeploy.json ●

```
1    arm!①
         □ arm!②                          Resource Group Templa…
         □ arm!mg                         Management Group Temp…
         □ arm!s                          Subscription Template…
         □ arm!t                          Tenant Template (Azur…
         □ armp!                          Parameters Template (…
```

Figure 4-2. *Azure Resource Manager snippet*

Once you select the resource group template, you will see the ARM template, as shown in Figure 4-3.

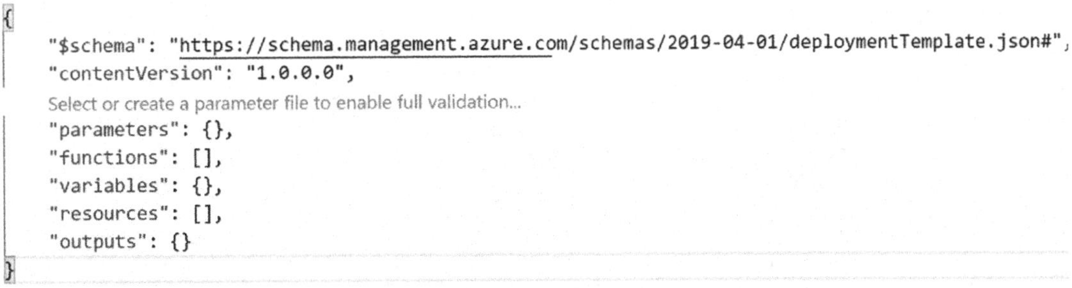

```
{
    "$schema": "https://schema.management.azure.com/schemas/2019-04-01/deploymentTemplate.json#",
    "contentVersion": "1.0.0.0",
    Select or create a parameter file to enable full validation…
    "parameters": {},
    "functions": [],
    "variables": {},
    "resources": [],
    "outputs": {}
}
```

Figure 4-3. *ARM template from snippet*

As you can see in Figure 4-3, the snippet contains the core elements of an ARM template; it also includes schema and contentVersion.

Now let's create a new resource, under the resources section, to define a new storage account.

Creating a Storage Account on Your ARM Template

Now we will expand the resources section. Inside the square brackets, type storage. You will see that the ARM extension provides a snippet to create a storage account, as shown in Figure 4-4.

```
"functions": [],
"variables": {},
"resources": [storage,
"outputs": {}
```

Figure 4-4. *ARM template, storage account snippet*

Select arm-storage, as shown in Figure 4-4.

This will generate the snippet to create an storage account, including all the objects needed to define this resource. Once you select the storage account snippet, your ARM template should look like Figure 4-5.

```
{
    "$schema": "https://schema.management.azure.com/schemas/2019-04-01/deploymentTemplate.json#",
    "contentVersion": "1.0.0.0",
    Select or create a parameter file to enable full validation...
    "parameters": {},
    "functions": [],
    "variables": {},
    "resources": [{
        "name": "storageaccount1",
        "type": "Microsoft.Storage/storageAccounts",
        "apiVersion": "2019-06-01",
        "tags": {
            "displayName": "storageaccount1"
        },
        "location": "[resourceGroup().location]",
        "kind": "StorageV2",
        "sku": {
            "name": "Premium_LRS",
            "tier": "Premium"
        }
    }],
    "outputs": {}
}
```

Figure 4-5. *Storage account in ARM template*

Note that the schema refers to an outdated API; ensure you adopt best practices and use the latest stable API version in the schema.

Now that we have defined the storage account resource in our ARM template, we can customize this type of resource. This storage account can contain different data objects such as blob files, queues, tables, and disks; also note that there are different types of storage accounts that vary according to their features. Here are some examples:

- General-purpose v2 accounts

- General-purpose v1 accounts

- BlockBlobStorage accounts

- FileStorage accounts

- BlobStorage accounts

In addition, your organization might need a specific type of redundancy level for the storage account. The redundancy level property for the storage account can be defined in the ARM template. Some of the redundancy options for the storage account include the following:

- Locally redundant storage (LRS)

- Zone-redundant storage (ZRS)

- Georedundant storage (GRS)

- Geozone-redundant storage (GZRS) (in preview as of this writing)

All the properties listed can be defined in the ARM template in a declarative way; we can also leverage parameters for this template.

Although we will cover how you can work with parameters in your ARM template in Chapter 6, right now you can assign a parameter that will be passed to the storage account name and the storage account type.

To pass these values as parameters, you only need to define the object, as shown in Listing 4-1.

Listing 4-1. ARM Template, Storage Account with Parameters

```
"resources": [{
    //Pass on the storage account name as parameter
    "name": "[parameters('storageAccountName')]",
    "type": "Microsoft.Storage/storageAccounts",
    "apiVersion": "2019-06-01",
    "tags": {
        "displayName": "storageaccount1"
    },
    "location": "[resourceGroup().location]",
    "kind": "StorageV2",
```

```
    "sku": {
        //Pass on the storage account type as parameter
        "name": "[parameters('storageAccountType')]"
    }
}],
```

Note that storageAccountName and storageAccountType are defined as parameters.

The value options of both of these parameters, storageAccountName and storageAccountType, can be defined in the same ARM template in the parameters section, as shown in Listing 4-2.

Listing 4-2. ARM Template, Definition of the Parameters for a Storage Account

```
{
  "$schema": "https://schema.management.azure.com/schemas/2019-04-01/
  deploymentTemplate.json#",
  "contentVersion": "1.0.0.0",
  "parameters": {
      "storageAccountName": {
          "type": "string",
          "metadata": {
              "description": "My new storage account"
          }
      },
      "storageAccountType":{
          "type": "string",
          "metadata": {
              "description": "Storage Account Type: Standard_LRS"
          },
          "allowedValues": [
              "Standard_LRS",
              "Standard_GRS",
              "Standard_ZRS",
              "Premium_LRS"
          ],
```

```
            "defaultValue": "Standard_LRS"

        }
    },
    "functions": [],
```

So now, where do we define the actual values of these parameters? The actual values of both of these parameters, `storageAccountName` and `storageAccountType`, can be defined either in the same ARM template or in a separate file that will be dedicated to the definition of the actual values of the parameters.

For larger deployments and to keep your templates organized, it is best to have a separate definition file for all the parameters that you plan to utilize; name it `azuredeploy.parameters.json`.

The parameters file will include only the definition of the actual values of the parameters you need to pass. This parameters file is a `.json` file with a similar structure to the ARM template file, meaning that the parameters file will have properties defined such as `schema` and `contentVersion`, as well as a `parameters` section, as shown in Listing 4-3.

Listing 4-3. Parameters File for ARM Template, Definition of the Actual Parameters for a Storage Account

```
{
    "$schema": "https://schema.management.azure.com/schemas/2019-04-01/
    deploymentParameters.json#",
    "contentVersion": "1.0.0.0",
    "parameters": {
        "storageAccountName": {
            "value": "mystorageaccount"
        },
        "storageAccountType": {
            "value": "Standard_GRS"
        }
    }
}
```

Note   You can utilize the reserved word `armp!` to quickly generate the parameters file. Click Create New File in Visual Studio Code, and save the file as `azuredeploy.parameters.json`. Then type `armp`, as shown in Figure 4-6, and you will see the snippet for the parameters file.

```
storage-account > {} param.json
  1    armp
           □ armp!                    Azure Resource Manager (ARM) Parame...
```

Figure 4-6. *Snippet for the parameters file for the ARM template*

Once you create a new file in Vistual Studio Code and save it as `azuredeploy.parameters.json`, the ARM extension will detect the format, and then you will be able to use the code snippets. Listing 4-4 shows an example of the parameters file.

Listing 4-4. Parameters File for ARM Template

```
{
    "$schema": "https://schema.management.azure.com/schemas/2019-04-01/
    deploymentParameters.json#",
    "contentVersion": "1.0.0.0",
    "parameters": {
    }
}
```

Note that the parameters file has a simple structure, and for this specific case we have defined `storageAccountName` and `storageAccountType` with their actual values that will be passed to the ARM template during the deployment phase.

As of now, we have two files, shown here:

- Our ARM template (`azuredeploy.json`)

- Our parameters file (`azuredeploy.parameters.json`)

Listing 4-5 shows the definition of the ARM template.

Listing 4-5. ARM Template, with the Definition to Deploy the Storage Account to Your Azure Subscription

```
{
    "$schema": "https://schema.management.azure.com/schemas/2019-04-01/
    deploymentTemplate.json#",
    "contentVersion": "1.0.0.0",
    "parameters": {
        "storageAccountName": {
                "type": "string",
                "metadata": {
                    "description": "My new storage account"
                }
            },
            "storageAccountType":{
                "type": "string",
                "metadata": {
                    "description": "Storage Account Type: Standard_LRS"
                },
                "allowedValues": [
                    "Standard_LRS",
                    "Standard_GRS",
                    "Standard_ZRS",
                    "Premium_LRS"
                ],
                "defaultValue": "Standard_LRS"

            }
    },
    "functions": [],
    "variables": {},
    "resources": [{
        //Pass on the storage account name as parameter
        "name": "[parameters('storageAccountName')]",
        "type": "Microsoft.Storage/storageAccounts",
        "apiVersion": "2019-06-01",
```

```
        "tags": {
            "displayName": "storageaccount1"
        },
        "location": "[resourceGroup().location]",
        "kind": "StorageV2",
        "sku": {
            //Pass on the storage account type as parameter
            "name": "[parameters('storageAccountType')]"
        }
    }],
    "outputs": {}
}
```

Listing 4-6 shows the definition of the parameters file.

Listing 4-6. Parameters File, with Definition of the Parameters for a
Storage Account

```
{
    "$schema": "https://schema.management.azure.com/schemas/2019-04-01/
    deploymentParameters.json#",
    "contentVersion": "1.0.0.0",
    "parameters": {
        "storageAccountName": {
            "value": "mystorageaccount"
        },
        "storageAccountType": {
            "value": "Standard_GRS"
        }
    }
}
```

Once we have defined the resources we want to include in our ARM template, the
next step is to deploy this storage account to our Azure subscription.

Deploying Your First ARM Template

Now that we have defined the resources that we want to deploy to Azure, it is time to deploy the ARM template that includes the definition of the storage account to our Azure subscription.

We will leverage Windows Terminal and PowerShell 7.x to deploy our first template. We assume you are already logged in to your Azure subscription and that you have the Owner or Contributor role. Create a new resource group with the command shown in Listing 4-7.

Listing 4-7. PowerShell Command to Create a New Resource Group in Your Azure Subscription

```
New-AzResourceGroup -Name "storage-resource-group" -Location "westus"
```

You should see that the resource group has been created after a few seconds, as shown in Figure 4-7.

```
PS C:\Users\dave\ArmTemplates> New-AzResourceGroup -Name "storage-resource-group" -Location "westus"

ResourceGroupName : storage-resource-group
Location          : westus
ProvisioningState : Succeeded
Tags              :
ResourceId        : /subscriptions/                               /resourceGroups/storage-resource-group
```

Figure 4-7. *Console output, definition of resource group created in the Azure subscription*

Now that the resource group has been created, we will go to the directory where the ARM template is located, in this case `ArmTemplates/storage-account`, and deploy the ARM template in that resource group, as every resource must be deployed in a resource group. We will target this deployment to the resource group level using the command shown in Listing 4-8.

Listing 4-8. PowerShell Command to Perform a New Resource Group Deployment

```
New-AzResourceGroupDeployment -Name "storage-account-deployment"
-ResourceGroupName "storage-resource-group" -TemplateFile
.\azuredeploy.json -TemplateParameterFile .\azuredeploy.parameters.json
```

Once you deploy the ARM template, after a few seconds you should be able to see in the output that your resource has been successfully created, as shown in Figure 4-8.

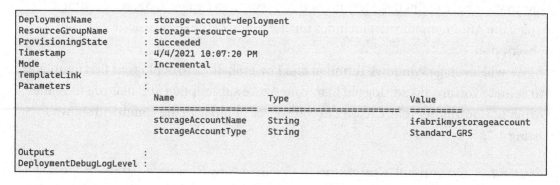

```
DeploymentName        : storage-account-deployment
ResourceGroupName     : storage-resource-group
ProvisioningState     : Succeeded
Timestamp             : 4/4/2021 10:07:20 PM
Mode                  : Incremental
TemplateLink          :
Parameters            :
                        Name                    Type                        Value
                        ====================    ========================    ==========
                        storageAccountName      String                      ifabrikmystorageaccount
                        storageAccountType      String                      Standard_GRS

Outputs               :
DeploymentDebugLogLevel :
```

Figure 4-8. *PowerShell output, storage account created in Azure*

Note that the storage account name must be globally unique. Ensure you define in the parameters file a unique name for the storage account.

The Azure portal shows relevant information related to this deployment, so open the Azure portal using the following URL: `https://portal.azure.com`. Then go to the resource group called `storage-resource-group` that was recently created, as shown in Figure 4-9.

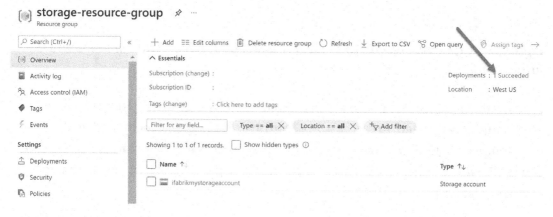

Figure 4-9. *Azure portal, resource group page*

Notice that the Azure portal shows whether the deployment succeeded or whether there was any error during the deployment phase. You can review the details of the deployment by clicking the Deployments output label, as shown in Figure 4-9.

Then you will be directed to the Deployments page where you will be able to review the deployments history and details related to each deployment. This way, you can easily check on your most recent deployments and review the related events, as shown in Figure 4-10.

Figure 4-10. *Azure portal, Deployments page*

It is possible to drill down into the details; specifically, by clicking the deployment name, you will be able to see the template that was provisioned and also deploy the template again from the Azure portal, as shown in Figure 4-11.

Figure 4-11. *Azure portal, Template page*

The process described earlier to provision resources in Azure using an ARM template gives you a better idea of the workflow of the deployment process of ARM templates and the flexibility to define the desired services and components that will be part of your environment in Azure.

So, how does Azure translate how and which resources have to be provisioned? Let's take a look at the deployment workflow of an ARM template.

Deployment Workflow of Your First ARM Template

The basic unit, that we need to define is our ARM template file which will comprise the definition of the resources, functions, variables, and outputs desired in the deployment. ARM templates can include a small part of your entire environment, meaning that you can create multiple templates and dependencies to achieve the desired configuration of your environment in Azure.

Once you have your template ready, Azure Resource Manager will take care of the resources that are to be created through REST API operations. Each operation is handled by a specific Azure resource provider. In this chapter, we provisioned an Azure storage account, which relies on the `Microsoft.Storage` resource provider.

Each service will mostly depend on a resource provider. The resource provider will then process the REST API operation. For instance, in our storage account, the request for the resource provider is the code shown in Listing 4-9.

Listing 4-9. REST API Operation for the Creation of the Azure Storage Account

```
PUT
https://management.azure.com/subscriptions/{Your-subscriptionId}/
resourceGroups/{Your-resourceGroupName}/providers/Microsoft.Storage/
storageAccounts/yourstorageaccount?api-version=2019-06-01
REQUEST BODY
{
  "location": "westus",
  "sku": {
    "name": "Standard_GRS"
  },
  "kind": "StorageV2",
  "properties": {}
}
```

In this chapter, we utilized PowerShell to provision our ARM template and used Visual Studio Code with the ARM extension to define our ARM templates; however, you have a variety of options to work on the definition and provisioning process of your ARM templates, including the following:

- Azure CLI

- Azure portal

- PowerShell

- REST API

- GitHub

- Azure Cloud Shell

- Azure DevOps

- Terraform

- Pulumi,

Summary

In this chapter, we reviewed the basic structure of an ARM template file and parameters file, and we showed a practical example of how to define a storage account and how to pass parameters during the deployment phase. We also reviewed the code snippets that you can utilize through Visual Studio Code to speed up the creation process of your ARM templates and parameters files.

Then, we deployed the storage account in an Azure subscription and reviewed the deployment workflow of the ARM template.

Now that we have deployed our first ARM template, it is time to deep dive into the different scopes for your deployments.

CHAPTER 5

Deployment Scopes

In Chapter 4, we reviewed how to build your first Azure Resource Manager (ARM) template from scratch and how to deploy it to your Azure subscription within the scope of a resource group. This chapter will cover the various scopes in which you can target an Azure Resource Manager deployment and the differences between the scoped deployments.

The following are some of the topics included in this chapter:

- Understanding deployment scope

- Targeting your deployment to a resource group, subscription, management group, or tenant

- Working across scopes

The first step is to understand what *deployment* means in the Azure Resource Manager context. Azure Resource Manager was initially intended to have a consistent management layer in Azure to handle the creation, update, deletion, authentication, and authorization of requests, all through a unique API to achieve a consistent output through all the tools that can be utilized to perform deployment requests in Azure.

This means you can use your preferred tool such as Azure PowerShell, Azure CLI, REST clients, or the Azure portal to provision the services in Azure that you need for your environment, and Azure Resource Manager will handle the requests to complete the tasks needed whether you need to create, update, or delete a resource.

A *resource* is meant to be any item that can be managed and available in Azure, such as a storage account, virtual machine, web app, subscription, resource group, and so on.

Therefore, it is essential to be aware that you can specify the scope of the deployment of your ARM template. There are various scopes that you can target for your deployment, including the following:

- Management groups

- Subscriptions

© David Rendón 2022
D. Rendón, *Building Applications with Azure Resource Manager (ARM)*,
https://doi.org/10.1007/978-1-4842-7747-8_5

- Resource groups

- Resources

Figure 5-1 highlights the four levels of scope.

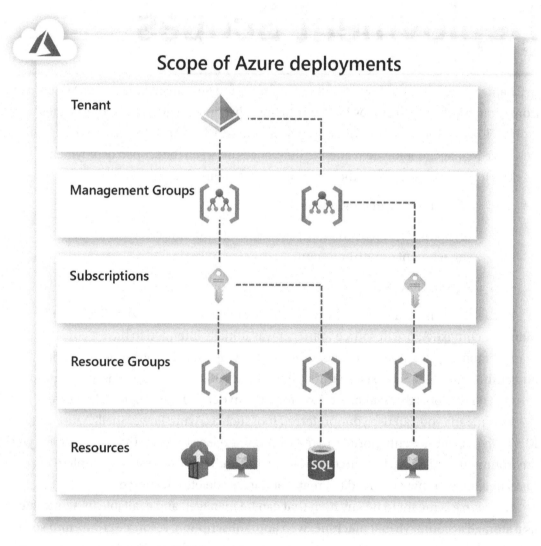

Figure 5-1. *Scopes of Azure deployments*

Depending on your needs, you can deploy your ARM templates to a specific tenant, management group, subscription, or resource group.

To better understand the different deployment scopes, let's proceed to work on some practical examples. In this chapter, we will look at the definitions of the deployment scopes supported by your ARM templates, including resource groups, subscriptions, management groups, and tenants.

Note   You can always combine these scopes in your ARM template as needed, and for every scope, you will need to have the proper permissions to create resources.

Targeting Your Deployment to a Resource Group

As mentioned at the beginning of this chapter, one of the deployment options is to target your deployment to a resource group. This is useful when working with resources with the same life-cycle management and that are deployed in the same resource group.

You can use the PowerShell command shown in Listing 5-1 to specify the deployment scope to a resource group.

Listing 5-1. PowerShell Command to Deploy to a Resource Group

```
New-AzResourceGroupDeployment -ResourceGroupName <resource-group-name>
-TemplateFile <path-to-template-or-bicep>
```

Using the command shown in Listing 5-1, you will be able to deploy your ARM template to the same resource group as many times as needed. Also, note that this command allows you to define either an ARM template or a Bicep file to deploy your resources.

Let's use the ARM template from Chapter 4 as our base template; in this ARM template, we defined a new storage account and a parameters file that includes our storage account's name and type properties.

To provision this ARM template, we will use the command shown in Listing 5-2.

Listing 5-2. PowerShell Command to Deploy an ARM Template to a Resource Group Scope

```
New-AzResourceGroupDeployment -Name "storage-account-deployment"
-ResourceGroupName "storage-resource-group" -TemplateFile .\azuredeploy
.json -TemplateParameterFile .\azuredeploy.parameters.json
```

As you can see in the previous code, we specify the deployment scope at the resource group level. This is the scope defined by default in Azure Resource Manager.

As a best practice, it is always good to provide a unique name to your deployments; this will allow you to better manage the history of deployments in your environment and quickly identify a specific deployment.

To provide a unique name to each of your deployments, you could assign a date value to your deployment name, as shown in Listing 5-3.

Listing 5-3. PowerShell Script to Add a Date Value to a Deployment

```
$date = Get-Date -Format "MM-dd-yyyy"
$deploymentName = "ExampleDeployment"+"$date"
```

Now, what's the real benefit of adding a date value to your deployment and having a unique name for each deployment? Let's use the following use case: the DevOps team from iFabrik must deploy four storage accounts to the same resource group in their Azure subscription to maintain a dedicated storage account per department. Each storage account will be utilized to store multiple files from these departments.

Suppose the engineers from this team decide to perform a deployment to provision a storage account and execute this deployment multiple times using the same deployment name. In that case, the result will be that there will be only one storage account.

Figure 5-2 shows the output of deploying a storage account using the same deployment name multiple times.

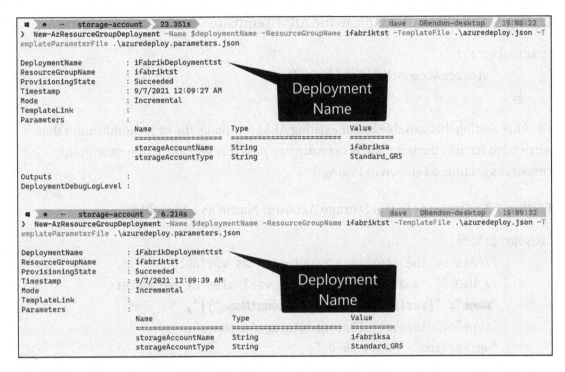

Figure 5-2. *Output of deploying a storage account*

Why did this happen? Well, when there's no definition of a unique deployment name, you immediately execute the deployment multiple times using the same deployment name. In reality, you are just overwriting the existing deployment.

On the other hand, two deployments via the same deployment name, using different storage account names, will result in two different storage accounts.

By specifying a unique name for each of your deployments, you will be able to perform concurrent deployments without running into any naming conflicts. In this case, by adding the date as a stamp to the deployment name, they will have a unique name for each deployment. This way, the DevOps team will be able to deploy the four storage accounts needed and avoid any conflict with the existing deployments. Also, the engineers from the DevOps team will be able to quickly find any specific deployment in the deployment history.

The other important piece here is that storage accounts must also have a unique name; therefore, we have to modify our ARM template to validate that each deployment has a unique name for the storage account.

To ensure we have a unique name for the storage account, we will define a variable in our ARM template and will leverage the uniqueString function that we will review in further chapters, as shown in Listing 5-4.

Listing 5-4. Adding a Variable to the ARM Template

```
"variables": {
        "storageAccountName": "ifabriksa"
    },
```

After adding this variable to our existing ARM template, the only modification that we need to have in the template is to ensure we pass this variable to the name in the resources section, as shown in Listing 5-5.

Listing 5-5. Passing On the Storage Account Name as a Variable

```
"resources": [{
        //Pass on the storage account name as variable
        // Use "[" and "]" to reference variables or parameters
        "name": "[variables('storageAccountName')]",
        "type": "Microsoft.Storage/storageAccounts",
        "apiVersion": "2019-06-01",
        "tags": {
            "displayName": "storageaccount1"
        },
        "location": "[resourceGroup().location]",
        "kind": "StorageV2",
        "sku": {
            //Pass on the storage account type as parameter
            "name": "[parameters('storageAccountType')]"
        }
    }],
```

Once we have these modifications in our ARM template, we will be able to deploy the same ARM template multiple times, even concurrently, without running into any naming conflicts. We will not override the existing storage account.

In reality, most of the time using the uniqueString function in a name is impractical since one of the IaC pillars is to ensure the same resource can be deployed repeatedly and as necessary.

The code in Listing 5-6 specifies the deployment scope to a resource group and provides a unique name to the deployment.

Listing 5-6. PowerShell Script to Add a Date Value to a Deployment

```
$date = Get-Date -Format "MM-dd-yyyy"
$deploymentName = "iFabrikDeployment"+"$date"
New-AzResourceGroupDeployment `
  -Name $deploymentName `
  -ResourceGroupName iFabrikRG `
  TemplateFile .\azuredeploy.json -TemplateParameterFile
  .\azuredeploy.parameters.json
```

Once you execute this script, you will find that the deployment contains the date value, and you will be able to execute the script multiple times and concurrently if needed.

You can get the new ARM template that we will use for this deployment from the following URL:

```
https://github.com/daveRendon/iac/tree/main/templates/storage-account-v2
```

In Listing 5-7 you will find the code to deploy a storage account. We will use this as an example to perform a deployment. Then, using PowerShell, we will target the deployment to a resource group level.

Listing 5-7. ARM Template to Deploy a Storage Account with a Unique ID

```
{
    "$schema": "https://schema.management.azure.com/schemas/2019-04-01/
    deploymentTemplate.json#",
    "contentVersion": "1.0.0.0",
    "parameters": {
        "storageAccountName": {
                "type": "string",
                "metadata": {
                    "description": "The name of the storage account, prefix
                    string to add to a generated string that is unique to
                    the resourceGroup."
                }
        },
        "storageAccountType":{
                "type": "string",
```

```
            "metadata": {
                "description": "Storage Account Type: Standard_LRS"
            },
            "allowedValues": [
                "Standard_LRS",
                "Standard_GRS",
                "Standard_ZRS",
                "Premium_LRS"
            ],
            "defaultValue": "Standard_LRS"

        }
    },
    "functions": [],
    "variables": {
        "storageAccountName": "[toLower( concat( parameters('storageAccount
        Name'), uniqueString(resourceGroup().id) ) )]"
    },
    "resources": [{
        //Pass on the storage account name as variable
        "name": "[variables('storageAccountName')]",
        "type": "Microsoft.Storage/storageAccounts",
        "apiVersion": "2019-06-01",
        "tags": {
            "displayName": "storageaccount1"
        },
        "location": "[resourceGroup().location]",
        "kind": "StorageV2",
        "sku": {
            //Pass on the storage account type as parameter
            "name": "[parameters('storageAccountType')]"
        }
    }],
    "outputs": {}
}
```

Listing 5-8 shows the parameters file definition.

Listing 5-8. Parameters File to Deploy a Storage Account with a Unique ID

```
{
    "$schema": "https://schema.management.azure.com/schemas/2019-04-01/
    deploymentParameters.json#",
    "contentVersion": "1.0.0.0",
    "parameters": {
        "storageAccountName": {
            "value": "ifabriksa"
        },
        "storageAccountType": {
            "value": "Standard_GRS"
        }
    }
}
```

Figure 5-3 shows the result of provisioning the ARM template using the script previously described.

```
DeploymentName          : iFabrikDeployment04-09-2021
ResourceGroupName       : iFabrikRG
ProvisioningState       : Succeeded
Timestamp               : 4/10/2021 1:16:37 AM
Mode                    : Incremental
TemplateLink            :
Parameters              :
                          Name                      Type                      Value
                          ====================      ========================  ==========
                          storageAccountName        String                    ifabriksa
                          storageAccountType        String                    Standard_GRS
```

Figure 5-3. *ARM template deployment result*

Note   Azure stores the deployment data in the location defined in the resource group.

Now that we have reviewed how to target the deployment scope to a resource group from the operation, we will review how you can target other resource groups that live in the same Azure subscription.

Target Your Deployment Scope to Other Resource Groups in the Same Subscription

Another common use case when working in Azure environments is the ability to provision services across different resource groups that live in the same Azure subscription. You can do so by defining a new object in your ARM template and including the resourceGroup property as shown in Listing 5-9.

Listing 5-9. ARM Template with Nested Deployment Target

```
{
    "$schema": "https://schema.management.azure.com/schemas/2019-04-01/
    deploymentTemplate.json#",
    "contentVersion": "1.0.0.0",
    "resources": [
        {
            "type": "Microsoft.Resources/deployments",
            "apiVersion": "2020-06-01",
            "name": "nestedDeployment",
            "resourceGroup": "myAltResourceGroup",
            "properties": {
                "mode": "Incremental",
                "template": {
                    <resource-group-resources>
                }
            }
        }
    ],
    "outputs": {}
}
```

Note   Ensure that you specify the resource group and that the resource group is created before the deployment phase.

Let's go through a practical example of how you can deploy a storage account to multiple resource groups in the same subscription. We will use the previous ARM template as our base template to deploy our resources.

Use Case: Deploy a Storage Account to Multiple Resource Groups in the Same Subscription

In this use case, the iFabrik DevOps team needs to provision two storage accounts across different resource groups. Each storage account must have a unique identifier, and resources can be provisioned on the same deployment.

The first step is to open our previous ARM template; we will add new parameters in the parameters section.

Note   You can leverage the code snippet to add a new parameter in your ARM template. You can type new-parameter and press Enter to quickly add your parameters.

Once you have your ARM template, we will type new-parameter and press Enter to quickly add the new parameter, as shown in Figure 5-4.

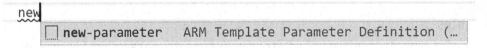

Figure 5-4. *Adding a parameter in the ARM template*

This will create the snippet shown in Listing 5-10.

Listing 5-10. Parameter Definition

```
"parameter1": {
            "type": "string",
            "metadata": {
                "description": "description"
            }
        }
    }
```

We will add two new parameters, secondResourceGroup and secondStorageLocation, as shown in Listing 5-11.

Listing 5-11. Parameters Definition

```
        "secondResourceGroup": {
            "type": "string",
            "metadata": {
                "description": "description"
            }
        },
    }
```

Now that we have these parameters defined, the next step is to add a variable for our second storage account. Listing 5-12 highlights the definition for our second storage account.

Listing 5-12. Definition of the Variables for Two Storage Accounts in ARM Template

```
"variables": {
        "storageAccountName1": "[toLower( concat( parameters('storageAccount
        Name'), uniqueString(resourceGroup().id) ) )]",
            "storageAccountName2": "[toLower( concat( parameters('
            storageAccountName'), uniqueString(parameters('second
            ResourceGroup')) ) )]"
    },
```

Now that we have defined the variables for the storage accounts, we will add the definition for the second storage account in the resources section of the ARM template. We will use the snippet by using new-arm-nested-template, as shown in Figure 5-5.

```
ne|
{   ☐ arm-nested-template-inner
    ☐ arm-nested-template…    Nested (inline) Outer-Scoped…
```

Figure 5-5. *Adding a nested template outer-scoped*

This snippet will help us create the definition of properties in our nested template. Once you press Enter, you will add the additional object definition, as shown in Listing 5-13.

Listing 5-13. Nested Deployment Snippet

```
{
        "name": "nestedDeployment1",
        "type": "Microsoft.Resources/deployments",
        "apiVersion": "2020-10-01",
        "properties": {
            "expressionEvaluationOptions": {
                "scope": "inner"
            },
            "mode": "Incremental",
            "parameters": {
            },
            "template": {
                "$schema": "https://schema.management.azure.com/
                schemas/2019-04-01/deploymentTemplate.json#",
                "contentVersion": "1.0.0.0",
                "parameters": {},
                "variables": {},
                "resources": [],
                "outputs": {}
            }
        }
    }
```

The next step is to define the second resource group; we will add the resourceGroup object and pass it as a parameter, as shown in Listing 5-14.

Listing 5-14. Defining the Second Resource Group in the ARM Template

```
{
        "name": "nestedDeployment1",
        "type": "Microsoft.Resources/deployments",
        "apiVersion": "2020-10-01",
        "resourceGroup": "[parameters('secondResourceGroup')]",
        "properties": {
            "expressionEvaluationOptions": {
                "scope": "inner"
            },
            "mode": "Incremental",
            "parameters": {},
            "template": {
                "$schema": "https://schema.management.azure.com/
                schemas/2019-04-01/deploymentTemplate.json#",
                "contentVersion": "1.0.0.0",
                "parameters": {},
                "variables": {},
                "resources": [],
                "outputs": {}
            }
        }
}
```

Now we will work on the definition of the second storage account in the `resources` section of the nested template. Expand the `resources` section, type `arm-storage`, and select the storage snippet shown in Figure 5-6.

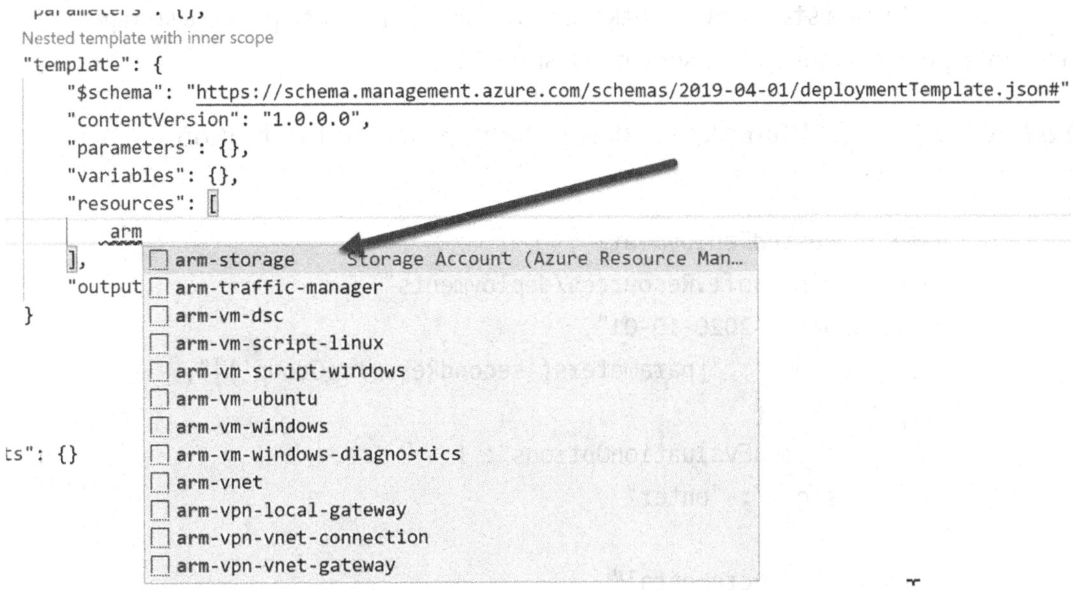

```
par ameters · {}}
```
Nested template with inner scope
```
"template": {
    "$schema": "https://schema.management.azure.com/schemas/2019-04-01/deploymentTemplate.json#"
    "contentVersion": "1.0.0.0",
    "parameters": {},
    "variables": {},
    "resources": [
        arm
    ],
    "output
}
```
```
ts": {}
```

arm-storage   Storage Account (Azure Resource Man...
arm-traffic-manager
arm-vm-dsc
arm-vm-script-linux
arm-vm-script-windows
arm-vm-ubuntu
arm-vm-windows
arm-vm-windows-diagnostics
arm-vnet
arm-vpn-local-gateway
arm-vpn-vnet-connection
arm-vpn-vnet-gateway

Figure 5-6. *Adding a storage snippet*

This action will define the properties for a new storage account, as shown in Listing 5-15.

Listing 5-15. Storage Account Snippet in Nested Template

```
"resources": [
                {
                    "name": "storageaccount1",
                    "type": "Microsoft.Storage/storageAccounts",
                    "apiVersion": "2019-06-01",
                    "tags": {
                        "displayName": "storageaccount1"
                    },
                    "location": "[resourceGroup().location]",
                    "kind": "StorageV2",
                    "sku": {
                        "name": "Premium_LRS",
                        "tier": "Premium"
                    }
                }
            ],
```

Next we will pass `storageAccountName2` as a variable and also pass the storage account type as a parameter, as shown in Listing 5-16.

Listing 5-16. Nested Template with New Storage Account Definition

```
{
        "name": "nestedDeployment1",
        "type": "Microsoft.Resources/deployments",
        "apiVersion": "2020-10-01",
        "resourceGroup": "[parameters('secondResourceGroup')]",
        "properties": {
            "expressionEvaluationOptions": {
                "scope": "outer"
            },
            "mode": "Incremental",
            "parameters": {},
            "template": {
                "$schema": "https://schema.management.azure.com/schemas/
                2019-04-01/deploymentTemplate.json#",
                "contentVersion": "1.0.0.0",
                "parameters": {},
                "variables": {},
                "resources": [
                    {
                        //Pass on the storage account name as variable
                        "name": "[variables('storageAccountName2')]",
                        "type": "Microsoft.Storage/storageAccounts",
                        "apiVersion": "2019-06-01",
                        "tags": {
                            "displayName": "storageaccount2"
                        },
                        "location": "[resourceGroup().location]",
                        "kind": "StorageV2",
                        "sku": {
                            //Pass on the storage account type as parameter
                            "name": "[parameters('storageAccountType')]"
```

```
                    }
                }
            ],
            "outputs": {}
        }
    }
}
],
```

Now all we have to do is to add the secondResourceGroup definition in the parameters file, as shown in Listing 5-17.

Listing 5-17. Parameters File

```
{
    "$schema": "https://schema.management.azure.com/schemas/2019-04-01/
    deploymentParameters.json#",
    "contentVersion": "1.0.0.0",
    "parameters": {
        "storageAccountName": {
            "value": "ifabriksa"
        },
        "storageAccountType": {
            "value": "Standard_GRS"
        },
        "secondResourceGroup": {
            "value": "iFabrikSecondRG"
        }
    }
}
```

Now let's go ahead and perform a new deployment of the ARM template using the script shown in Listing 5-18.

Listing 5-18. Deployment to Multiple Resource Groups in the Same Subscription

```
New-AzResourceGroupDeployment -Name $deploymentName -ResourceGroupName
iFabrikRG -TemplateFile .\azuredeploy.json -TemplateParameterFile
.\azuredeploy.parameters.json
```

Once the deployment is complete, you should see that the two storage accounts were successfully created in two different resource groups in the same subscription, as shown in Figure 5-7.

```
DeploymentName        : iFabrikDeployment04-09-2021
ResourceGroupName     : iFabrikRG
ProvisioningState     : Succeeded
Timestamp             : 4/10/2021 2:45:27 AM
Mode                  : Incremental
TemplateLink          :
Parameters            :
                        Name                      Type                          Value
                        ====================      ==========================    ==========
                        storageAccountName        String                        ifabriksa
                        storageAccountType        String                        Standard_GRS
                        secondResourceGroup       String                        iFabrikSecondRG
```

Figure 5-7. *Deployment results*

Note that we have defined the deployment scope to the resource group in the operation, and we have used a nested template to define the additional resource group to deploy our storage account.

Probably you have already thought of an additional deployment scope option, which is the ability to define the scope to a resource group that lives in a different subscription. Yes, it is possible to define the deployment scope to target a resource group that lives in a different subscription

Targeting Your Deployment to a Resource Group in a Different Subscription

This deployment scope option is a bit similar to the last one we reviewed. In this case, we can use a nested template and include two new properties, subscriptionID and resourceGroup, as shown in Listing 5-19.

Listing 5-19. Definition of subscriptionID and resourceGroup Properties in ARM Template

```
{
      "name": "nestedDeployment1",
      "type": "Microsoft.Resources/deployments",
      "apiVersion": "2020-10-01",
      "resourceGroup": "[parameters('secondResourceGroup')]",
      "subscriptionId": "xxxxxxxx-xxxx-xxxx-xxxx-xxxxxxxx",
      "properties": {
          "expressionEvaluationOptions": {
              "scope": "outer"
          },
          "mode": "Incremental",
          "parameters": {},
          "template": {
              "$schema": "https://schema.management.azure.com/
              schemas/2019-04-01/deploymentTemplate.json#",
              "contentVersion": "1.0.0.0",
              "parameters": {},
              "variables": {},
              "resources": [
                  {
                      //Pass on the storage account name as variable
                      "name": "[variables('storageAccountName2')]",
                      "type": "Microsoft.Storage/storageAccounts",
                      "apiVersion": "2019-06-01",
                      "tags": {
                          "displayName": "storageaccount2"
                      },
                      "location": "[resourceGroup().location]",
                      "kind": "StorageV2",
                      "sku": {
                          //Pass on the storage account type as parameter
                          "name": "[parameters('storageAccountType')]"
                      }
```

```
                }
            ],
            "outputs": {}
        }
    }
}
```

Now that we have gone through the resource group deployment scope and its multiple variants, it is time to look at some additional use cases to target deployments in a subscription scope.

Targeting Your Deployment to a Subscription

When targeting your deployments to a subscription, you must specify the target at the operation level. This means we can use our existing ARM template and utilize the command shown in Listing 5-20 to define the subscription scope during the deployment operation.

Listing 5-20. PowerShell Script to Perform a Deployment in a Given Subscription

```
New-AzSubscriptionDeployment `
  -Name mySubscriptionDeployment `
  -Location westus `
  -TemplateUri <your-template> `
  -rgName myResourceGroup `
  -rgLocation westus
```

Note You can also use the alias New-AzSubscriptionDeployment.

For this kind of deployment, note that there is a location defined in the script because you must specify a location for the deployment that is immutable and independent of the location of the resources you plan to deploy. The information related to the deployment is stored as metadata in the resource group targeted.

Targeting Your Deployment to Multiple Subscriptions

Let's analyze the following use case. The iFabrik DevOps team uses two Azure subscriptions in the same tenant. They have to deploy shared resources like DNS and networking services to each of these subscriptions.

Instead of manually creating the resources needed per subscription for this kind of task, it is possible to define the deployment scope for multiple subscriptions in the same tenant in the ARM template.

Like the case where we deployed the storage accounts across multiple resource groups, we can leverage nested templates, specify the `subscriptionID` property in the ARM template, and define the location in this nested template.

Listing 5-21 shows the example of the nested ARM template that the iFabrik DevOps team could utilize to provision the two storage accounts in two different subscriptions, one storage account per subscription in the same deployment.

Listing 5-21. ARM Template to Deploy Two Storage Accounts, One per Subscription

```
{
        "name": "nestedDeployment1",
        "type": "Microsoft.Resources/deployments",
        "apiVersion": "2020-10-01",
        "resourceGroup": "[parameters('secondResourceGroup')]",
        "subscriptionId": "xxxxxxxx-xxxx-xxxx-xxxx-xxxxxxxxxxxx",
        "location": "westus",
        "properties": {
            "expressionEvaluationOptions": {
                "scope": "outer"
            },
            "mode": "Incremental",
            "parameters": {},
            "template": {
                "$schema": "https://schema.management.azure.com/
                schemas/2019-04-01/deploymentTemplate.json#",
                "contentVersion": "1.0.0.0",
                "parameters": {},
```

```
            "variables": {},
            "resources": [
                {
                    //Pass on the storage account name as variable
                    "name": "[variables('storageAccountName2')]",
                    "type": "Microsoft.Storage/storageAccounts",
                    "apiVersion": "2019-06-01",
                    "tags": {
                        "displayName": "storageaccount2"
                    },
                    "location": "[resourceGroup().location]",
                    "kind": "StorageV2",
                    "sku": {
                        //Pass on the storage account type as parameter
                        "name": "[parameters('storageAccountType')]"
                    }
                }
            ],
            "outputs": {}
        }
    }
}
```

To perform this deployment, we will utilize the script shown in Listing 5-22.

Listing 5-22. Azure Subscription Deployment Using PowerShell

```
$date = Get-Date -Format "MM-dd-yyyy"
$deploymentName = "iFabrikDeployment"+"$date"
New-AzSubscriptionDeployment -Name $deploymentName -Location eastus
-TemplateFile .\azuredeploy.json -TemplateParameterFile
.\azuredeploy.parameters.json
```

Note   You need to ensure you have the right permissions and roles assigned to be able to provision resources to a different subscription. You can deploy resources to multiple subscriptions within the same tenant.

It is also possible to target your deployment to a specific management group. Think of management groups as containers that will help you have better management capabilities for your Azure subscriptions in your tenant.

Targeting Your Deployment to a Management Group

In each Azure account hierarchy, management groups are above the subscription level. Therefore, you will have a root management group, and the next level is a management group. You can nest multiple management groups or have multiple subscriptions below a management group, as shown in Figure 5-8.

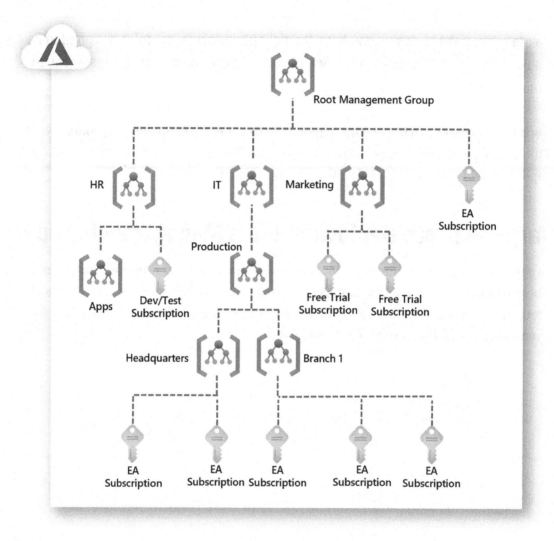

Figure 5-8. *Management group hierarchy*

That said, it is possible to define the deployment scope to a specific management group by using the command shown in Listing 5-23.

Listing 5-23. PowerShell Command to Deploy to a Management Group

```
New-AzManagementGroupDeployment `
  -Name demoMGDeployment `
  -Location "West US" `
  -ManagementGroupId "myMG" `
  -TemplateUri <your-template>
```

By default, when you define the resources you want to deploy in the resources section of your ARM template, those resources will be included in the default management group, as shown in Listing 5-24.

Listing 5-24. Example of the Scope for Management Groups in an ARM Template

```
{
    "$schema": "https://schema.management.azure.com/schemas/2019-04-01/
    deploymentTemplate.json#",
    "contentVersion": "1.0.0.0",
    "parameters": {},
    "functions": [],
    "variables": {},
    "resources": [
        <Management Group resources>
    ],
    "outputs": {}
}
```

You can also target your resources to a different management group in the same subscription by using nested templates, defining the property scope, and passing on the value in a variable using the format Microsoft.Management/managementGroups/ <your-management-group-name>.

Let's see an example of an ARM template that defines the scope to a different management group; see Listing 5-25. In this template, we will define a parameter for the management group. We will add a variable to pass on the scope property, and then we will add the nested template in which we will define the scope property and the location for our deployment.

Listing 5-25. Scope Deployment to a Different Management Group

```
{
    "$schema": "https://schema.management.azure.com/schemas/2019-08-01/
    managementGroupDeploymentTemplate.json#",
    "contentVersion": "1.0.0.0",
    "parameters": {
```

```
        "managementGroupName": {
            "type": "string"
        }
    },
    "variables": {
        "managementGroupId": "[concat('Microsoft.Management/
        managementGroups/', parameters('managementGroupName'))]"
    },
    "resources": [
        {
            "type": "Microsoft.Resources/deployments",
            "apiVersion": "2019-10-01",
            "name": "nestedDeployment",
            "scope": "[variables('managementGroupId')]",
            "location": "eastus",
            "properties": {
                "mode": "Incremental",
                "template": {
                    // Define the resources for the management group
                }
            }
        }
    ],
    "outputs": {}
}
```

Note   To create management groups in your template, you should define a different schema: `"$schema": "https://schema.management.azure.com/ schemas/2019-08-01/managementGroupDeploymentTemplate.json#"`.

Now that we've gone through the scope for management groups, the last option we will review is the tenant deployment scope.

Targeting Your Deployment to a Tenant

In the context of Azure, a *tenant* represents a dedicated instance of Azure Active Directory (Azure AD), and it refers to a single organization. Within a tenant we can configure users, groups, and applications to be able to perform identity and access management functions.

You can define the deployment scope to a tenant by using the schema shown in Listing 5-26.

Listing 5-26. Tenant Deployment Scope

```
"$schema":"https://schema.management.azure.com/schemas/2019-08-01/
tenantDeploymentTemplate.json#"
```

By using this schema, you can define your resources under the `resources` section of your ARM template, and they will be applied to a tenant scope. It is also possible to combine the scopes. For example, if needed, you could define the schema for the tenant scope and then scope to a specific management group later in your template.

You can do this by defining a variable in the template that references the management group name and then use a nested template that defines the scope for the management group and the location, as shown in Listing 5-27.

Listing 5-27. Scope to Management Groups Within a Tenant

```
{
    "$schema": "https://schema.management.azure.com/schemas/2019-08-01/
    tenantDeploymentTemplate.json#",
    "contentVersion": "1.0.0.0",
    "parameters": {
        "managementGroupName": {
            "type": "string"
        }
    },
    "variables": {
        "managementGroupId": "[concat('Microsoft.Management/
        managementGroups/', parameters('managementGroupName'))]"
    },
```

```
    "resources": [
        {
            "type": "Microsoft.Resources/deployments",
            "apiVersion": "2020-06-01",
            "name": "nestedManagementGroup",
            "scope": "[variables('managementGroupId')]",
            "location": "eastus",
            "properties": {
                "mode": "Incremental",
                "template": {
                    //Your Management Group Resources
                }
            }
        }
    ],
    "outputs": {}
}
```

When working at a tenant level, you can apply configurations such as policies and role assignments at a global level. It is recommended that you leverage a service principal to deploy templates and avoid any permission conflicts during the deployment operation.

Targeting to a subscription level, you can better secure and prevent cross-subscription deployments when not applicable.

You can use the PowerShell command in Listing 5-28 to deploy your ARM template and scope it at a tenant level.

Listing 5-28. PowerShell Command to Deploy Template at Tenant Level

```
New-AzTenantDeployment `
  -Name iFabrikTenantDeployment `
  -Location "West US" `
  -TemplateUri "Your-template-location"
```

As you can see, we have the flexibility to define the scope at multiple levels of the hierarchy of Azure Resource Manager and combine scopes as needed.

Summary

In this chapter, we reviewed how we can define the scope of our deployment at different levels including at the resource group, subscription, management group, and tenant levels.

Also, we can work across these scopes by defining the proper schema and leveraging nested templates in which we will define the additional scope that we want to work with; we then pass the variables needed by referring to the name and/or ID of the resources.

In the next chapter, we will review in detail what are we referring to when we talk about *parameters* and how you can leverage them in your ARM templates.

CHAPTER 6

Working with Parameters on Your ARM Template

This chapter will cover how to integrate parameters in your Azure Resource Manager (ARM) templates. We will go over how to create an Azure Resource Manager template with parameters, how to define parameter values, show concrete examples to emphasize the different ways you can use parameters within an ARM template so that you can understand better how parameters work, and describe how to leverage variables on your ARM templates based on the environment's needs.

These are some of the topics covered in this chapter:

- Introduction to parameters in your ARM template

- Creating unique identifiers for your parameters

- Utilizing objects as parameters in your ARM template

We can define multiple resources in our ARM templates and specify the value and type of our resources; for example, in our last template, we defined the storage account type and the location for our storage account. Similarly, we can leverage parameters to define the value or type of a specific resource that we need to include in our ARM template.

Introduction to Parameters in Your ARM Template

Parameters are a great way to provide values for resources in our ARM template. Using parameters comes in handy when considering complex deployments as we can reuse them as needed for multiple environments.

81

© David Rendón 2022
D. Rendón, *Building Applications with Azure Resource Manager (ARM)*,
https://doi.org/10.1007/978-1-4842-7747-8_6

When you work with ARM templates, it is a best practice to modularize your ARM templates. Having a modular approach will allow you to reuse an ARM template across multiple environments. Parameters will help you to handle your ARM template in a more dynamic way. For instance, when deploying multiple virtual machines, you will probably need to specify the size of the virtual machine and the disk type.

Hard-coding these types of values in your ARM templates will limit the ability to reuse them for multiple purposes.

Instead, we can leverage parameters, use a separate file to define the values of the parameters, and pass these values in your ARM template to be more dynamic inside your ARM template.

This will give you the flexibility to inject values in your ARM template as needed and save you some time when working with multiple definitions of resources in more complex environments.

Figure 6-1 highlights the definition of the parameters that should be included in the ARM template and, in a separate file, the definition of the actual values or references for the parameters.

Figure 6-1. *Definition of ARM template (left) and parameters file (right)*

Note   Parameter values are resolved by Azure Resource Manager before the deployment operation and can be included in the ARM template or Bicep file.

Parameters can include one of the following data types:

- array
- bool
- int
- object
- secureObject
- secureString
- string

Working with the array Data Type

Let's take a look at a definition of an array; see Listing 6-1.

Listing 6-1. Parameters, Array Definition

```
"parameters": {
  "myArray": {
    "type": "array",
    "defaultValue": [
      1,
      2,
      3
    ]
  }
},
```

A quick and simple example can be the definition of the allowed values for your storage account; see Listing 6-2.

Listing 6-2. Parameters, Array Definition for Storage Account Types

```
"storageAccountType":{
                "type": "string",
                "allowedValues": [
                    "Standard_LRS",
                    "Standard_GRS",
                    "Standard_ZRS",
                    "Premium_LRS"
                ],
                "defaultValue": "Standard_LRS"

        }
```

In the previous code, we have defined an array for the storage account type. Note that we can define a value per line and include the property for the default value in case no value is declared during the deployment operation.

It is also possible to include different element types as elements in your array; see Listing 6-3 for an example.

Listing 6-3. Array with Different Types

```
"parameters": {
  "yourMixedArray": [
    "[resourceGroup().name]",
    1,
    false,
    "this is a simple array example with elements of different types"
  ]
}
```

Now that we have reviewed a quick example of arrays, let's look at the definition for bool values.

Working with the bool Data Type

While the `bool` type usually refers to a function in an ARM template, we can define it in the `parameters` section and provide a default value, as shown in Listing 6-4.

Listing 6-4. Parameters, bool Value

```
"parameters": {
  "exampleBool": {
    "type": "bool",
    "defaultValue": true
  }
},
```

Now let's take a quick look at specifying integer values.

Working with the int Data Type

When working with integers or `bool,` there's no need to use quotation marks, as shown in Listing 6-5.

Listing 6-5. Parameters, Working with Integers

```
"parameters": {
  "exampleInt": {
    "type": "int",
    "defaultValue": 1
  }
}
```

We can also define the allowed values for the parameter in an array of `int` values.

Let's check a quick example: We need to deploy an application gateway instance. Therefore, we have to define the "gateway capacity" for this parameter. We could define a type `int` and also define an array for the "allowed values," as shown in Listing 6-6.

Listing 6-6. Parameters, int Type and Array

```
"applicationGatewayCapacity": {
    "type": "int",
    "allowedValues": [
        1,
        2,
        3,
```

```
      4,
      5,
      6,
      7,
      8,
      9,
      10
    ],
    "defaultValue": 4,
    "metadata": {
      "description": "Specifies the number of the application gateway
      instances."
    }
  },
```

As you can see in the previous code, we can define the type as an integer while adding an array of the possible values specified to the resource. It is also important to always add the defaultValue when working with this type of array.

What if we need to define a different type of object that can include custom values? Well, we also have the option to leverage the object data type.

Working with the object Data Type

The parameter type object in your ARM template can help you define custom values and multiple properties where a comma separates each property. The definition of this data type always starts with a left brace and ends with a right brace, and you can define custom keys and values, as shown in Listing 6-7.

Listing 6-7. Definition of Data Type: object in the parameters Section of an ARM Template

```
"parameters": {
  "exampleObject": {
    "type": "object",
    "defaultValue": {
      "name": "object name",
```

```
      "id": "123-abc",
      "isCurrent": false,
      "tier": 1
    }
  }
}
```

When should we consider using this object type? That's a valid question that you probably are thinking about already.

This data type can help you simplify the definition of the parameters that should be specified on the resources. As a quick example, we can consider the deployment of a virtual network.

An Azure virtual network usually includes the actual definition of the Azure virtual network, the network address prefixes, the subnet names, and the address prefixes for the subnets.

Although you could use a parameter for each property for your Azure virtual network, you can leverage the object type to include all the properties and subproperties for the virtual network in a single parameter.

In your ARM template, you can define the object type as vnetSettings and then specify all the parameters values in the parameters file, as shown in Listing 6-8.

Listing 6-8. Definition of the object Type in the ARM Template

```
"parameters": {
    "vnetSettings":{"type":"object"}
},
```

Then you can define the actual parameter values for the vnetSettings in your parameters file. Listing 6-9 highlights this example.

Listing 6-9. Use of object Data Type to Define a Virtual Network Properties in the Parameters File

```
"parameters":{
    //Properties of this object, specified in the ARM template
    "vnetSettings":{
        "value":{
            //subproperty
```

```
        "name":"yourVnet",
        //subproperty
        "addressPrefixes": [
            {
                "name": "firstPrefix",
                "addressPrefix": "10.0.0.0/16"
            }
        ],
        //subproperty
        "subnets":[
            {
                "name": "firstSubnet",
                "addressPrefix": "10.0.0.0/24"
            },
            {
                "name":"secondSubnet",
                "addressPrefix":"10.0.1.0/24"
            }
        ]
    }
  }
}
```

By using object types, you can simplify the definition of the parameters and be more dynamic in your ARM templates. Note that now we will need to pass on the values defined in the resources section of the ARM template.

We will deep dive into how you can reference these values in the resources section in your ARM template later in this chapter. Now let's review the string data type.

Working with the string Data Type

Strings are the most common data type used in ARM templates. Listing 6-10 highlights the use of the string type in the parameters section of the ARM template.

Listing 6-10. Definition of string in Parameters

```
"parameters": {
  "exampleString": {
    "type": "string",
    "defaultValue": "this is my string"
  }
},
```

A quick example of the use of strings is when deploying a new virtual machine, you can define the authentication type, which can include values like sshPublicKey or password, as shown in Listing 6-11.

Listing 6-11. Use of string Data Type

```
"authenticationType": {
      "type": "string",
      "defaultValue": "sshPublicKey",
      "allowedValues": [
        "sshPublicKey",
        "password"
      ],
      "metadata": {
        "description": "Type of authentication to use on the Virtual
        Machine. SSH key is recommended."
      }
    },
```

Note that we have defined the type string and included a default value, which is the sshPublicKey for our new virtual machine, and you can define the allowed values as an array and add values like sshPublicKey or password, as shown in the previous code.

At this point, I hope you are getting more familiar with how you can work with parameters in your ARM templates. A prevalent question that often comes up with secrets or passwords is, how can we pass on these secrets as parameters without exposing the actual secret value?

We can leverage two data types, secureObject and secureString, to pass values in sensitive parameters in the environment. These parameter values are not exposed nor stored in deployment history. Let's see how we can work with these two data types.

Working with the secureString Data Type

Working with the secureString data type is similar to the string type. The secureString data type is often utilized to pass on passwords and secrets securely.

Listing 6-12 highlights how you can define a secureString in your parameters.

Listing 6-12. Use of secureString

```
"parameters": {
  "password": {
    "type": "secureString"
  }
}
```

As you can see, we define a secureString similarly to how we define a string. Let's review a quick example. Consider the use case when you're deploying a virtual machine and need to pass the password for the administrator of that virtual machine. It is possible to use the secureString for this case, as shown in Listing 6-13.

Listing 6-13. Using secureString for the Password of a Virtual Machine Administrator

```
"vmAdminPassword": {
      "type": "securestring",
      "metadata": {
        "description": "Set this value for the VM admin user password"
      }
```

Now, how do we pass on the password value? That's a good point; we can define in the parameters file the parameter and reference the actual value of the password.

In the parameters file, we can add a parameter value as shown here:

```
"vmAdminPassword": {
    "defaultValue": "P!!w0rda1234",
        "type": "securestring"
  },
```

It is a best practice to leverage Key Vault, which will be reviewed in Chapter 15; Key Vault is a secret management service available in Azure to reference the passwords of a virtual machine, as shown in Listing 6-14.

Listing 6-14. Referencing Key Vault for the Password of the Virtual Machine

```
"vmAdminPassword": {
  "reference": {
    "keyVault": {
        "id": "/subscriptions/{guid}/resourceGroups/{your-group-name}/
        providers/Microsoft.KeyVault/vaults/{your-vault-name}"
                },
        "secretName": "<the password secret from the keyVault> e.g.
        vmAdminPassword"
            }
},
```

You could also include some of the values like guid and vault-name as parameters in the parameters file to save some time updating those values in the next deployment.

The actual secret values that are referenced as parameters in your ARM template are not stored in the deployment history or exposed to the user. Therefore, using this reference for Key Vault is a secure tactic to leverage when working with this data type.

Now let's see how you can leverage the secureObject data type.

Working with the secureObject Data Type

The secureObject data type is typically utilized when there's a need to refer to a specific configuration of a resource type that can contain the definition of multiple properties or subproperties and that can include sensitive information.

A quick example of this data type includes the definition of a parameter that can include the reference for the password of a database or even multiple secrets in the same secureObject definition so that the engineer can reuse the same parameter values in the template as needed.

The code in Listing 6-15 highlights the use of the `secureObject` data type to create a range of secrets that can be stored in a Key Vault service and then refer to this Key Vault for the rest of the deployment.

Listing 6-15. Use of secureObject

```
"secretsObject": {
  "type": "secureObject",
  "defaultValue": {
    "secrets": [
      {
        "secretName": "mySecret1",
        "secretValue": "secretVaule1"
      },
      {
        "secretName": "mySecret2",
        "secretValue": "secretValue2"
      }
    ]
  }
}
```

At this point, we have gone through multiple use cases, and probably you already noticed that the more parameters we define, the more careful we must be when defining unique identifiers for those parameters.

Note   When there is no need to specify the value of properties during the deployment operation, it is preferred to leverage the use of variables or hard-code the values for those properties.

Let's take a look at how we can create unique identifiers for the parameters we intend to use in our ARM templates.

Creating Unique Identifiers (IDs) for Your Parameters

Let's look at how we can create unique identifiers for the parameters we intend to use in our ARM templates.

Leveraging unique identifiers (IDs) for your parameters is a great way to easily identify parameter values for resource names and settings that might vary depending on the environment.

In previous chapters, we reviewed how you could add a unique ID for the deployment operation by using a variable that included the timestamp, which is a good practice that will help you quickly identify a specific deployment operation.

The critical question here is how we can guarantee that our parameter ID is globally unique? Azure Resource Manager provides various functions that we can leverage to create unique IDs for our parameters. These functions include the following:

- guid: This will create a value based on the parameters' values that can be used as a globally unique identifier.

- newGuid: This returns a value that can be utilized as a unique globally unique identifier.

While you would think that both functions work similarly, it is essential to note that guid should be used when there's a need to generate the same GUID for a given environment.

newGuid will be helpful in those cases in which there's a need to have a different ID each time you perform a deployment.

Another important difference is that newGuid will not take any parameter as a form factor to create the ID. When you perform a guid call for the same parameter, it will return the same ID every single time.

Let's look at the following example that includes a parameter that defines a parameter called guidValue and references the newGuid function. If you deploy this template, you will see in the output a value called guidOutput with a unique value, as shown in Listing 6-16.

Listing 6-16. Use of newGuid Function

```
{
  "$schema": "https://schema.management.azure.com/schemas/2019-04-01/
  deploymentTemplate.json#",
  "contentVersion": "1.0.0.0",
  "parameters": {
    "guidValue": {
      "type": "string",
      //use of newGuid function
      "defaultValue": "[newGuid()]"
    }
  },
  "resources": [
  ],
  "outputs": {
    "guidOutput": {
      "type": "string",
      "value": "[parameters('guidValue')]"
    }
  }
}
```

Figure 6-2 shows the output obtained from the previous ARM template.

guidOutput

8e3b57a0-c3a7-48b7-9761-03824c4db7e1

Figure 6-2. *Output from newGuid function*

How can we actually use this newGuid function? Let's take a practical example. In this example, we will refer to our previous ARM template that creates a new storage account.

In this ARM template, we will include the newGuid function to create a unique ID for our storage account, as shown in Listing 6-17.

Listing 6-17. ARM Template That Creates a Storage Account with Unique ID Using newGuid Function

```
{
    "$schema": "https://schema.management.azure.com/schemas/2019-04-01/
    deploymentTemplate.json#",
    "contentVersion": "1.0.0.0",
    "parameters": {
        "storageAccountName": {
                "type": "string",
                "metadata": {
                    "description": "The name of the storage account, prefix
                    string to add to a generated string that is unique to
                    the resourceGroup."
                }
        },
        "storageAccountType":{
            "type": "string",
            "metadata": {
                "description": "Storage Account Type: Standard_LRS"
            },
            "allowedValues": [
                "Standard_LRS",
                "Standard_GRS",
                "Standard_ZRS",
                "Premium_LRS"
            ],
            "defaultValue": "Standard_LRS"

        },
        "guidValue": {
            "type": "string",
            "defaultValue": "[newGuid()]",
            "metadata": {
                "description": "Unique globally value"
            }
```

```
            }
    },
    "functions": [],
    "variables": {
        "myStorageAccountName": "[toLower( concat( parameters(
        'storageAccountName'), uniqueString(parameters('guidValue')) ) )]"
    },
    "resources": [{
        //Pass on the storage account name as variable
        "name": "[variables('myStorageAccountName')]",
        "type": "Microsoft.Storage/storageAccounts",
        "apiVersion": "2019-06-01",
        "tags": {
            "displayName": "storageaccount1"
        },
        "location": "[resourceGroup().location]",
        "kind": "StorageV2",
        "sku": {
            //Pass on the storage account type as parameter
            "name": "[parameters('storageAccountType')]"
        }
    }],
    "outputs": {
        "outputStorageAccount": {
            "type": "string",
            "value": "[variables('myStorageAccountName')]"
        }
    }
}
```

As you can see, we are reusing our previous template, and we only added the new parameter and defined the newGuid function as a default value in the parameters section.

Listing 6-18 shows the parameters file related to the previous ARM template.

Listing 6-18. Parameters File

```
{
    "$schema": "https://schema.management.azure.com/schemas/2019-04-01/
    deploymentParameters.json#",
    "contentVersion": "1.0.0.0",
    "parameters": {
        "storageAccountName": {
            "value": "ifabriksa"
        },
        "storageAccountType": {
            "value": "Standard_GRS"
        }
    }
}
```

Note we didn't have to make any changes to the parameters file. Now to deploy our ARM template, we will be using PowerShell with the commands shown in Listing 6-19.

Listing 6-19. ARM Template Deployment

```
//Deployment definition
$date = Get-Date -Format "MM-dd-yyyy"
$deploymentName = "iFabrikDeployment"+"$date"

//Deploy to Resource Group
New-AzResourceGroupDeployment -Name $deploymentName -ResourceGroupName
iFabrikRG -TemplateFile .\azuredeploy.json -TemplateParameterFile
.\azuredeploy.parameters.json
```

Figure 6-3 shows the output from the deployment.

```
DeploymentName        : iFabrikDeployment04-24-2021
ResourceGroupName     : iFabrikRG
ProvisioningState     : Succeeded
Timestamp             : 4/25/2021 2:06:58 AM
Mode                  : Incremental
TemplateLink          :
Parameters            :
                        Name                     Type                         Value
                        ====================     =========================    ==========
                        storageAccountName       String                       ifabriksa
                        storageAccountType       String                       Standard_GRS
                        guidValue                String                       b3bcd8d4-5787-43ba-9271-7378d679aac4

Outputs               :
                        Name                     Type                         Value
                        ====================     =========================    ==========
                        outputStorageAccount     String                       ifabriksar53d4dt7q4pma
```

Figure 6-3. *Output from ARM template deployment*

The output shows the actual value of the storage account name compounded by the default name defined in the template as a parameter plus the unique identifier provided by the newGuid function.

You can refer to the following GitHub repository to review the ARM template utilized in the previous example: https://github.com/daveRendon/iac/tree/main/templates/create-storage-account-using-newGuid.

Now that we have reviewed how to utilize unique identifiers for our parameters, let's see how we can leverage objects as parameters in the ARM template.

Utilizing Objects as Parameters in Your ARM Template

Once you define the parameters using the object type, you can reference them in the resources section of your ARM template.

How can we reference the parameters' values in the ARM template? To reference the parameter values, we are going to leverage functions.

While we will dedicate an entire chapter to functions in ARM templates, we will go to the resources section in the ARM template now and delete the hard-coded values for the resource.

Let's use the following use case: the iFabrik team needs to deploy a virtual network with two subnets in the same Azure subscription and provide the developer team with the ability to define in a flexible way the address prefix and the name of the virtual network and subnets during the deployment operation.

To achieve this task, the iFabrik team can create an ARM template that includes the definition of parameters with object types and a separate file for the parameter values.

Let's reuse the example from the earlier section "Working with the object Data Type." In the ARM template we will define a parameter that leverages an object type that will help the dev team define the virtual network properties, as shown in Listing 6-20.

Listing 6-20. Definition of an Object in the Parameters Section in the ARM Template

```
"parameters": {
    "vnetSettings":{"type":"object"}
},
```

The next step is to create the parameters file and include the definition of the parameters' values for the virtual network, as shown in Listing 6-21.

Listing 6-21. Creation of Parameters File with the object Data Type

```
"parameters":{
    //Properties of this object, specified in the ARM template
    "vnetSettings":{
        "value":{
            //subproperty
            "name":"yourVnet",
            //subproperty
            "addressPrefixes": [
                {
                    "name": "firstPrefix",
                    "addressPrefix": "10.0.0.0/16"
                }
            ],
            //subproperty
            "subnets":[
                {
                    "name": "firstSubnet",
                    "addressPrefix": "10.0.0.0/24"
                },
```

```
                {
                    "name":"secondSubnet",
                    "addressPrefix":"10.0.1.0/24"
                }
            ]
        }
    }
}
```

Through the definition of the object for the virtual network parameter, the dev team will be able to modify the parameter values as best needed for the customization of the virtual network and its properties including the virtual network name, the address prefixes for the virtual network, the subnet names, and the address prefix for each of the subnets.

The last piece to complete our ARM template will be to reference the parameter values to the resources. Back in the ARM template, we can go to the resources section and then reference the parameter values using functions, which basically is done through a function, escaping the JSON ([), which tells Azure there is a function/parameter/variable to use. Then, use the function parameters and provide the object name and the property or subproperty, as shown in Listing 6-22.

Listing 6-22. Utilize objects as Parameters in Your ARM Template

```
//resources section of the ARM template
"resources": [
    {
        "apiVersion": "2015-06-15",
        "type": "Microsoft.Network/virtualNetworks",
        //delete hard-coded values, add square brackets [], use function
        parameters, refer object and property/subproperty
        "name": "[parameters('vnetSettings').name]",
        "location":"[resourceGroup().location]",
        "properties": {
          "addressSpace":{
                "addressPrefixes": [
//access to subproperties
"[parameters('vnetSettings').addressPrefixes[0].addressPrefix]"
```

```
            ]
        },
        "subnets":[
            {
                "name":"[parameters('vnetSettings').subnets[0].name]",
                "properties": {
                    "addressPrefix": "[parameters('VNetSettings').
                    subnets[0].addressPrefix]"
                }
            },
            {

                "name":"[parameters('vnetSettings').subnets[1].name]",
                "properties": {
                    "addressPrefix": "[parameters('vnetSettings').
                    subnets[1].addressPrefix]"
                }
            }
        ]
    }
  }
]
```

Leveraging objects as parameters is beneficial when working with multiple resources that need a specific definition of properties and subproperties and that can be defined beforehand or during the deployment operation.

Summary

This chapter reviewed how you can leverage parameters in your ARM template and why it is important to understand the different data types available for the parameters.

We also reviewed practical examples and best practices for passing parameters values in your ARM template and how you should leverage them to modularize your ARM templates so that they can be reused as many times as needed with little to no modification at all.

CHAPTER 7

Using Variables in Your ARM Template

This chapter will cover how to use variables to simplify the definition of your Azure Resource Manager (ARM) template; we will go over how to create an Azure Resource Manager template with variables and how to reference values and configuration variables. This chapter will also cover how to create multiple values for a variable in your template and how to integrate the copy function to perform iterations.

These are some of the topics in this chapter:

- Introduction to variables in your ARM template

- How to reference variable values

- How to leverage configuration variables

- Variable iteration

Let's do a quick recap of the template file structure; as you remember, the ARM template includes the following sections: schema, contentVersion, parameters, functions, variables, resources, and outputs. See Listing 7-1.

© David Rendón 2022
D. Rendón, *Building Applications with Azure Resource Manager (ARM)*,
https://doi.org/10.1007/978-1-4842-7747-8_7

Listing 7-1. ARM Template File Structure

```
{
    "$schema": "https://schema.management.azure.com/schemas/2019-04-01/
    deploymentTemplate.json#",
    "contentVersion": "1.0.0.0",
    "parameters": {},
    "functions": [],
    "variables": {},
    "resources": [],
    "outputs": {}
}
```

Now let's see how we can work with the variables section of our ARM template.

Introduction to Variables in Your ARM Template

Variables in your ARM templates behave the same way as variables in programming languages. You can use variables to store data values. The main difference between using variables rather than parameters is that there's no need to specify a data type for the variables you define.

The actual variable type will be inferred from the resolved value, and you can construct variables from parameters values. Isn't that great?

Let's look at how you can define variables in your ARM template. Listing 7-2 shows the definition of a variable named storageName and a value, in this case, ifabriksa.

Listing 7-2. Definition of a Variable in ARM Template

```
{
    "$schema": "https://schema.management.azure.com/schemas/2019-04-01/
    deploymentTemplate.json#",
    "contentVersion": "1.0.0.0",
    "parameters": {},
    "functions": [],
    "variables": {
        "storageName": "ifabriksa"
    },
```

```
    "resources": [],
    "outputs": {}
}
```

While we can hard-code the value of the variable, the main objective of using variables in ARM templates is to be able to reuse them as needed in our templates. Therefore, we have multiple options to define variables.

We can use parameters as a form factor for our variables, leverage functions to get parameter values, and create a unique string for our variable; we can also leverage arrays to define variables or define objects as variables. Another option to define variables is to use the copy element to represent multiple instances of our variable.

Simply put, there are multiple ways to define a variable, including the following:

- Hard-coding values

- Using parameters as a form factor

- Using arrays

- Using objects

- Using the copy element

Let's see how you can leverage parameters as a form factor to define variables in your ARM template.

Parameters as a Form Factor

We can define parameters in our ARM template and then use this value from the parameter to construct our variable using the concat function. In the following example, we will define a parameter for the storage name, and then in the variables section, we will use the concat function to define the variable. See Listing 7-3.

Listing 7-3. Define a Variable from a Parameter

```
"parameters": {
  "storageName": {
    "defaultValue": "ifabriksa",
    "type": "string"
  }
```

```
},
"variables": {
  "myVariable": "[concat(parameters('storageName'), 'addtoparam')]"
}
```

As highlighted in the previous code, you can define a parameter in your ARM template and then pass its actual value to a variable and concatenate it to create a unique identifier value.

Let's do a quick stop here; since we can pass parameters values to define a variable, would it be possible to define variables and use another variable as a form factor? Yes, it is possible. Listing 7-4 denotes the definition of a variable, which then will be used to define a different variable through the concat function.

Listing 7-4. Definition of a Variable Using the concat Function

```
"parameters": {
  "storageName": {
    "defaultValue": "ifabriksa",
    "type": "string"
  }
},
"variables": {
  "myVariable": "variable",
  "newVariable": "[concat(variables('myVariable'), '-addtovar') ]"
}
```

Now that we have seen how variables can be dynamically constructed in our ARM template using the concat function, let's see how we can leverage arrays in variables.

Use of Arrays

It is possible to define arrays as variables in your ARM template. To define an array, we need to specify the variable's name, and then we can provide the values in the array.

The ARM template in Listing 7-5 uses an array as a variable, and then we include the array values as the output.

Listing 7-5. Use of Arrays

```
{
    "$schema": "https://schema.management.azure.com/schemas/2019-04-01/
    deploymentTemplate.json#",
    "contentVersion": "1.0.0.0",
    "parameters": {},
    "functions": [],
    "variables": {
        "arrayVariable": [
            1,
            2,
            3,
            4
        ]
    },
    "resources": [],
    "outputs": {
        "arrayOutput": {
            "type": "array",
            "value": "[variables('arrayVariable')]"
        }
    }
}
```

If you deploy this template, although we are not defining any resource, you will be able to see the array values as the output, as shown in Figure 7-1.

arrayOutput

[1,2,3,4]

Figure 7-1. *Output from array*

Use of Objects

Variables can also be defined as objects in the ARM template. This becomes helpful when working with dynamic values that have to be referenced in larger deployments.

The ARM template shown in Listing 7-6 provides an example of how you can define a variable object, and then we will define the object as the output.

Listing 7-6. Working with Variable Objects

```
{
    "$schema": "https://schema.management.azure.com/schemas/2019-04-01/
    deploymentTemplate.json#",
    "contentVersion": "1.0.0.0",
    "parameters": {},
    "functions": [],
    "variables": {
        "objectVariable": {
            "property1": "value1",
            "property2": "value2"
        }
    },
    "resources": [],
    "outputs": {
        "objectOutput": {
            "type": "object",
            "value": "[variables('objectVariable')]"
        }
    }
}
```

Working with variable objects can help you define variables for resources that can include multiple properties and subproperties; by leveraging objects, you can avoid writing multiple times the values for the same properties.

This leads to our following scenario, where you probably want to deploy the same resource multiple times and simplify the task of manually defining multiple variables for the same resource type. For that, we can use the copy element that we will address in the following section.

With this basis, you now have more clearance on the multiple ways variables can be defined in an ARM template. Let's see how we can reference the value of a variable to the resources section of the ARM template.

How to Reference Variables Values

Working with multiple variables in more complex environments can be tricky; therefore, it is of high importance to leverage variables defined by a parameter or by another variable for those values that might be used more than once in your ARM template.

Listing 7-7 shows a quick example of how we can reference variable values in the resources section of the ARM template. Note that we are using the previous example in Listing 7-3. In this case, we are going to define the storage account in the resources section of the ARM template, and we will reference the variable in the name property of the storage account.

Listing 7-7. Referencing the Value for the Variable

```
"variables": {
  "storageName":"[concat(toLower(parameters('storageNamePrefix')),
  uniqueString(resourceGroup().id))]"
},
"resources": [
  {
    "type": "Microsoft.Storage/storageAccounts",
    "name": "[variables('storageName')]",
    }
]...
```

When the variable is to be used just one time or twice, then probably a hard-coded value is a good approach; however, it makes much more sense to dynamically construct variables using functions like in the example in Listing 7-3 ("concatToParam": "[concat(parameters('storageName'), '-addtoparam')]"), where we used the concat function to define a variable when we plan to use the variables multiple times in an ARM template.

As you can see, referencing variable values in the resources section of the ARM template looks really simple; in the previous examples, we utilized some functions like concat to construct our variable. However, bear in mind that the reference and list functions cannot be used when declaring a variable.

Imagine the following use case where the iFabrik team is currently leveraging two environments to roll out updates. One is the staging environment, and the second one is the production environment.

As previously mentioned in this chapter, variables can also be defined as an object that can contain multiple properties and/or subproperties. Therefore, we can leverage variables as objects to define the properties that should be part of the environment. Those would be configuration variables.

How to Leverage Configuration Variables

Consider configuration variables as presets of properties defined in an object that should be implied and included when deploying to a specific environment.

Returning to the same example in which iFabrik is leveraging the staging and production environments, we could define a variable as an object that can contain certain properties attached for staging only, and then define a separate variable with properties that must contain specific prerequisites for production.

Listing 7-8 shows how to use configuration variables for both the staging environment and the production environment.

Listing 7-8. Configuration Variables

```
{
  "$schema": "https://schema.management.azure.com/schemas/2019-04-01/
  deploymentTemplate.json#",
    "contentVersion": "1.0.0.0",
    "parameters": {
      "environmentType": {
        "type": "string",
        "allowedValues":[
                "staging",
                "production"
              ],
```

```
    "metadata": {
    "description": "Environment type (staging or production)"
        }
      }
  },
  "functions": [],
  "variables": {
      "environmentConfig": {
          "staging":{
              "instanceType":"small",
              "instanceCount":"1"
          },
          "production":{
              "instanceType":"large",
              "instanceCount":"3"
          }
      }
  },
  "resources": [],
  "outputs": {
      "instanceType": {
          "type": "string",
          "value": "[variables('environmentConfig')
          [parameters('environmentType')].instanceType]"
      },
      "instanceCount": {
          "type": "string",
          "value": "[variables('environmentConfig')
          [parameters('environmentType')].instanceCount]"
      }
  }
}
```

When deploying this template from the Azure portal, you will notice that you are going to be able to target a specific environment type, and it will contain the predefined properties previously configured, as shown in Figure 7-2.

Template

Customized template ⧉
0 resources

Edit template   Edit parameters

Project details

Select the subscription to manage deployed resources and costs. Use resource groups like folders to organize and manage all your resources.

Subscription * ⓘ   iFabrik   ⌄

└──── Resource group * ⓘ   (New) Configuration-Variables   ⌄
                                   Create new

Instance details

Region * ⓘ   Brazil South   ⌄

Environment Type * ⓘ   ⌃

                                   staging

                                   production

[Review + create]   [< Previous]   [Next : Review + create >]

Figure 7-2. *Template deployment*

After deploying this template, you can go to the output section, and you will see the configuration defined for that environment type, as shown in Figure 7-3.

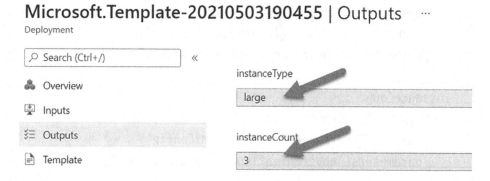

Microsoft.Template-20210503190455 | Outputs   ⋯
Deployment

🔍 Search (Ctrl+/)   «

                                    instanceType
♣ Overview
                                    large
🖳 Inputs

≡ Outputs   instanceCount

📄 Template   3

Figure 7-3. *ARM template output of configuration variable*

By leveraging configuration variables, we can ensure the iFabrik team is targeting the next release to the right environment and that this environment includes the preset of properties that are compliant with it.

This scenario addresses how configuration variables can be utilized and leads to a question you probably already thought of: how can we leverage variable values to deploy the same amount of resources without manual intervention during the deployment operation? In other words, how can we iterate? Let's discuss variable iteration.

Variable Iteration

Picture the following use case in which the iFabrik team needs to deploy multiple data disks with the same properties including same disk size.

In this case, it makes more sense to dynamically construct those values rather than just hard-coding all the values. But how can we dynamically specify the number of elements of a variable during the deployment operation? That's where the copy element comes in handy.

Bear with me, the copy element will allow you to create multiple values for a variable in the ARM template; this way you can avoid the definition of the variable multiple times in your ARM template.

In other words, by using the copy element, you can just define the object called copy and then include the properties: name, count, and input. This will allow you to create the value of a variable as many times as needed.

Listing 7-9 highlights the basic use of the copy element in your ARM template.

Listing 7-9. Using the copy Element

```
"copy": [
  {
    "name": " ",
    "count": ,
    "input":
  }
]
```

It is possible to leverage the copy element for the resources, for the properties in a given resource, and for the outputs in your ARM template.

In Listing 7-9 there are three relevant properties:

- name: This will be the identifier of your loop.

- count: This will help you specify how many iterations are needed for the variable.

- input: This defines the properties that should be repeated. It can include a single property, an array, or an object with properties and/ or subproperties.

Now let's look at a quick example of how we can define an array of values. In the ARM template shown in Listing 7-10, we will create a new parameter called itemCount and set the default value to 5. Then we will define a new variable defined by the copy element, and will reference the itemCount in the property count. For the input property, we will pass the array count.

Listing 7-10. Array of String Values

```
{
    "$schema": "https://schema.management.azure.com/schemas/2019-04-01/
    deploymentTemplate.json#",
    "contentVersion": "1.0.0.0",
    "parameters": {
        "itemCount": {
            "type": "int",
            "defaultValue": 5,
            "metadata": {
                "description": "itemCount Parameter"
            }
        }
    },
    "functions": [],
    "variables": {
        "copy": [
            {
                "name":"myArray",
                "count":"[parameters('itemCount')]",
```

```
        "input":"[concat('item', copyIndex('myArray',1))]"
      }
    ]
  },
  "resources": [],
  "outputs": {
    "arrayOutput": {
      "type": "array",
      "value": "[variables('myArray')]"
    }
  }
}
```

Now we can deploy this ARM template as a custom template, as shown in Figure 7-4.

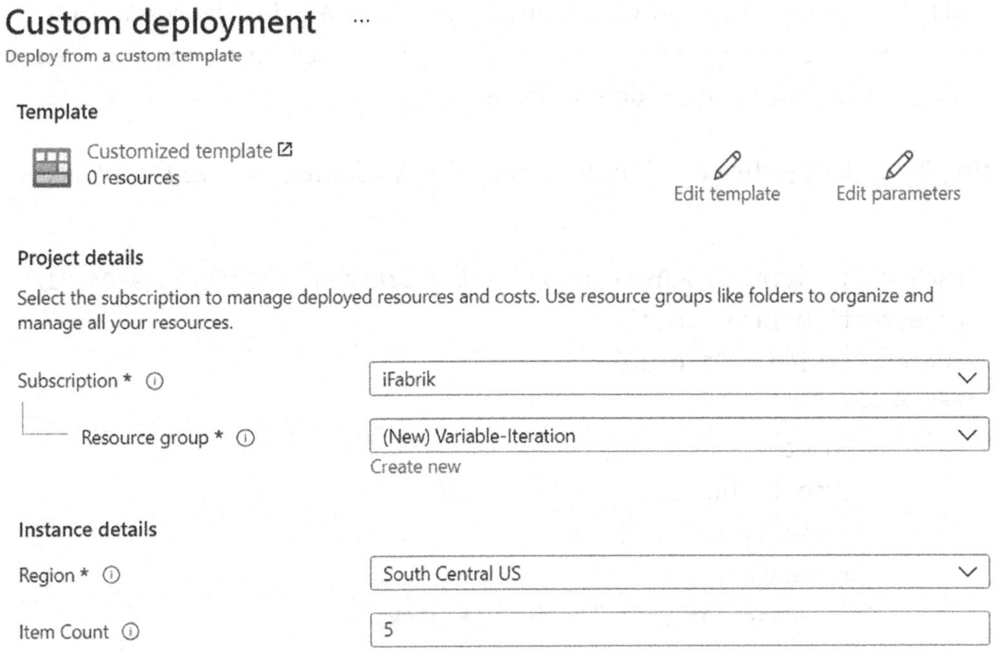

Figure 7-4. *Custom deployment*

The output of this ARM template shows the values of the array, as shown in Figure 7-5.

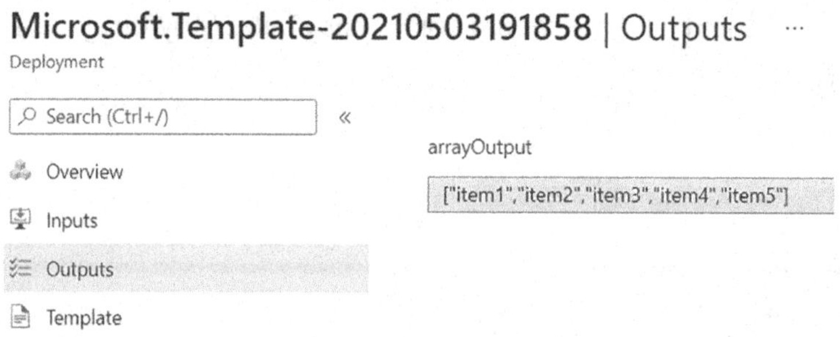

Microsoft.Template-20210503191858 | Outputs ···
Deployment

arrayOutput

["item1","item2","item3","item4","item5"]

Figure 7-5. *Output from array*

As you can tell, for larger environments, using a copy element can become really helpful. To solve the challenging case in which the iFabrik team needs to deploy five data disks with the same properties including the same disk size, we could leverage the copy element.

In the template shown in Listing 7-11, we are using the copy element to deploy an array of objects that contains the definition of the properties of five data disks. Note that we are not actually deploying the data disk, but rather demonstrating how the copy element can help you create multiple variables.

Listing 7-11. Using the copy Element to Define Variables for Five Data Disks

```
{
    "$schema": "https://schema.management.azure.com/schemas/2019-04-01/
    deploymentTemplate.json#",
    "contentVersion": "1.0.0.0",
    "parameters": {
        "diskCount": {
            "type": "int",
            "defaultValue": 5,
            "metadata": {
                "description": "Number of disks"
            }
        }
    },
    "functions": [],
    "variables": {
        "copy": [
```

```
        {
            "name":"disk",
            "count":"[parameters('diskCount')]",
            "input": {
                "name":"[concat('dataDisk', copyIndex('disk',1))]",
                "diskSizeGb":"1",
                "diskIndex":"[copyIndex('disk')]"
            }
        }
    ]
},
"resources": [],
"outputs": {
    "result": {
        "type": "array",
        "value": "[variables('disk')]"
    }
}
}
```

In the previous code, we are defining a parameter with data type int and a default value set to 5. We also defined a variable using the copy element that includes the name, the count (referenced from the parameter), and the input that includes the objects.

Figure 7-6 shows the output of the previous ARM template.

Figure 7-6. *ARM template output of the variables for the five data disks*

Listing 7-12 shows the complete output from the array.

Listing 7-12. ARM Template Output of the Variables for the Five Data Disks

```
[{"name":"dataDisk1","diskSizeGb":"1","diskIndex":0},{"name":"dataDisk2",
"diskSizeGb":"1","diskIndex":1},{"name":"dataDisk3","diskSizeGb":"1",
"diskIndex":2},{"name":"dataDisk4","diskSizeGb":"1","diskIndex":3},
{"name":"dataDisk5","diskSizeGb":"1","diskIndex":4}]
```

Using the copy element, you can simplify the creation of multiple values for variables in your ARM template. As you probably noticed, the more variables we use in the ARM template, the clearer we have to define them. It is highly recommended to use the camelCase convention; standardizing the naming of variables and parameters is a best practice when authoring ARM templates.

Summary

In this chapter, we reviewed the multiple ways you can define variables and reference them in your ARM template's resources section. We also went through practical examples of how configuration variables can be utilized. Lastly, we took a look at the copy element as a critical component to creating more than one value for variables in your ARM template, along with practical examples.

In the next chapter, we will take a deep dive into understanding the resources section of your Azure Resource Manager template.

CHAPTER 8

Working with the Resources Section of Your ARM Template

This chapter will provide a better understanding of the resources section of your Azure Resource Manager (ARM) template; we will go over how to create child resources and conditional deployments and how to set dependency values and location values.

In addition, we will cover how you can define a postdeployment configuration and automation tasks on Azure virtual machines.

These are some of the topics in this chapter:

- Understanding the resources section in your ARM template

- Working with child resources

- Conditional deployments

Chapter 6 reviewed how you can work with the parameters section of an ARM template; then, in Chapter 7, we covered how to utilize variables. In this chapter, we will focus on the resources section of the ARM template.

Listing 8-1 highlights the ARM template file structure and the section we will focus on in this chapter.

© David Rendón 2022
D. Rendón, *Building Applications with Azure Resource Manager (ARM)*,
https://doi.org/10.1007/978-1-4842-7747-8_8

Listing 8-1. ARM Template File Structure

```
{
    "$schema": "https://schema.management.azure.com/schemas/2019-04-01/
    deploymentTemplate.json#",
    "contentVersion": "1.0.0.0",
    "parameters": {},
    "functions": [],
    "variables": {},
    "resources": [],
    "outputs": {}
}
```

Understanding the resources Section in Your ARM Template

The resources section in your ARM template is where you will define the actual services or components that you want to deploy in your environment.

Every single item you define in this section is considered a resource, such as IP addresses, network security groups, virtual networks, etc.

Some of the resources can be deployed independently, and others depend on an existing resource before they can be deployed; therefore, it is essential to understand how resources can be defined.

When defining the resources we want to deploy, we need to provide the resource provider and type information. This means that if we deploy a storage account, we will need to define the resource type and the resource provider, in this case, Microsoft.Storage/storageAccounts.

Note that all resource types are defined in the following format: {resource-provider}/{resource-type}.

The declaration of a new resource in your ARM template from scratch is pretty simple; we can start by defining the resource type and the API version under the resources section of the ARM template, as shown in Listing 8-2.

Listing 8-2. Setting the Resource Type and API Version of a Storage Account

```
{
    "$schema": "https://schema.management.azure.com/schemas/2019-04-01/
    deploymentTemplate.json#",
    "contentVersion": "1.0.0.0",
    "parameters": {},
    "functions": [],
    "variables": {},
    "resources": [
        {
            "type": "Microsoft.Storage/storageAccounts",
            "apiVersion": "2019-06-01",
...
```

Does this mean that we have to learn all the resource providers and API versions out there?

Not at all! You can leverage the ARM snippets to create the definition of any resource. When working with the ARM extension in Visual Studio Code, you can type arm-Resource-Type and see the snippet for the desired resource type.

Figure 8-1 highlights how to use snippets to create a storage account.

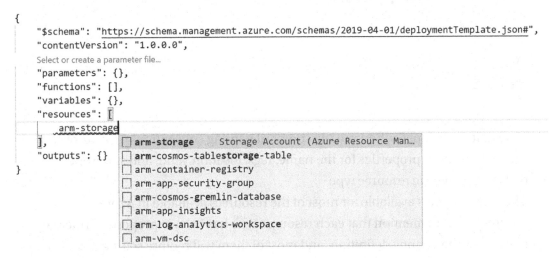

Figure 8-1. *Creation of a storage account using the ARM extension in Visual Studio Code*

When leveraging snippets, you will see that it includes all the properties needed to define and deploy this resource, as shown in Listing 8-3.

Listing 8-3. Snippet for the Storage Account

```
{
    "$schema": "https://schema.management.azure.com/schemas/2019-04-01/
    deploymentTemplate.json#",
    "contentVersion": "1.0.0.0",
    "parameters": {},
    "functions": [],
    "variables": {},
    "resources": [
        {
            "name": "storageaccount1",
            "type": "Microsoft.Storage/storageAccounts",
            "apiVersion": "2019-06-01",
            "location": "[resourceGroup().location]",
            "kind": "StorageV2",
            "sku": {
                "name": "Premium_LRS",
                "tier": "Premium"
            }
        }
    ],
    "outputs": {}
}
```

Note that the snippet adheres to the standard naming convention of the resource definition; it includes properties for the name, tags, location, kind, and subproperties needed for this specific resource type.

There are snippets available for most of the resources available in Azure.

It is important to mention that each resource type has its own properties, rules, and restrictions for the naming definition, and most of them will require setting a location.

Most of the resources must have at least the following properties present in the resource definition:

- `type`

- `apiVersion`

- `name`

- `location`

Resource-specific properties depend on the resource type that you are looking to deploy.

For example, let's deploy the previous ARM template in an existing resource group in our Azure subscription. We will update the resource name and hard-code the name to `storageaccountiac`. Figure 8-2 shows the output from the deployment.

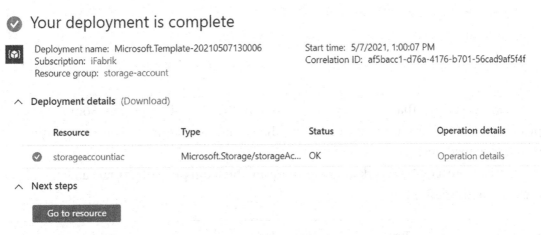

Figure 8-2. *ARM template deployment result*

We have defined a resource in the `resources` section of the ARM template and have successfully deployed it.

Another simple example is the definition of a network interface; under the `resources` section, we can define the network interface, as shown in Listing 8-4.

Listing 8-4. Definition of a Network Interface

```
{
    "name": "networkInterface1",
    "type": "Microsoft.Network/networkInterfaces",
    "apiVersion": "2019-11-01",
    "location": "[resourceGroup().location]",
```

```
"properties": {
    "ipConfigurations": [
        {
            "name": "ipConfig1",
            "properties": {
                "privateIPAllocationMethod": "Dynamic",
                "subnet": {
                    "id": "[resourceId('Microsoft.Network/
                          virtualNetworks/subnets',
                          'virtualNetwork1', 'subnet1')]"
                }
            }
        }
    ]
}
}
```

In this case, note that the resource can contain specific subproperties. Some properties and subproperties are optional, while others are required. This varies from resource to resource.

In the context of a network interface, here are the main properties that can be included in the definition:

Name	Type	Required	Value
name	string	Yes	The name of the network interface
type	enum	Yes	For JSON, Microsoft.Network/networkInterfaces
apiVersion	enum	Yes	For JSON, 2020-07-01
location	string	Yes	Resource location
tags	object	No	Resource tags
extendedLocation	object	No	The extended location of the network interface
properties	object	Yes	Properties of the network interface
resources	array	No	tapConfigurations

Now let's look at a use case where the iFabrik team needs to provision a virtual machine in a specific subnet in an existing environment in Azure.

The `apiVersion` and the resource type will always be included in the definition of the resource. These two values will determine the additional properties available for the resource. The `apiVersion` value refers to the actual version of the resources, and you don't automatically get any updates for the resource provider.

Some resources can be defined only within the context of another. In this case, a subnet cannot exist if there is no virtual network previously defined. This is known as a *parent-child* relationship.

Working with Child Resources

Working with resources that can be defined only within the context of another resource in your ARM template without the proper definition between them can lead you to a deployment failure.

Therefore, it is essential to understand the concepts of child resources and parent resources.

To deploy a virtual machine in a subnet, we would need to validate the existence of a virtual network. So first, let's take a look at the definition of a virtual network and subnets.

The virtual network can be defined as the parent resource, while the subnets can be defined as child resources.

We have two ways to specify child resources in the ARM template.

- Specify a child resource within a parent resource

- Specify a child resource outside of a parent resource

Let's see the difference between these options.

Specify a Child Resource Within a Parent Resource

In this method, you will define a parent resource in the `resources` section of the ARM template, and then to add the child resource, you will define another JSON object within the parent resource.

Listing 8-5 specifies the definition of a child resource within a parent resource.

Listing 8-5. Specify Child Resources Within a Parent Resource

```
{
    "$schema": "https://schema.management.azure.com/schemas/2019-04-01/
    deploymentTemplate.json#",
    "contentVersion": "1.0.0.0",
    "parameters": {},
    "functions": [],
    "variables": {},
    "resources": [
        {
            <parent-resource>
             "resources": [
                <child-resource>
        ]
        }
    ],
    "outputs": {}
}
```

Think of the previous example, where you have to provision a virtual network. Each virtual network can have multiple subnets. You can define the virtual network as a parent resource and include the desired subnet definition as a child resource.

Listing 8-6 highlights the definition of a virtual network as a parent resource and two subnets as child resources within the parent resource.

Listing 8-6. Definition of Child Resource Within a Parent Resource

```
{
    "$schema": "https://schema.management.azure.com/schemas/2019-04-01/
    deploymentTemplate.json#",
    "contentVersion": "1.0.0.0",
    "parameters": {},
    "functions": [],
    "variables": {},
    "resources": [
        {
```

```
        "name": "virtualNetwork1",
        "type": "Microsoft.Network/virtualNetworks",
        "apiVersion": "2019-11-01",
        "location": "[resourceGroup().location]",
        "tags": {
            "displayName": "virtualNetwork1"
        },
        "properties": {
            "addressSpace": {
                "addressPrefixes": [
                    "10.0.0.0/16"
                ]
            },
            "subnets": [
                {
                    "name": "Subnet-1",
                    "properties": {
                        "addressPrefix": "10.0.0.0/24"
                    }
                },
                {
                    "name": "Subnet-2",
                    "properties": {
                        "addressPrefix": "10.0.1.0/24"
                    }
                }
            ]
        }
    }
    ],
    "outputs": {}
}
```

In this case, the child resources (the two subnets) are dependent on the parent resource (the virtual network). Parent resources must be defined before the child resources.

As a tip, you can leverage the ARM snippet for virtual networks by typing `arm-vnet`, and it will create the definition of the virtual network as a parent resource and subnets as child resources, as shown in Figure 8-3.

```
{
    "$schema": "https://schema.management.azure.com/schemas/2019-04-01/deploymentTemplate.json#",
    "contentVersion": "1.0.0.0",

    "parameters": {},
    "functions": [],
    "variables": {},
    "resources": [
        {
            2 children: Subnet-1 (subnets), Subnet-2 (subnets)
            "name": "virtualNetwork1",  ◀━━━━━━━━
            "type": "Microsoft.Network/virtualNetworks",
            "apiVersion": "2019-11-01",
            "location": "[resourceGroup().location]",
            "tags": {
                "displayName": "virtualNetwork1"
            },
            "properties": {
                "addressSpace": {
                    "addressPrefixes": [
                        "10.0.0.0/16"
                    ]
                },
                "subnets": [
                    {
                        Parent: virtualNetwork1 (virtualNetworks)
                        "name": "Subnet-1",  ◀━━━━━━
                        "properties": {
                            "addressPrefix": "10.0.0.0/24"
                        }
                    },
                    {
                        Parent: virtualNetwork1 (virtualNetworks)
                        "name": "Subnet-2",  ◀━━━━━━
                        "properties": {
                            "addressPrefix": "10.0.1.0/24"
                        }
                    }
                ]
            }
        }
    ],
    "outputs": {}
}
```

Figure 8-3. *ARM snippet for virtual network*

As you can see in Figure 8-3, when working with child resources within a parent resource, there's no need to include the resource type in the child resource.

Now let's see how you can work with child resources defined outside of a parent resource.

Specify a Child Resource Outside of a Parent Resource

To specify a child resource outside of a parent resource, we can follow the structure highlighted in Listing 8-7.

Listing 8-7. Specify a Child Resource Outside of a Parent Resource

```
{
    "$schema": "https://schema.management.azure.com/schemas/2019-04-01/
    deploymentTemplate.json#",
    "contentVersion": "1.0.0.0",
    "parameters": {},
    "functions": [],
    "variables": {},
    "resources": [
            {
                <parent-resource>
            },
            {
                <child-resource>
            }
        ],
    "outputs": {}
}
```

When working with child resources outside of a parent resource, we will have to define the resource type in the child resource.

Figure 8-4 highlights the definition of a virtual network as a parent resource and a subnet as a child resource outside of a parent resource.

```
{
    "$schema": "https://schema.management.azure.com/schemas/2019-04-01/deploymentTemplate.json#",
    "contentVersion": "1.0.0.0",

    "parameters": {},
    "functions": [],
    "variables": {},
    "resources": [
        {
                    1 child: Subnet1 (subnets)
                    "type": "Microsoft.Network/virtualNetworks",
                    "apiVersion": "2018-10-01",
                    "name": "virtualNetwork1",
                    "location": "[resourceGroup().location]",
                    "properties": {
                    "addressSpace": {
                        "addressPrefixes": [
                        "10.0.0.0/16"
                        ]
                    }
                    }
        },
        {
                    Parent: virtualNetwork1 (virtualNetworks)
                    "type": "Microsoft.Network/virtualNetworks/subnets",
                    "apiVersion": "2018-10-01",
                    "name": "virtualNetwork1/Subnet1",
                    "properties": {
                    "addressPrefix": "10.0.0.0/24"
                    }
        }
    ],
    "outputs": {}
}
```

Figure 8-4. *Example of child resource outside of the parent resource*

To define the resource, type `Microsoft.Network/virtualNetworks/subnets` in the child resource. In this specification option, we don't need to follow the strict parent-child order.

When should we specify a child resource outside of a parent resource?

Let's say you deploy a virtual network and a single subnet in the ARM template as there are no requirements to define additional subnets in this ARM template for the initial deployment.

Later, you are asked to deploy additional subnets in the same virtual network. In this case, it is helpful to specify the child resources outside of a parent resource, as you wouldn't need to define the parent resource again. The parent resource is not deployed in the same ARM template.

Another good use case is when there's a need to create multiple child resources; you could leverage the copy element to simplify creating more than one child resource.

Following the same line, what if we need to force the deployment to include two subnets whenever a virtual network is defined? How can we create this condition on the ARM template? Let's see how conditional deployments can help us on this task.

Conditional Deployments

How can we include a condition in an ARM template to decide whether a resource should be deployed? You can leverage conditional deployments so that based on the parameters defined, you will be able to deploy a different set of resources. We can address two approaches in this situation.

The first one is that we can have Azure Resource Manager check implicitly whether a resource defined in your ARM template already exists in your environment in Azure. This helps you better reason the logic that can be implemented in the ARM template.

If the ARM template contains the definition of a resource that already exists in your Azure environment, then it will not be deployed.

Take the following example: the iFabrik team needs to provide their clients with the ability to create and assign a public IP address to a virtual machine. They will be able to create a new public IP address, and Azure Resource Manage will validate the preexistence of this resource in the environment. If the IP address already exists, then this resource will not be deployed.

The second approach is to deploy a set of resources to a specific environment, based on the parameters included in the ARM template. This is known as *branching logic*.

You have probably already thought of the following question: what if the resource specified in the conditional deployment already exists? As mentioned earlier in this chapter, Azure Resource Manager will check if a resource already exists in your environment. If that's the case, then you can apply different logic.

This logic can be applied using the condition construct.

Deploy the condition Construct

You can explicitly add the logic in your ARM template or have Azure Resource Manager validate the logic. We can achieve this using the condition construct.

This `condition` construct is a property that will help you include the logic in the ARM template to evaluate whether to deploy or configure a particular resource in your environment.

To utilize the `condition` construct, you can define it in the `resources` section of the ARM template, as shown in Listing 8-8.

Listing 8-8. Deploy condition

```
"resources" : [
  {
    "condition": "[parameters('shouldDeployStorageAccount')]"
  }
]...
```

The `condition` construct is a property that you can define in the `resources` section of the ARM template. It will evaluate if the value is a `true` or `false` value or if the expression to be considered is a `true` or `false` value.

We can pass parameter values as shown in the previous example, pass variable values, or perform a function to evaluate the condition.

The `condition` construct is a property that will evaluate whether the value is `true` or `false` or if the expression to be evaluated is `true` or `false`.

In the following example, we will add the `condition` construct in the `resources` section of the ARM template to evaluate an expression value and validate whether a storage account should be deployed. Instead of assigning a strict `true` or `false` value, we will use a function to evaluate `true`. We will specify the logic for the conditional deployment of a storage account, and based on the parameters passed at the deployment time, the resource will be deployed or not. See Figure 8-5.

```
{
    "$schema": "https://schema.management.azure.com/schemas/2019-04-01/deploymentTemplate.json#",
    "contentVersion": "1.0.0.0",

    "parameters": {
        "shouldDeployStorageAccount": {
            "type": "string",
            "defaultValue": "new",
            "allowedValues": [
                "new",
                "existing"
            ]

        },
        "storageAccountName": {
            "type": "string"
        }
    },
    "functions": [],
    "variables": {},
    "resources": [
        {
        "condition": "[equals(parameters('shouldDeployStorageAccount'), 'new')]",
        "type": "Microsoft.Storage/storageAccounts",
        "apiVersion": "2019-06-01",
        "name": "[parameters('storageAccountName')]",
        "location": "eastus",
        "sku": {
            "name": "Standard_LRS",
            "tier": "Standard"
        },
        "kind": "StorageV2",
        "properties": {
            "accessTier": "Hot"
        }
    }
    ],
    "outputs": {}
}
```

Figure 8-5. *Evaluating an expression value*

If you deploy this ARM template, at deployment time, you will be able to choose whether you want to create a new storage account or use an existing one, as shown in Figure 8-6.

Custom deployment ···

Deploy from a custom template

Customized template ⎁
1 resource

   Edit template   Edit parameters

Project details

Select the subscription to manage deployed resources and costs. Use resource groups like folders to organize and manage all your resources.

Subscription * ⓘ

iFabrik ⌄

Resource group * ⓘ

(New) iFabrik ⌄

Create new

Instance details

Region * ⓘ

East US ⌄

Should Deploy Storage Account

existing ⌃

Storage Account Name *

new

existing

Figure 8-6. Custom deployment ARM template in the Azure portal

The same principle can be utilized to create a conditional deployment like the ARM template shown in Listing 8-9, which includes a parameter value to define two environment types: testing and production environments. It will also define a web application based on a condition.

The condition evaluates if the environment type is `Production` or `Testing`.

If the members of the team select `Production`, they will be able to provision a web application that is Linux-based and target the App Service Plan with specific compute resources.

On the other hand, if the team members select `Testing`, they will be able to provision only two App Service Plans with specific compute resources.

Based on the environment defined at deployment time, the iFabrik team will provision a different set of resources.

In other words, depending on the parameters that are passed on to the ARM template at deployment, you can define a specific set of resources to be deployed.

Listing 8-9. Conditional Deployment to Create a Linux Web Application in the Production Environment

```
{
  "$schema": "https://schema.management.azure.com/schemas/2019-04-01/
  deploymentTemplate.json#",
  "contentVersion": "1.0.0.0",
  "parameters": {
    "environmentType": {
            "type": "string",
            "allowedValues": [
                "Production",
                "Testing"
            ],
            "defaultValue": "Production"
        },

    "webAppName": {
      "type": "string",
      "defaultValue": "ifabrik",
      "minLength": 2
    }

  },
  "variables": {
    "linuxFxVersion": "php|7.4",
    "skuProduction": "S1",
    "skuTesting": "F1",
    "appServicePlanPortalNameProduction": "[concat('AppServicePlan-Prod-',
    parameters('webAppName'))]",
    "appServicePlanPortalNameTesting": "[concat('AppServicePlan-Test-',
    parameters('webAppName'))]"

  },
  "resources": [
    {
      "type": "Microsoft.Web/serverfarms",
```

```
    "apiVersion": "2020-06-01",
    "name": "[variables('appServicePlanPortalNameProduction')]",
    "location": "[resourceGroup().location]",
    "sku": {
      "name": "[variables('skuProduction')]"
    },
    "kind": "linux",
      "properties": {
        "reserved": true
      }

  },
  {
    "type": "Microsoft.Web/serverfarms",
    "apiVersion": "2020-06-01",
    "name": "[variables('appServicePlanPortalNameTesting')]",
    "location": "[resourceGroup().location]",
    "sku": {
      "name": "[variables('skuTesting')]"
    },
    "kind": "linux",
      "properties": {
        "reserved": true
      }

  },

  {
    "condition": "[equals(parameters('environmentType'), 'Production')]",
    "type": "Microsoft.Web/sites",
    "apiVersion": "2020-06-01",
    "name": "[parameters('webAppName')]",
    "location": "[resourceGroup().location]",
    "dependsOn": [
```

```
    "[resourceId('Microsoft.Web/serverfarms', variables('appServicePlan
    PortalNameProduction'))]",
    "[resourceId('Microsoft.Web/serverfarms', variables('appServicePlan
    PortalNameTesting'))]"
  ],
  "properties": {
    "siteConfig": {
      "linuxFxVersion": "[variables('linuxFxVersion')]"
    },

    "serverFarmId": "[resourceId('Microsoft.Web/serverfarms',
    variables('appServicePlanPortalNameProduction'))]"
  }

 }
]
}
```

When provisioning other resources such as virtual machines, we must include the definition of additional resources in the ARM template that the virtual machine depends on to be deployed, such as network interfaces, IP addresses, storage accounts, virtual networks, subnets, disk types, etc.

Summary

This chapter reviewed how to define the actual resources that will be part of your environment in Azure. We covered the basic definition of a resource and how you can leverage the Azure Resource Manager extension in Visual Studio Code to speed up the definition of resources.

This chapter also addressed how to specify parent and child resources in your ARM template and the main differences when specifying a child resource within a parent resource and outside of a parent resource.

At the end of this chapter, we discussed how you can leverage conditional deployments and add logic in the ARM template to decide whether a resource should be deployed.

The next chapter will cover how you can get more control over the order in which resources can be deployed.

## CHAPTER 9

Understanding Dependencies in Your ARM Template

In Chapter 8, we reviewed how to define the resources that will be part of your environment. This chapter will cover how to create multiple dependent resources to understand better the deployment order and how Azure Resource Manager (ARM) evaluates dependencies across various resources. This chapter will also focus on how you can define dependencies in your ARM template.

Specifically, the chapter will cover the following:

- Understanding the order for deploying resources in ARM templates
- Setting resource dependencies and location
- Circular dependencies

How can we define the order of all the resources needed to deploy a virtual machine in the ARM template? In addition to the specification of parent and child resources and conditional deployments, we can leverage the definition of dependencies in the ARM template.

Setting Resource Dependencies and Location

Now let's see how you can define the order of the resources that will be deployed in your ARM template. There are two relevant components to better control the deployment order of the resources defined in the ARM template: the location and the dependsOn construct.

139

© David Rendón 2022
D. Rendón, *Building Applications with Azure Resource Manager (ARM)*,
https://doi.org/10.1007/978-1-4842-7747-8_9

Resource Location

Most of the resources that can be deployed in Azure require a location to be provided at deployment time or to be predefined in the ARM template.

While this also applies to resource groups, remember that resources can span Azure regions, so you can define the location for a resource group to be the East US region and have the resources deployed in a different region.

The resource group will store metadata about the resources you provision within that resource group. However, resources that depend on one another should use the same location. For example, think of a virtual machine deployment; in this case, we would need to define the same location for all the components such as the virtual network, network interfaces, etc.

While you can hard-code the value for the location in your ARM template, it is handy to reference the location rather than a parameter value when working with larger environments.

This parameter value can be dynamically assigned by utilizing the resourceGroup function. This function is commonly utilized to create resources in the same location defined as the resource group.

Listing 9-1 highlights the use of the resourceGroup function to define the location for a parameter value.

Listing 9-1. Using the resourceGroup Function to Define the Location for a Parameter Value

```
{
    "$schema": "https://schema.management.azure.com/schemas/2019-04-01/
    deploymentTemplate.json#",
    "contentVersion": "1.0.0.0",
    "parameters": {
        "location": {
            "type": "string",
            "defaultValue": "[resourceGroup().location]",
            "metadata": {
                "description": "default value for the location"
            }
        }
    },
```

```
    "functions": [],
    "variables": {},
    "resources": [],
    "outputs": {}
}
```

There are additional properties for the resourceGroup function that you can leverage based on your needs. At the moment, we will focus only on the location property; however, for further reference, please refer to this link:

https://docs.microsoft.com/en-us/dotnet/api/microsoft.azure.management
.resourcemanager.models.resourcegroup?view=azure-dotnet

Resource Dependencies

To better control the deployment order of the resources defined in the ARM template, you can use the dependsOn construct.

This construct will help you define the order of the resources deployed in the ARM template.

Suppose we need to deploy a virtual machine. In that case, we have to ensure that some resources already exist in the environment or can be created before we perform the actual deployment of the virtual machine resource.

Therefore, you can utilize the dependsOn construct to define the order in which resources should be deployed explicitly.

Azure Resource Manager will handle the deployment of these resources. If there are no dependencies between the resources defined in the ARM template, those resources will be deployed in parallel.

Listing 9-2 highlights the use of the dependsOn construct.

Listing 9-2. Using the dependsOn Construct

```
"resources": [
  {
    "name": "<Resource that needs to exist first>"
  },
  {
    "name": "anotherResource",
```

```
    "dependsOn": [
      "<Resource that needs to exist first>"
    ]
  }
]
```

The dependsOn construct can be defined as a property and can include an array of strings. The resources defined inside this array will be conditionally deployed. See Figure 9-1.

```
"dependsOn": [
    //"[resourceId('<Resource Provider>', parameters('<parameterValue>'))]",
    "[resourceId('Microsoft.Network/virtualNetworks/', parameters('ifabrikVirtualNetwork'))]",
    "[resourceId('Microsoft.Network/loadBalancers/', parameters('ifabrikLoadBalancer'))]"
]
```

Figure 9-1. *Using the dependsOn construct with arrays*

Figure 9-1 specifies the dependent resources included in the array. The resources are referred to by their unique ID obtained from the resourceId function that combines the namespace, type, and parameter value.

You can also define dependencies between parent and child resources explicitly using the dependsOn construct, as shown in Listing 9-3.

Listing 9-3. Dependencies Between Parent and Child Resources

```
"resources": [
  {
    "name": "Your-Parent-Resource",
    "resources": [{
      "dependsOn": ["Your-Parent-Resource"],
      "name": "Your Child Resource"
    }]
  }
]
```

Azure Resource Manager will not create dependencies between parent and child resources; therefore, you need to define this dependency explicitly.

Now that we have reviewed how the dependsOn construct works, here are some fundamental questions:

- How can we use dependencies to better author our ARM templates?

- How can we validate the correct order of resources that will be deployed?

- Most importantly, do we have to memorize the resources and their dependencies?

Practice: Provisioning a Virtual Machine Considering Resource Dependencies

If you're new to Azure Resource Manager and authoring templates, the best option for you is to think of your ARM template as a whole document that will define your environment in smaller pieces.

Picture the scenario of a virtual machine. A virtual machine needs certain pieces or resources to function correctly. Such resources can include the following:

- A virtual network

- A network interface

- A storage account

- An IP address

- A network security group

- The virtual machine itself

Of course, the virtual machine is the primary resource we want to deploy.

Once you map all the resources needed to deploy the primary resource, start by drawing a diagram, placing the primary resource at the top, adding the other resources to the bottom, and making relationships between those resources.

For a virtual machine, we can start a diagram like Figure 9-2.

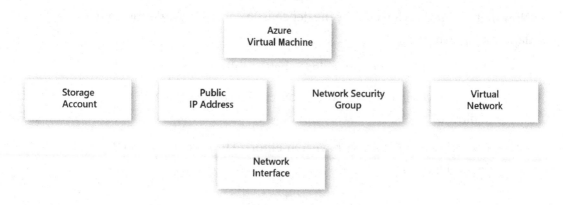

Figure 9-2. *Resources needed to deploy a virtual machine*

Now consider the dependencies between those resources. You can attach a network interface to the virtual machine, which is usually connected to a subnet in the virtual network. Then, a public IP address can be associated with the network interface. Also, you can assign a network security group to allow specific traffic through the virtual machine in the virtual network.

Then, the diagram will look like Figure 9-3.

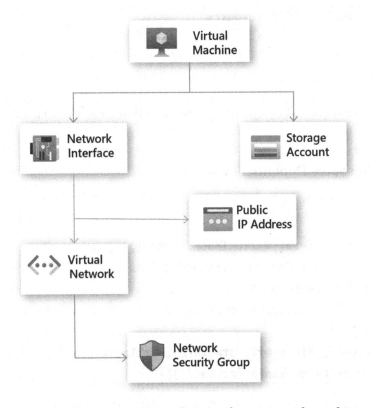

Figure 9-3. *Diagram of resource dependencies for a virtual machine*

Now we have a better idea of the potential dependencies that should be considered in the ARM template. We will create a new ARM template and define the parameter values for the resources mentioned earlier.

In the resources section of the ARM template, we will create a parent and a child resource dependency. Thus, we can start by defining the virtual machine as resource-dependent on the network interface. See Listing 9-4.

Listing 9-4. Creating a Parent-Child Resource Dependency

```
"resources": [
        {
            "name": "parent-resource",
            "resources": [{
            "dependsOn": ["parent-resource"],
```

```
        "name": "child resource"
      }]
    }
  ]
```

The parent resource will be our virtual machine that depends on a network interface. See Listing 9-5.

Listing 9-5. Resource Dependency Definition

```
"resources":[
  {
    "name": "[parameters('virtualMachineName')]",
    "type": "Microsoft.Compute/virtualMachines",
    "apiVersion": "2021-03-01",
    "location": "[parameters('location')]",
    "dependsOn": [
      "[resourceId('Microsoft.Network/networkInterfaces/',
      parameters('networkInterfaceName'))]"
          ],
...
```

Now we will define the properties for this resource. Remember that each resource has its own properties that have to be defined in the resource section of the ARM template. For this virtual machine, we will determine the following properties:

- Hardware profile

- Storage profile

- Network profile

- Operating system profile

- Diagnostics profile

- Plan

- Zones

Listing 9-6 highlights the definition of the properties for the virtual machine.

Listing 9-6. Virtual Machine, Properties Definition

```
"properties": {
     "hardwareProfile": {
     "vmSize": "[parameters('virtualMachineSize')]"
               },
       "storageProfile": {
          "osDisk": {
              "createOption": "fromImage",
              "managedDisk": {
                   "storageAccountType": "[parameters('osDiskType')]"
                     }
                 },
                 "imageReference": {
                 "publisher": "microsoftwindowsserver",
                 "offer": "microsoftserveroperatingsystems-previews",
                 "sku": "windows-server-2022",
                 "version": "latest"
                   }
               },
         "networkProfile": {
             "networkInterfaces": [
               {
               "id": "[resourceId('Microsoft.Network/networkInterfaces',
                    parameters('networkInterfaceName'))]"
                     }
                 ]
               },
      "osProfile": {
      "computerName": "[parameters('virtualMachineComputerName')]",
      "adminUsername": "[parameters('adminUsername')]",
      "adminPassword": "[parameters('adminPassword')]"

                 },
      "diagnosticsProfile": {
                   "bootDiagnostics": {
```

```
                        "enabled": true
                    }
                }
            },
        "plan": {
        "name": "windows-server-2022",
        "publisher": "microsoftwindowsserver",
        "product": "microsoftserveroperatingsystems-previews"
            },
        "zones": [
        "[parameters('zone')]"
                ]
        },
```

Then we will define the following resources: the network interface and its properties. Note that the network interface depends on the virtual network and the public IP address. See Listing 9-7.

Listing 9-7. Network Interface Definition

```
{
  "name": "[parameters('networkInterfaceName')]",
  "type": "Microsoft.Network/networkInterfaces",
  "apiVersion": "2018-10-01",
  "location": "[parameters('location')]",
  "dependsOn": [
    "[concat('Microsoft.Network/networkSecurityGroups/',
    parameters('networkSecurityGroupName'))]",
    "[concat('Microsoft.Network/virtualNetworks/',
    parameters('virtualNetworkName'))]",
    "[concat('Microsoft.Network/publicIpAddresses/',
    parameters('publicIpAddressName'))]"
            ],
  "properties": {
    "ipConfigurations": [
            {
```

```
"name": "ipconfig1",
"properties": {
"subnet": {
"id": "[variables('subnetRef')]"
              },
"privateIPAllocationMethod": "Dynamic",
"publicIpAddress": {
"id": "[resourceId(resourceGroup().name, 'Microsoft.Network/
       publicIpAddresses', parameters('publicIpAddressName'))]"
              }
          }
      }
    ],
    "networkSecurityGroup": {
        "id": "[variables('nsgId')]"
    }
  }
},
```

The next step is to include the definition of the network security group; see Listing 9-8.

Listing 9-8. Network Security Group Definition

```
{
  "name": "[parameters('networkSecurityGroupName')]",
  "type": "Microsoft.Network/networkSecurityGroups",
  "apiVersion": "2019-02-01",
  "location": "[parameters('location')]",
  "properties": {
     "securityRules": "[parameters('networkSecurityGroupRules')]"
         }
      },
```

Now let's proceed with the definition of the virtual network and subnets; see Listing 9-9.

Listing 9-9. Definition of Virtual Network and Subnets

```
{
  "name": "[parameters('virtualNetworkName')]",
  "type": "Microsoft.Network/virtualNetworks",
  "apiVersion": "2019-09-01",
  "location": "[parameters('location')]",
  "properties": {
    "addressSpace": {
        "addressPrefixes": "[parameters('addressPrefixes')]"
              },
        "subnets": "[parameters('subnets')]"
            }
        },
```

Lastly, we will add the definition of the public IP address; see Listing 9-10.

Listing 9-10. Definition of Public IP Address

```
{
 "name": "[parameters('publicIpAddressName')]",
 "type": "Microsoft.Network/publicIpAddresses",
 "apiVersion": "2019-02-01",
 "location": "[parameters('location')]",
 "properties": {
     "publicIpAllocationMethod": "[parameters('publicIpAddressType')]"
        },
 "sku": {
     "name": "[parameters('publicIpAddressSku')]"
           },
     "zones": [
             "[parameters('zone')]"
             ]
         }
```

Now we will define the parameters; see Listing 9-11.

Listing 9-11. Definition of Parameters in the ARM Template

```
"location": {
    "type": "string"
},
"networkInterfaceName": {
    "type": "string"
},
"networkSecurityGroupName": {
    "type": "string"
},
"networkSecurityGroupRules": {
    "type": "array"
},
"subnetName": {
    "type": "string"
},
"virtualNetworkName": {
    "type": "string"
},
"addressPrefixes": {
    "type": "array"
},
"subnets": {
    "type": "array"
},
"publicIpAddressName": {
    "type": "string"
},
"publicIpAddressType": {
    "type": "string"
},
"publicIpAddressSku": {
    "type": "string"
},
"virtualMachineName": {
```

```
            "type": "string"
        },
        "virtualMachineComputerName": {
            "type": "string"
        },
        "virtualMachineRG": {
            "type": "string"
        },
        "osDiskType": {
            "type": "string"
        },
        "virtualMachineSize": {
            "type": "string"
        },
        "adminUsername": {
            "type": "string"
        },
        "adminPassword": {
            "type": "secureString"
        },
        "zone": {
            "type": "string"
        }
```

Once we have the resources and parameters sections of our template, let's work on the definition of the variables. See Listing 9-12.

Listing 9-12. Definition of Variables in the ARM Template

```
"variables": {
  "nsgId": "[resourceId(resourceGroup().name, 'Microsoft.Network/
  networkSecurityGroups', parameters('networkSecurityGroupName'))]",
  "vnetId": "[resourceId(resourceGroup().name,'Microsoft.Network/
  virtualNetworks', parameters('virtualNetworkName'))]",
    "subnetRef": "[concat(variables('vnetId'), '/subnets/',
  parameters('subnetName'))]"
    },
```

Lastly, we will create a parameters file to pass the actual values; see Listing 9-13.

Listing 9-13. Definition of Parameter Values in the Parameters File

```
{
    "$schema": "https://schema.management.azure.com/schemas/2015-01-01/
    deploymentParameters.json#",
    "contentVersion": "1.0.0.0",
    "parameters": {
        "location": {
            "value": "eastus"
        },
        "networkInterfaceName": {
            "value": "ifabrikNic"
        },
        "networkSecurityGroupName": {
            "value": "ifabrikNsg"
        },
        "networkSecurityGroupRules": {
            "value": [
                {
                    "name": "RDP",
                    "properties": {
                        "priority": 300,
                        "protocol": "TCP",
                        "access": "Allow",
                        "direction": "Inbound",
                        "sourceAddressPrefix": "*",
                        "sourcePortRange": "*",
                        "destinationAddressPrefix": "*",
                        "destinationPortRange": "3389"
                    }
                }
            ]
        },
```

```
    "subnetName": {
        "value": "default"
    },
    "virtualNetworkName": {
        "value": "ifabrik-vnet"
    },
    "addressPrefixes": {
        "value": [
            "10.0.0.0/16"
        ]
    },
    "subnets": {
        "value": [
            {
                "name": "default",
                "properties": {
                    "addressPrefix": "10.0.0.0/24"
                }
            }
        ]
    },
    "publicIpAddressName": {
        "value": "ifabrik-pip"
    },
    "publicIpAddressType": {
        "value": "Static"
    },
    "publicIpAddressSku": {
        "value": "Standard"
    },
    "virtualMachineName": {
        "value": "ifabrik-vm"
    },
    "virtualMachineComputerName": {
        "value": "ifabrik-vm"
    },
```

```
    "virtualMachineRG": {
        "value": "ifabrikRg"
    },
    "osDiskType": {
        "value": "StandardSSD_LRS"
    },
    "virtualMachineSize": {
        "value": "Standard_D16as_v4"
    },
    "adminUsername": {
        "value": "azureuser"
    },
    "adminPassword": {
        "value": null
    },
    "zone": {
        "value": "1"
    }
  }
}
```

You can find this template at the following URL:

https://github.com/daveRendon/iac/tree/main/chapter-9/
create%20virtual%20machine%20using%20resource%20dependencies

Note   To deploy this example, you might have to run `az vm image list --all --output table --publisher 'microsoftwindowsserver' --sku 'windows-server-2022'`. The secure string can be passed during deployment.

If you deployed the ARM template shown earlier, you should see your virtual machine successfully deployed along with the following resources defined in the ARM template: network interface, virtual network, public IP address, virtual network and subnet, network security group, and the disk, as shown in Figure 9-4.

☐ 🖼 ifabrik-pip	Public IP address
☐ 🖥 ifabrik-vm	Virtual machine
☐ 💾 ifabrik-vm_OsDisk_1_7115a1aca2c445909b1dfcf58ea105de	Disk
☐ ⟨·⟩ ifabrik-vnet	Virtual network
☐ 🗔 ifabrikNic	Network interface
☐ 🛡 ifabrikNsg	Network security group

Figure 9-4. *Virtual machine deployment*

This example might sound simple, but it helps you better understand resource dependencies and how you can start working on the definition of the resources that are dependent on another one.

We can take a similar use case: the iFabrik team needs to deploy two web applications running as application services. Each application service will have its own application service plan. Also, consider that the second web application will run a service dependent on the first web application.

We have a case where we could find ourselves with the following template error: "circular dependency detected."

Using Circular Dependencies

Circular dependencies mean that you might have resources defined in your ARM template that depend on multiple resources in such a way that it is likely that your deployment might not start or be successfully provisioned. For instance, say you have these three resources:

- A web app

- A source control

- An app service plan

The web app depends on the app service plan, the source control depends on the web app, and the app service plan depends on the source control.

Figure 9-5 highlights this circular dependency.

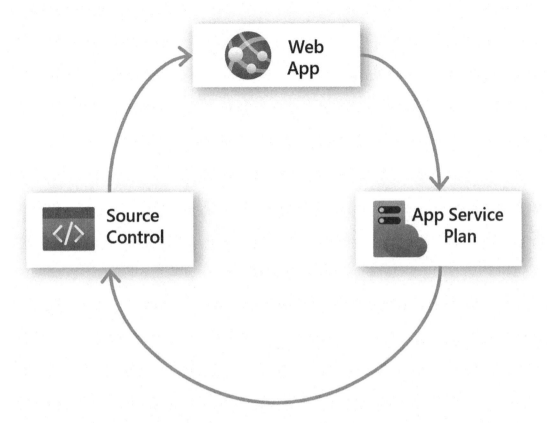

Figure 9-5. *Circular dependencies*

Suppose you find yourself with a circular dependency preventing you from successfully completing a deployment. In that case, the recommendation is to remove potential dependsOn properties that might cause the problem and work with child resources instead as an alternative.

Summary

This chapter reviewed how to better control the deployment order of the resources defined in your ARM template by using the dependsOn property. We also went through an example of resource dependencies to deploy a virtual machine and showed how you can handle circular dependencies in your ARM template.

In the next chapter, we will go over the use of multiple functions and work with various value types such as strings and numeric values in your ARM template.

CHAPTER 10

Using Functions in Your ARM Template

This chapter will focus on using logical operations and expressions in your Azure Resource Manager (ARM) template. We will go over the scope of the functions available and the most common functions utilized in ARM templates. This chapter will also cover how to create your own custom ARM template function.

The topics in this chapter include the following:

- Understanding ARM template functions

- Examples of ARM template functions

- Creating your own ARM template function

Although we used some ARM template functions in previous chapters, it is important to fully understand the ARM template functions that we can leverage to work with various values such as strings and numeric values.

ARM templates are based on the JSON language. The ARM language includes richer expressions that we can leverage to refer to values or evaluate expressions in our ARM templates.

While a variety of ARM template functions can be utilized, we will focus on the most relevant ones.

Understanding Functions in ARM Templates

ARM template functions are expressions available in the ARM language that will allow you to define logical operations and evaluate expressions in your ARM templates.

159

© David Rendón 2022
D. Rendón, *Building Applications with Azure Resource Manager (ARM)*,
https://doi.org/10.1007/978-1-4842-7747-8_10

In general, ARM template functions will help you do the following:

- Creating reusable ARM templates

- Speeding up the naming process of variables, parameters, and resources

- Facilitating the use of unique identifiers by defining prefixes and appending them to a resource

We can categorize the ARM template functions available into ten categories, listed here:

- Array functions

- Comparison functions

- Date functions

- Deployment functions

- Logical functions

- Numeric functions

- Object functions

- Resource functions

- String functions

So, how can we declare a function in an ARM template? Let's start by understanding the fundamentals of an ARM function.

Declaring an ARM Template Function

Functions are declared in the ARM template, and depending on your needs, they can be defined in the `parameters`, `variables`, `resources`, and `output` sections of the ARM template.

To declare a function, you start by adding quotes, and then inside the quotes, you add square braces, [ ]. This will denote that whatever is inside the square braces will be interpolated.

Then, we provide the name of the function and add parentheses. Inside the parentheses, we will provide the parameters, variables, or string values needed to pass the function.

Listing 10-1 highlights the basic structure of an ARM template function.

Listing 10-1. ARM Template Function Definition

```
"[functionName(param1,param2)]"
```

Note   Instead of passing a parameter value, it is possible to include a nested function.

The ARM template shown in Listing 10-2 includes the definition of a function in the parameters section that will use the location from the existing resource group.

Listing 10-2. ARM Function Definition

```
{
  "$schema": "https://schema.management.azure.com/schemas/2019-04-01/
  deploymentTemplate.json#",
    "contentVersion": "1.0.0.0",
    "parameters": {
        "location": {
            "type": "string",
            "defaultValue": "[resourceGroup().location]"
        }
    },
    "functions": [],
    "variables": {},
    "resources": [],
    "outputs": {
        "location": {
            "type": "string",
            "value": "[parameters('location')]"
        }
    }
}
```

In the example shown in Listing 10-2, we are using two functions: one function in the parameters section that will get the location value from the resource group, and a second function in the output section that will show the location value from the resource group. Figure 10-1 shows the output.

```
DeploymentName        : iFabrikDeployment06-21-2021
ResourceGroupName     : iFabrikRG
ProvisioningState     : Succeeded
Timestamp             : 6/22/2021 1:28:03 AM
Mode                  : Incremental
TemplateLink          :
Parameters            :
Outputs               :
                        Name              Type                          Value
                        ==============    ==========================    ==========
                        location          String                        eastus
```

Figure 10-1. *ARM function output*

This might look like a basic example; however, pulling the location is useful for those cases where we need to deploy our environment in the same location. Rather than passing the location name every single time, we can reference the location from the resource group.

Example: Creating an Azure Storage Account Using ARM Template Functions

In this example, we will leverage Azure ARM template functions to create a storage account. While we could hard-code some of the values for our storage account, such as the storage account name, location, or SKU, we are going to leverage some of the common Azure ARM template functions. See Figure 10-2.

```
{
    "$schema": "https://schema.management.azure.com/schemas/2019-04-01/deploymentTemplate.json#",
    "contentVersion": "1.0.0.0",
    Parameter file: "azuredeploy.parameters.json" | Change...
    "parameters": {
        Value: "ifabriksa"
        "storageAccountName": {
            "type": "string",
            "metadata": {
                "description": "The name of the storage account."
            }
        }
    },
    "variables": {
        "storageAccountType": "Standard_GRS",
        // use of "toLower" function to convert the specified string to lower case.
        // use of "concat" function as nested function to combine multiple string values and return the concatenated string.
        // use of "uniqueString" function to creates a deterministic hash string based on the values provided as parameters.
        "storageAccountName1": "[toLower( concat( parameters('storageAccountName'), uniqueString(resourceGroup().id) ) )]"
    },
    "resources": [
        {
            //Pass on the storage account name as variable
            "name": "[variables('storageAccountName1')]",
            "type": "Microsoft.Storage/storageAccounts",
            "apiVersion": "2019-06-01",
            "tags": {
                "displayName": "storageaccount1"
            },
            "location": "[resourceGroup().location]",
            "kind": "StorageV2",
            "sku": {
                //Pass on the storage account type as variable
                "name": "[variables('storageAccountType')]"
            }
        }
    ],
    "outputs": {}
}
```

Figure 10-2. *ARM template that creates a storage account*

In the ARM template shown in Figure 10-2, we are using the following ARM template functions:

- toLower(): This will help us to convert the storage account name string to lowercase.

- concat(): This will combine multiple string values and return a concatenated string.

- uniqueString(): This will help us to create a unique hash string based on the id property of the resource group.

- resourceGroup(): For this specific template, we are getting the location property from the resource group.

You can access the template shown in Figure 10-2 using the following URL:

```
https://github.com/daveRendon/iac/blob/main/chapter-10/
storage-account-using-functions/azuredeploy.json
```

Now let's take the previous ARM template as a baseline, and we will consider the use case where we need to deploy multiple storage accounts.

Example: Creating Multiple Azure Storage Accounts Using ARM Template Functions

In the example shown in Figure 10-3, we will use the `concat()` function, and we will use the `copyIndex()` function as a nested function to create the iteration needed to deploy the required number of storage accounts. See Figure 10-3.

```
{
    "$schema": "https://schema.management.azure.com/schemas/2019-04-01/deploymentTemplate.json#",
    "contentVersion": "1.0.0.0",
    Parameter file: "azuredeploy.parameters.json" | Change...
    "parameters": {
        Value: "ifabriksa"
        "storageAccountNamePrefix": {
            "type": "string",
            "metadata": {
                "description": "The name of the storage account."
            }
        },
        Using default value
        "storageCount": {
            "type": "int",
            "defaultValue": 3
        }
    },
    "variables": {
        "storageAccountType": "Standard_LRS",
        // use of "toLower" function to convert the specified string to lower case.
        // use of "concat" function as nested function to combine multiple string values and return the concatenated string.
        // use of "uniqueString" function to creates a deterministic hash string based on the values provided as parameters.
        "storageAccountName": "[toLower( concat( parameters('storageAccountNamePrefix'), uniqueString(resourceGroup().id) ) )]"
    },
    "resources": [
        {
            "type": "Microsoft.Storage/storageAccounts",
            "apiVersion": "2019-04-01",
            // use of "concat" function to combine multiple string values and return the concatenated string.
            // use of "copyIndex" function to return the index of an iteration loop
            "name": "[concat(copyIndex(), variables('storageAccountName'))]",
            "location": "[resourceGroup().location]",
            "sku": {
                "name": "[variables('storageAccountType')]"
            },
            "kind": "Storage",
            "properties": {},
            "copy": {
                "name": "storagecopy",
                "count": "[parameters('storageCount')]"
            }
        }
    ]
}
```

Figure 10-3. *ARM template that creates multiple storage accounts*

As you can see in Figure 10-3, we can pass on the number of storage accounts as a parameter and provide the prefix of the storage account name.

We are also leveraging the copyIndex() function to return the current iteration in the loop along with the copy object. This function can take two parameters: loopName and offset.

The loopName parameter is the actual name of the loop that gets the iteration, while the offset parameter is the number added to the zero-based iteration value.

Note that the name of the storage account reflects the zero-based iteration value, as shown in Figure 10-4.

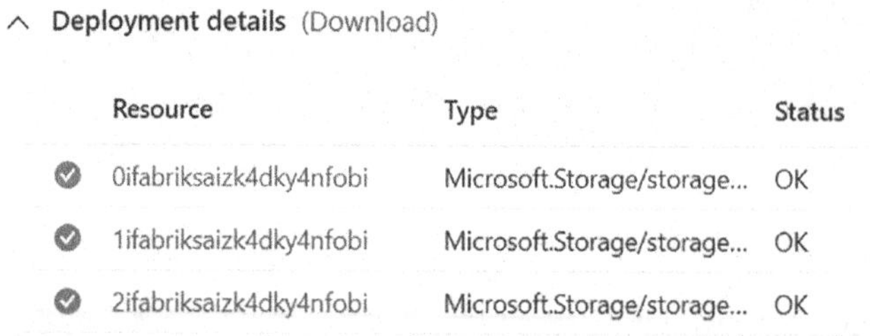
Deployment details (Download)

Resource	Type	Status
0ifabriksaizk4dky4nfobi	Microsoft.Storage/storage...	OK
1ifabriksaizk4dky4nfobi	Microsoft.Storage/storage...	OK
2ifabriksaizk4dky4nfobi	Microsoft.Storage/storage...	OK

Figure 10-4. *Deployment details from the ARM template that creates multiple storage accounts*

The previous ARM template code can be found here:

`https://github.com/daveRendon/iac/tree/main/chapter-10/create-n-storage-accounts`

Working with ARM template functions can help you also with conditional deployments and validate whether a specific resource should be deployed or not at all.

The following ARM template provides an example of a conditional deployment using the `equals()` function.

Example: Conditional Deployment for Web Applications Using ARM Template Functions

In the next ARM template, we will leverage conditional deployments to provision a Linux-based or Windows-based web application based on the parameters passed at deployment time.

Let's analyze the structure of this ARM template; it includes the following:

- Parameters
    - `platform`
    - `webAppName`
    - `location`
    - `sku`
    - `repoUrl`
    - `helloWorld`

- Variables

  - language

  - linuxVersion

  - linuxOffer

  - windowsOffer

  - appServicePlanPortalName

  - gitRepoReference

  - gitRepoUrl

  - configReferenceWindows

- Resources

  - App service plan

  - App service

  - Source controls

Based on the platform selected at deployment time, we will be able to provision an app service plan on a Windows-based or Linux-based computer and an app service.

Listing 10-3 highlights the parameters section of the ARM template.

Listing 10-3. ARM Template, parameters Section

```
"parameters": {
    "platform": {
            "type": "string",
            "allowedValues": [
                "Win",
                "Linux"
            ],
            "metadata": {
                "description": "Select the OS type to deploy."
            }
        },
```

```
"webAppName": {
  "type": "string",
  "defaultValue": "[concat('webApp-', uniqueString
  (resourceGroup().id))]",
  "minLength": 2,
  "metadata": {
    "description": "Web app name."
  }
},
"location": {
  "type": "string",
  "defaultValue": "[resourceGroup().location]",
  "metadata": {
    "description": "Location for all resources."
  }
},
"sku": {
  "type": "string",
  "defaultValue": "F1",
  "metadata": {
    "description": "The SKU of App Service Plan."
  }
},
"repoUrl": {
  "type": "string",
  "defaultValue": " ",
  "metadata": {
    "description": "Optional Git Repo URL"
  }
},
"helloWorld": {
  "type": "bool",
  "defaultValue": false,
  "metadata": {
```

```
        "description": "true=deploy a sample Hello World app."
      }
    }
},
```

Listing 10-4 highlights the variables section of the ARM template.

Listing 10-4. ARM Template, variables Section

```
"variables": {
  "language": ".net",
  "linuxVersion": "DOTNETCORE|3.0",
  "linuxOffer": "linux",
  "windowsOffer": "windows",
  "appServicePlanPortalName": "[concat('AppServicePlan-',
  parameters('webAppName'))]",
  "gitRepoReference": {
    ".net": "https://github.com/Azure-Samples/
    app-service-web-dotnet-get-started",
    "node": "https://github.com/Azure-Samples/nodejs-docs-hello-world",
    "php": "https://github.com/Azure-Samples/php-docs-hello-world",
    "html": "https://github.com/Azure-Samples/html-docs-hello-world"
    },
  "gitRepoUrl": "[if(bool(parameters('helloWorld')),
  variables('gitRepoReference')[toLower(variables('language'))],
  parameters('repoUrl'))]",
"configReferenceWindows": {
  ".net": {
   "comments": ".Net app. No additional configuration needed."
     },
   "html": {
   "comments": "HTML app. No additional configuration needed."
     },
   "php": {
       "phpVersion": "7.4"
     },
```

169

```
"node": {
    "appSettings": [
      {
        "name": "WEBSITE_NODE_DEFAULT_VERSION",
        "value": "12.15.0"
      }
    ]
  }
},
```

In this section of the ARM template, we are leveraging logical functions such as if() and bool(), as well as string functions such as toLower().

The function evaluates the value from the parameter helloWorld. If the Boolean of the converted value is true, then the ARM template will deploy a sample Hello World app.

Then through the use of the toLower() function in [toLower(variables('language'))] we ensure that the string is converted to lowercase. Finally, we pass the repoURL parameter.

Now let's analyze the resources section of the ARM template, as shown in Listing 10-5.

Listing 10-5. ARM Template, resources Section

```
"resources": [
    {
      "type": "Microsoft.Web/serverfarms",
      "apiVersion": "2020-06-01",
      "name": "[variables('appServicePlanPortalName')]",
      "location": "[parameters('location')]",
      "sku": {
        "name": "[parameters('sku')]"
      },
      "kind": "[if(equals(parameters('platform'), 'Linux'),
      variables('linuxOffer'), variables('windowsOffer'))]"

    },
```

```
{
  "type": "Microsoft.Web/sites",
  "apiVersion": "2020-06-01",
  "name": "[parameters('webAppName')]",
  "location": "[parameters('location')]",

  "dependsOn": [
    "[resourceId('Microsoft.Web/serverfarms', variables('appServicePlan
    PortalName'))]"
  ],
  "properties": {
    "serverFarmId": "[resourceId('Microsoft.Web/serverfarms', variables
    ('appServicePlanPortalName'))]",
    "siteConfig":"[if(equals(parameters('platform'), 'Linux'),
    variables('linuxVersion'), variables('configReferenceWindows'))]"
  },
  "resources": [
    {
      "condition": "[contains(parameters('repoUrl'),'http')]",
      "type": "sourcecontrols",
      "apiVersion": "2020-06-01",
      "name": "web",
      "location": "[parameters('location')]",
      "dependsOn": [
        "[resourceId('Microsoft.Web/sites', parameters('webAppName'))]"
      ],
      "properties": {
        "repoUrl": "[parameters('repoUrl')]",
        "branch": "master",
        "isManualIntegration": true
      }
    }
  ]
}
]
}
```

Note that we are using a couple of functions in this ARM template; first, in the `kind` property for the server farm, we are validating whether the platform is Linux based using the logical function `if` and the comparison function `equals`. Then we pass on the variables depending on each use case.

We are also using a similar approach for the `siteConfig` property: we validate the platform and then pass along the variables based on the evaluation of the value of the platform.

Lastly, we declare a condition to deploy a source control only if the parameter for the `repoURL` parameter is passed during deployment time.

While there are multiple ways to deploy a template, Listing 10-6 shows an example of how to deploy this ARM template via Azure PowerShell.

Listing 10-6. PowerShell Script to Deploy ARM Template

```
$date = Get-Date -Format "MM-dd-yyyy"
$deploymentName = "iFabrikDeployment"+"$date"
New-AzResourceGroupDeployment -Name $deploymentName -ResourceGroupName
iFabrik -TemplateFile .\azuredeploy.json -TemplateParameterFile
.\azuredeploy.parameters.json
```

Figure 10-5 highlights the output from this deployment.

```
DeploymentName          : iFabrikDeployment06-25-2021
ResourceGroupName       : iFabrik
ProvisioningState       : Succeeded
Timestamp               : 6/26/2021 1:04:21 AM
Mode                    : Incremental
TemplateLink            :
Parameters              :
                          Name               Type                          Value
                          ===============    ==========================    ==========
                          platform           String                        Win
                          webAppName         String                        webApp-4lotfgeetgbes
                          location           String                        eastus
                          sku                String                        F1
                          repoUrl            String
                          helloWorld         Bool                          False
```

Figure 10-5. *ARM template output*

We can also deploy this ARM template using the Azure portal through a custom deployment, as shown in Figure 10-6.

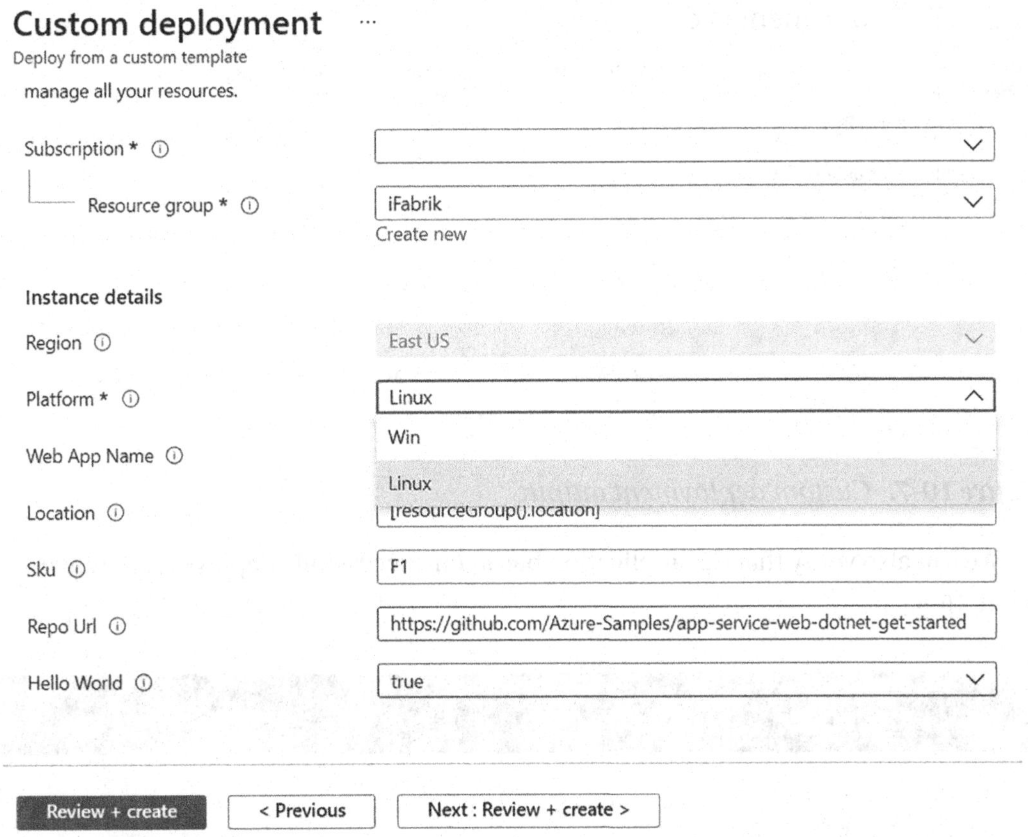

Custom deployment   ...

Deploy from a custom template

manage all your resources.

Subscription * ⓘ	⌄
└── Resource group * ⓘ	iFabrik ⌄
	Create new

Instance details

Region ⓘ	East US ⌄
Platform * ⓘ	Linux ⌃
Web App Name ⓘ	Win
	Linux
Location ⓘ	[resourceGroup().location]
Sku ⓘ	F1
Repo Url ⓘ	https://github.com/Azure-Samples/app-service-web-dotnet-get-started
Hello World ⓘ	true ⌄

Review + create	< Previous	Next : Review + create >

Figure 10-6. *Custom deployment using the Azure portal*

Note that in this custom deployment we are going to provision a Linux-based app service, and we will pass on a repository, which means we will create an app service plan, a Linux-based app service, and a source control, as shown in Figure 10-7.

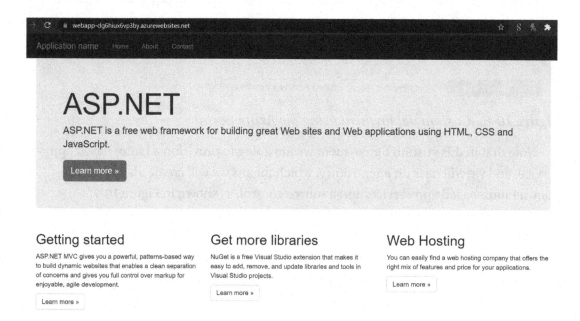

✅ Your deployment is complete

Deployment name: Microsoft.Template-20210625201807   Start time: 6/25/2021, 8:18:08 PM
Subscription: Correlation ID:
Resource group: iFabrik

∧ Deployment details (Download)

	Resource	Type	Status	Operation details
✅	webApp-dg6hiux6vp3by/	Microsoft.Web/sites/sourcecontrols	OK	Operation details
✅	webApp-dg6hiux6vp3by	Microsoft.Web/sites	OK	Operation details
✅	AppServicePlan-webApp-	Microsoft.Web/serverfarms	OK	Operation details

∧ Next steps

Figure 10-7. *Custom deployment output*

We can also verify that the application has been successfully deployed, as shown in Figure 10-8.

Figure 10-8. *Application running as app service*

The code related to the previous ARM template can be found here:

```
https://github.com/daveRendon/iac/tree/main/chapter-10/
conditional-deployment-webapp-using-functions
```

You should now be better able to understand how you can leverage ARM template functions for your deployments. So far, we have reviewed predefined functions. However, it is also possible to create your own ARM template functions. Let's see how you can start creating your own ARM template functions.

Creating Your Own Function

You might need a specific functionality or need to evaluate certain expressions that are not available as predefined functions. For those cases, you can create your own ARM template functions, usually called *user-defined functions.*

Remember the basic structure of the ARM template? There is a specific section for functions that we can leverage to create user-defined functions. See Listing 10-7.

Listing 10-7. ARM Template Structure

```
{
    "$schema": "https://schema.management.azure.com/schemas/2019-04-01/
    deploymentTemplate.json#",
    "contentVersion": "1.0.0.0",
    "parameters": {},
    "functions": [],
    "variables": {},
    "resources": [],
    "outputs": {}
}
```

Bear in mind that user-defined functions have some limitations:

- Parameters are not allowed to have default values.

- Variables cannot be accessed through the user-defined function.

- A user-defined function cannot call another user-defined function.

So, how can we declare a user-defined function?

Declaring User-Defined Functions

User-defined functions can be defined in the `functions` section of the ARM template. To define a function, we must include `namespace` as a property and the name of the function within a `members` property.

Each user-defined function includes two sections: a `parameters` section and the output section. Listing 10-8 highlights the structure of a user-defined function.

Listing 10-8. User-Defined Function Structure

```
"functions": [
    {
        "namespace": "<namespace-name>",
        "members": {
            "<function-name>": {
                "parameters": [
                    {
                        "name": "<parameter-name>",
                        "type": "<parameter-type>"
                    }
                ],
                "output": {
                    "type": "<output-type>",
                    "value": "<expression>"
                }
            }
        }
    }
],
```

The first step to declare our own function is to define the namespace. It is important to note that a namespace can contain multiple functions, and you can define multiple namespaces in the ARM template.

Once the namespace is defined, we need to provide a name for our function within the `members` section, as shown in Listing 10-9.

Listing 10-9. Definition of Function Name

```
"functions": [
    {
        "namespace": "<namespace-name>",
        "members": {
          "<function-name>": {
```

Now, the user-defined function has two sections: the `parameters` section and the output section. As mentioned, we can use parameters only in user-defined functions. Listing 10-10 highlights the `parameters` section and the `output` section.

Listing 10-10. The parameters and output Sections

```
"<function-name>": {
        "parameters": [
          {
              "name": "<parameter-name>",
              "type": "<parameter-type>"
          }
        ],
        "output": {
          "type": "<output-type>",
          "value": "<expression>"
        }
    }
```

In the `parameters` section, we will provide the input values to evaluate in our function. Note that this `parameters` section is basically a JSON array, and we can use any of the supported values for the parameter types such as arrays, Booleans, integers, objects, strings, secure strings, and secure objects.

The `output` section will include two properties: the data type and the value. The data type can be any JSON data type; the value will contain the actual evaluation of the expression.

Now that we have seen the basic structure of a user-defined function, let's review a practical example.

Example: Creating a Unique Prefix for Resources in Your Environment

In this example, we will create a user-defined function to standardize the naming convention for multiple resources. We will create multiple storage accounts, and all of them should have the same prefix, as well as a suffix that represents the resource name and the iteration number.

The deployment should contain the following resources:

- `ifabrik01storage`

- `ifabrik02storage`

- `ifabrik03storage`

The ARM template shown in Listing 10-11 includes a user-defined function to comply with the following naming convention for the storage accounts: prefix + iteration + storage.

We will start by adding two parameters: `storageAccountNamePrefix` and `storageCount`.

Listing 10-11. ARM Template, parameters Section

```
"parameters": {
    "storageAccountNamePrefix": {
        "type": "string",
        "metadata": {
          "description": "The prefix of the storage account."
            }
        },
    "storageCount": {
        "type": "int",
        "defaultValue": 3,
        "metadata": {
          "description": "Number of storage accounts to deploy"
            }
        }
    },
```

Then, we will add our user-defined function; we are declaring the namespace called iFabricStorageAccounts and the name uniqueName. Then we will define three parameters: prefix, increment, and resourceType. Lastly, we will define the output properties; we will include the type string, and the value will include the expression to evaluate. See Listing 10-12.

Listing 10-12. ARM Template, User-Defined Function

```
"functions": [
     {
       "namespace": "iFabrikStorageAccounts",
       "members": {
           "uniqueName": {
              "parameters": [
                   {
                      "name": "prefix",
                      "type": "string"
                   },
                   {
                      "name": "increment",
                      "type": "int"
                   },
                   {
                      "name": "resourceType",
                      "type": "string"
                   }
              ],
              "output": {
                   "type": "string",
                   "value": "[toLower(concat(parameters('prefix'),
                   parameters('increment'), parameters('resourceType')))]"
              }
           }
       }
     }
  ],
```

For the expression to evaluate, we are using a couple of predefined functions such as toLower(), and then we will concatenate the parameters: prefix, increment, and resourceType.

Now we will add the storageAccountType variable, as shown in Listing 10-13.

Listing 10-13. ARM Template Variable

```
"variables": {
       "storageAccountType": "Standard_LRS"
   },
```

Next we will create the storage account using the code in Listing 10-14.

Listing 10-14. ARM Template Resources

```
"resources": [
       {
           "type": "Microsoft.Storage/storageAccounts",
           "apiVersion": "2019-04-01",
           "name": "[iFabrikStorageAccounts.uniqueName(parameters('storage
           AccountNamePrefix'), copyIndex('storagecopy',1), 'storage')]",
           "location": "[resourceGroup().location]",
           "sku": {
               "name": "[variables('storageAccountType')]"
           },
           "kind": "Storage",
           "properties": {},
           "copy": {
               "name": "storagecopy",
               "count": "[parameters('storageCount')]"
           }
       }
   ]
}
```

Note that we are using the user-defined function in the "" property, as shown in Listing 10-15.

Listing 10-15. User-Defined Function

```
"name": "[iFabrikStorageAccounts.uniqueName(parameters(
'storageAccountNamePrefix'), copyIndex('storagecopy',1), 'storage')]",
```

To refer to the user-defined function, we first pass the namespace, then the name of the function, and then the parameters needed to evaluate the expression.

We can deploy this ARM template using PowerShell with the command shown in Listing 10-16.

Listing 10-16. Deploying ARM Template Using PowerShell

```
$date = Get-Date -Format "MM-dd-yyyy"
$deploymentName = "iFabrikDeployment"+"$date"
New-AzResourceGroupDeployment -Name $deploymentName -ResourceGroupName
iFabrik -TemplateFile .\azuredeploy.json -TemplateParameterFile
.\azuredeploy.parameters.json
```

Figure 10-9 highlights the result from this deployment.

```
DeploymentName       : iFabrikDeployment06-27-2021
ResourceGroupName    : iFabrik
ProvisioningState    : Succeeded
Timestamp            : 6/27/2021 5:35:58 PM
Mode                 : Incremental
TemplateLink         :
Parameters           :
                       Name                        Type                        Value
                       ==========================  ==========================  ==========
                       storageAccountNamePrefix    String                      ifabrik
                       storageCount                Int                         3
```

Figure 10-9. *ARM template deployment result*

We can also verify via PowerShell or using the Azure portal the name of the storage accounts recently provisioned, as shown in Figure 10-10.

Name ↑↓	Type ↑↓	Location ↑↓
ifabrik1storage	Storage account	East US
ifabrik2storage	Storage account	East US
ifabrik3storage	Storage account	East US

Figure 10-10. *Storage accounts*

The code related to the previous ARM template can be found at `https://github.com/daveRendon/iac/tree/main/chapter-10/user-defined-function`.

User-defined functions can be useful when working with multiple resources, and there's a need to evaluate custom expressions rather than relying only on the predefined functions.

In the previous example, we reviewed how you can create a user-defined function. Note that while user-defined functions can help you facilitate reuse in your ARM template, we might be limited in the use of this user-defined functions across ARM templates, as we need to declare the user-defined function in each of the templates we plan to use.

Summary

This chapter reviewed what ARM template functions are and how you can leverage predefined functions in your ARM templates.

We also went through some practical examples of using ARM template functions and then reviewed the potential use of user-defined functions.

Lastly, we created an ARM template that leverages user-defined functions to create multiple storage accounts.

In the next chapter, we will review how to specify the deployment of your resources and validate if we should update the existing resources in the ARM template or perform a complete update on them.

CHAPTER 11

Deployment Modes of Your ARM Template

In Chapter 5, we reviewed how to define the various scopes in which you can target an Azure Resource Manager (ARM) deployment. Sometimes we might have to deploy an ARM template and target the same environment at different scopes.

So, how can we specify if we want to overwrite an existing deployment? Is it possible to target the same environment at different scopes without impacting the existing resources?

This chapter will cover the Azure Resource Manager deployment modes and focus on the main differences between the incremental and complete modes. This chapter will also cover how to set the deployment mode and show examples of when to leverage incremental mode.

Specifically, the chapter will cover these topics:

- Understanding incremental mode

- Understanding complete mode

- Setting the deployment mode

Introduction to Scopes and Modes

Before we dive into deployment modes, let's understand the difference between deployment scopes and deployment modes. *Deployment scopes* allow you to define where the resources included in the ARM template will be deployed: to a subscription level, to a resource group, to a tenant level, etc.

Deployment modes allow you to specify how the resources in the ARM template will be provisioned, and there are only two modes: incremental mode and complete mode.

© David Rendón 2022
D. Rendón, *Building Applications with Azure Resource Manager (ARM)*,
https://doi.org/10.1007/978-1-4842-7747-8_11

183

When provisioning a virtual machine in Azure, we can specify a deployment scope and target the deployment to a resource group. Then, we might have to deploy an additional data disk for the same virtual machine or create and attach a new network interface. We can deploy a new ARM template that includes the configuration for the additional disk or the new network interface.

Deployment modes help us create new resources in the same environment, and based on the deployment mode that we define, this can impact the existing resources or not at all. By specifying the deployment mode, we can control how Azure Resource Manager handles resources in the environment that did not exist in the initial deployment.

For both cases, meaning incremental mode and complete mode, Resource Manager will attempt to create all the resources included in the ARM template. However, if a resource already exists in the environment and there are no updates or changes to the settings of a specific resource, Resource Manager will leave that resource unchanged.

On the contrary, if there is any update on the settings of a given resource, Resource Manager will update that resource with the new values. Note that if you attempt to update the properties of a resource, such as the location, you will notice an error in the deployment. The recommendation is to deploy a new resource instead and update the location.

Now let's understand how incremental mode works.

Understanding Incremental Mode

Incremental mode is the default option when we don't specify any deployment mode. When you define the resources in the ARM template and deploy the ARM template, Resource Manager will validate if those resources already exist in the resource group.

If those resources are new to the resource group, then Resource Manager will create them.

Suppose the ARM template contains resources that match the resources that already exist in the resource group. In that case, Resource Manager will attempt to make that resource look like what's in the template regarding the settings and properties. Here comes the tricky part.

When we deploy an ARM template that matches an existing resource in the resource group and we don't define properties for those resources, Resource Manager will not ignore those properties. They will be set to the default values.

In addition, if you have a resource that wasn't created during the initial deployment or if you updated the ARM template, anything that is not explicitly defined will be set to the default values.

As mentioned earlier in this chapter, not all the properties from the resources can be updated, such as the location.

Now, you might have an existing resource in the resource group that is not in the ARM template; in this case, Resource Manager will not attempt to modify this resource, and it will be not touched.

Incremental mode is usually considered a "safe mode" to deploy and update resources, mainly because Resource Manager will not try to delete resources that are not specified in the ARM template.

Now let's take a look at complete mode.

Understanding Complete Mode

Complete mode differs from incremental mode a bit as it will match what you're deploying in the ARM template to what you have in the resource group. For instance, when deploying an ARM template that targets a resource group, Resource Manager will take the ARM template and try to match the resources defined in the ARM template to the resources in the resource group in Azure.

Existing resources in Azure that are not defined in the ARM template will be removed.

As you can tell, we need to be careful when working with complete mode as it can impact existing resources in our environment.

There are some additional considerations when using complete mode. Resources provisioned using conditional deployments that evaluate to a false condition might be deleted depending on the version. For instance, if you're using a version previous to 2019-05-10, the resources will not be deleted; otherwise, they will be removed.

Consider the parent-child relationship resources; when you don't specify the parent resource in the ARM template, it will be deleted. The same applies to child resources; if the parent resource is not present in the ARM template, child resources will be removed.

Bear in mind that not all child resources are removed when they're not defined in the ARM template; it is recommended to take a look at the following URL to see how Resource Manager handles the deletion for specific resource types:

```
https://docs.microsoft.com/en-us/azure/azure-resource-manager/templates/
deployment-complete-mode-deletion
```

Now that we have explained incremental mode and complete mode, let's review a practical example to see how these two modes work.

Say we have the following resources in our resource group:

- An app service plan

- A website

- A source control

Our ARM template contains the following resources:

- An app service plan

- A website

- Azure Application Insights

If we use incremental mode, the resource group will have the following:

- An app service plan

- A website

- A source control

- Azure Application Insights

If we use complete mode, the resource group will have the following:

- An app service plan

- A website

- Azure Application Insights

Setting Deployment Mode

We can set the deployment mode using Azure CLI or PowerShell or define it in the ARM template.

To set the deployment mode using PowerShell, we can use the parameter mode, as shown in Listing 11-1.

Listing 11-1. Setting the Deployment Mode Using PowerShell

```
New-AzResourceGroupDeployment `
  -Mode Complete `
  -Name iFabrikDeployment `
  -ResourceGroupName iFabrikResourceGroup `
  -TemplateFile azuredeploy.json
```

To set the deployment mode using Azure CLI, we can leverage the code shown in Listing 11-2.

Listing 11-2. Setting the Deployment Mode Using Azure CLI

```
az deployment group create \
  --mode Complete \
  --name iFabrikDeployment \
  --resource-group iFabrikResourceGroup \
  --template-file azuredeploy.json
```

To set the incremental deployment mode when working with linked templates, we can define the mode as shown in Figure 11-1.

```
{
    "$schema": "https://schema.management.azure.com/schemas/2019-04-01/deploymentTemplate.json#",
    "contentVersion": "1.0.0.0",
    Select or create a parameter file...
    "parameters": {},
    "functions": [],
    "variables": {},
    "resources": [
        {
            "name": "linkedDeployment1",
            "type": "Microsoft.Resources/deployments",
            "apiVersion": "2020-10-01",
            "properties": {
                "mode": "Incremental",
                Linked template: ".\artifactsLocation\linkedTemplates\linkedTemplate.jsonartifactsLocationSasToken"
                "templateLink": {
                    "uri": "[concat('artifactsLocation', '/linkedTemplates/linkedTemplate.json', 'artifactsLocationSasToken')]",
                    "contentVersion": "1.0.0.0"
                },
                "parameters": {
                }
            }
        }
    ],
    "outputs": {}
}
```

Figure 11-1. *Setting incremental mode in an ARM template*

We can also define complete mode when working with linked templates, as shown in Figure 11-2.

```
{
    "$schema": "https://schema.management.azure.com/schemas/2019-04-01/deploymentTemplate.json#",
    "contentVersion": "1.0.0.0",
    Select or create a parameter file...
    "parameters": {},
    "functions": [],
    "variables": {},
    "resources": [
        {
            "name": "linkedDeployment1",
            "type": "Microsoft.Resources/deployments",
            "apiVersion": "2020-10-01",
            "properties": {
                "mode": "Complete",
                Linked template: ".\artifactsLocation\linkedTemplates\linkedTemplate.jsonartifactsLocationSasToken"
                "templateLink": {
                    "uri": "[concat('artifactsLocation', '/linkedTemplates/linkedTemplate.json', 'artifactsLocationSasToken')]",
                    "contentVersion": "1.0.0.0"
                },
                "parameters": {
                }
            }
        }
    ],
    "outputs": {}
}
```

Figure 11-2. *Setting complete mode in an ARM template*

There is an important consideration when you work with linked templates to provision a more complex solution. If the main ARM template is deployed in complete mode and linked templates are scoped to target the same resource group, all resources in the linked templates will be deployed in complete mode.

For linked templates, it is possible to define incremental mode only.

Summary

In this chapter, we reviewed the two deployment modes available to deploy our resources. We examined the main differences between them and how Resource Manager handles existing resources in the resource group.

In the next chapter, we will review how you can work with loops in your ARM template.

## CHAPTER 12

Working with Loops in Your ARM Template

This chapter will cover how to create multiple instances of the same resource in our ARM template. We will deep dive into using the copy element for resource iteration and for iteration for child resources. As you might have noticed, we reviewed variable iteration in Chapter 7, and we went through the essential uses of the copy element.

In this chapter, we will go over the following topics:

- Understanding the copy element in more depth

- Serial mode and parallel mode

- Resource dependencies in a loop

Usually, when working with larger environments in Azure, we might have to deploy a specific resource or a variety of resources multiple times. While we can hard-code the creation of resources multiple times, we can leverage loops in our ARM template to simplify the creation process of multiple resources.

We can leverage the copy element in our ARM template to iterate on a resource to deploy *N* versions of a resource or a set of resources that we need to deploy.

This way, we can deploy multiple versions of an identical resource with specific properties or settings but with different names. Now let's review how the copy element really works in the ARM template.

Understanding the copy Element

Resource Manager provides the ability to create loops in our ARM template by using the copy element so that we can create multiple instances of a resource.

© David Rendón 2022
D. Rendón, *Building Applications with Azure Resource Manager (ARM)*,
https://doi.org/10.1007/978-1-4842-7747-8_12

Picture the scenario in which you need to deploy multiple disks that will be attached to the same virtual machine.

Instead of defining each disk and its properties in the ARM template, we can leverage the copy element in our ARM template to create multiple copies of the same resource.

Think of this copy element as a function that will help you create loops in the ARM template to create as many copies of resources as you need. We can use the copy element for resources, variables, and outputs.

So, how can we define the copy element in the ARM template? The copy element is a fundamental JSON structure that includes three main properties: the name, the count, and the input value.

Listing 12-1 highlights the syntax of the copy element.

Listing 12-1. Syntax of the copy Element

```
"copy": {
  "name": "<name-of-loop>",
  "count": <number-of-iterations>,
  "input": <values-for-the-property>
}
```

In the previous listing, there are three main properties.

- name: This will be the identifier of your loop.

- count: This will help you specify how many iterations are needed for the resource.

- input: This defined the properties that should be repeated. It can include a single property, an array, or an object with properties and subproperties.

We can also have two additional properties: mode and batchSize.

The mode property refers to the preferred method to deploy multiple instances of a given resource. The mode property defines if the resources should be deployed in parallel or in sequence mode.

The batchSize property defines how many instances should be deployed at a time.

Now that we have reviewed the basic structure of the copy element, let's deep dive into more practical examples.

The copy Element in Action

We will start with a straightforward example of how you can leverage the copy element.

In this example, we will deploy multiple instances of the same item.

We will define a parameter called itemCount, which will be an integer value to specify the number of items that should be created.

Then, we will add the copy element in the variables section of our ARM template. Lastly, we will reference the array of items in the output section.

Figure 12-1 highlights the use of the copy element in the ARM template.

```
{
    "$schema": "https://schema.management.azure.com/schemas/2019-04-01/deploymentTemplate.json#",
    "contentVersion": "1.0.0.0",
    Select or create a parameter file to enable full validation...
    "parameters": {
        "itemCount": {
            "type": "int"
        }
    },
    "variables": {
        "copy": [
            {
                "name":"myArray",
                "count":"[parameters('itemCount')]",
                "input":"[concat('item', copyIndex('myArray',1))]"
            }
        ]
    },
    "resources": [],
    "outputs": {
        "arrayOutput": {
            "type": "array",
            "value": "[variables('myArray')]"
        }
    }
}
```

Figure 12-1. *ARM template with the copy element*

In the previous ARM template, we defined a parameter called itemCount; then, in the variables section, we included the structure of the copy element that contains the name of the loop myArray; the count, which is passed from the parameter value; and the input value.

The ARM template and the parameters file related to the previous example can be found here:

https://github.com/daveRendon/iac/blob/main/chapter-12/
copy-function-example/azuredeploy.json

For the input value, we are utilizing the function concat() that will return the concatenated array of items.

Note that we are also referring to the copyIndex() function; this function just keeps tracking which iteration we're on. The copyIndex() function is a zero-based function, which means it will start the iteration from 0,1,2...etc.

In this example, the number of iterations is specified in the count property, and we have defined the copyIndex value with an offset of 1. Therefore, we will create five items.

To deploy this ARM template, we need to pass only the parameter value for the itemCount, which can be any integer value.

In this example, we will use the value 5. The ARM template will not create any resource; it will only create a random item and show the array in the output section, as shown in Figure 12-2.

```
DeploymentName            : iFabrikDeployment06-30-2021
ResourceGroupName         : iFabrik
ProvisioningState         : Succeeded
Timestamp                 : 6/30/2021 11:38:04 PM
Mode                      : Incremental
TemplateLink              :
Parameters                :
                            Name             Type                        Value
                            ===============  ==========================  ==========
                            itemCount        Int                         5

Outputs                   :
                            Name             Type                        Value
                            ===============  ==========================  ==========
                            arrayOutput      Array                       [
                              "item1",
                              "item2",
                              "item3",
                              "item4",
                              "item5"
                            ]
```

Figure 12-2. *ARM template output*

That said, we can apply the same principle to create multiple storage accounts.

Example: Create N Storage Accounts

In the ARM template shown in Listing 12-2, we will create N storage accounts.

The ARM template contains two parameters: itemCount and storageAccountName.

Listing 12-2. ARM Template Parameters

```
"parameters": {
    "storageAccountName": {
        "type": "string",
        "metadata": {
            "description": "Storage Account Name"
        }
    },
    "itemCount": {
        "type": "int",
        "metadata": {
            "description": "# of items to deploy"
        }
    }
},
```

We will pass the storage account type as a variable, and following the baseline from our previous example, we will use the copy element to deploy multiple storage accounts. See Listing 12-3.

Listing 12-3. ARM Template, variables and resources Sections

```
"variables": {
    "storageAccountType": "Standard_LRS"
},
"resources": [
  {
  "name": "[toLower(concat(parameters('storageAccountName'),copyIndex(),'dev'))]",
    "copy":{
        "name": "storagecopy",
        "count": "[parameters('itemCount')]"
            },
```

```
        "type": "Microsoft.Storage/storageAccounts",
        "apiVersion": "2019-06-01",
        "tags": {
            "displayName": "storageaccount1"
        },
        "location": "[resourceGroup().location]",
        "kind": "StorageV2",
        "sku": {
            "name": "[variables('storageAccountType')]"
        }
    }
],
```

Note that we are using the copyIndex() function without any values, which means that the offset value will start from 0.

We are also defining the copy element after the property name. In this copy element, we are passing the name storagecopy and the count that is referenced from the parameter itemCount, and then we are specifying the properties of the actual storage accounts.

Lastly, we will leverage the copy element in the output section of the ARM template to show the storage account endpoints. See Listing 12-4.

Listing 12-4. ARM Template, output Section

```
"outputs": {
    "storageAccounts": {
        "type": "array",
        "copy": {
          "count": "[parameters('itemCount')]",
          "input": "[reference(toLower(concat(parameters('storageAccountName'),
          copyIndex(),'dev'))).primaryEndpoints.blob]"
            }
        }
    }
}
```

Figure 12-3 shows how the complete ARM template looks.

```
{
    "$schema": "https://schema.management.azure.com/schemas/2019-04-01/deploymentTemplate.json#",
    "contentVersion": "1.0.0.0",
Parameter file: "azuredeploy.parameters.json" | Change...
    "parameters": {
        Value: "ifabrik"
        "storageAccountName": {
            "type": "string",
            "metadata": {
                "description": "Storage Account Name"
            }
        },
        Value: 3
        "itemCount": {
            "type": "int",
            "metadata": {
                "description": "# of items to deploy"
            }
        }
    },
    "variables": {
        "storageAccountType": "Standard_LRS"
    },
    "resources": [
        {
            "name": "[toLower(concat(parameters('storageAccountName'),copyIndex(),'dev'))]",
            "copy":{
                "name": "storagecopy",
                "count": "[parameters('itemCount')]"
            },
            "type": "Microsoft.Storage/storageAccounts",
            "apiVersion": "2019-06-01",
            "tags": {
                "displayName": "storageaccount1"
            },
            "location": "[resourceGroup().location]",
            "kind": "StorageV2",
            "sku": {
                "name": "[variables('storageAccountType')]"
            }
        }
    ],
    "outputs": {
        "storageAccounts": {
            "type": "array",
            "copy": {
                "count": "[parameters('itemCount')]",
                "input": "[reference(toLower(concat(parameters('storageAccountName'),copyIndex(),'dev'))).primaryEndpoints.blob]"
            }
        }
    }
}
```

Figure 12-3. *ARM template*

Figure 12-3 highlights the use of the copy element in our ARM template. In Figure 12-4 you will find the deployment results.

```
DeploymentName          : iFabrikDeployment06-30-2021
ResourceGroupName       : iFabrik
ProvisioningState       : Succeeded
Timestamp               : 7/1/2021 2:12:13 AM
Mode                    : Incremental
TemplateLink            :
Parameters              :
                          Name                    Type                        Value
                          ====================    =========================   ==========
                          storageAccountName      String                      ifabrik
                          itemCount               Int                         3

Outputs                 :
                          Name                Type                        Value
                          ================    =========================   ==========
                          storageAccounts     Array                       [
                            "https://ifabrik0dev.blob.core.windows.net/",
                            "https://ifabrik1dev.blob.core.windows.net/",
                            "https://ifabrik2dev.blob.core.windows.net/"
                          ]
```

Figure 12-4. *ARM template that includes the output of the storage accounts deployed*

Note that because we're using copyIndex() without any offset value, the storage account count number starts from 0.

Ensure you use a unique name for each storage account.

Now, what if we want to deploy 20 storage accounts, but we don't need to deploy all of them at once? We can leverage the mode and batchSize properties in the copy element. The mode can be defined as serial or parallel.

Understanding Resource Iteration: Serial Mode and Parallel Mode

To have more control over our deployment, we can set the mode property to either serial or parallel mode.

By setting the mode property to serial, we can specify which resources are deployed in sequence at a time. For instance, say we want to deploy twenty storage accounts, but we want to ensure that only five storage accounts are created at a time.

Note that Resource Manager creates resources in parallel mode by default.

We will use our previous ARM template as a baseline to provide a practical example of how to leverage serial mode and parallel mode.

In Listing 12-5, we will create twenty storage accounts but only five at a time. We will leverage serial mode.

Listing 12-5. ARM Template That Utilizes Serial Mode

```
"copy":{
            "name": "storagecopy",
            "count": "[parameters('itemCount')]",
            "mode": "Serial",
            "batchSize": 3
        },
```

When we use serial mode, Resource Manager creates dependencies on the resources in the loop to ensure that resources are not created until the previous batch is completed.

Now let's modify the copy element and deploy our ARM template, as shown in Figure 12-5.

```
{
    "$schema": "https://schema.management.azure.com/schemas/2019-04-01/deploymentTemplate.json#",
    "contentVersion": "1.0.0.0",
    Parameter file: "azuredeploy.parameters.json" | Change...
    "parameters": {
        Value: "ifabrik"
        "storageAccountName": {
            "type": "string",
            "metadata": {
                "description": "Storage Account Name"
            }
        },
        Value: 5
        "itemCount": {
            "type": "int",
            "metadata": {
                "description": "# of items to deploy"
            }
        }
    },
    "variables": {
        "storageAccountType": "Standard_LRS"
    },
    "resources": [
        {
            "name": "[toLower(concat(parameters('storageAccountName'),copyIndex(),'dev'))]",
            "copy":{
                "name": "storagecopy",
                "count": "[parameters('itemCount')]",
                "mode": "Serial",
                "batchSize": 4
            },
            "type": "Microsoft.Storage/storageAccounts",
            "apiVersion": "2019-06-01",
            "tags": {
                "displayName": "storageaccount1"
            },
            "location": "[resourceGroup().location]",
            "kind": "StorageV2",
            "sku": {
                "name": "[variables('storageAccountType')]"
            }
        }
    ],
    "outputs": {
        "storageAccounts": {
            "type": "array",
            "copy": {
                "count": "[parameters('itemCount')]",
                "input": "[reference(toLower(concat(parameters('storageAccountName'),copyIndex(),'dev'))).primaryEndpoints.blob]"
            }
        }
    }
}
```

Figure 12-5. *ARM template with copy element and serial mode defined*

As you can see in the previous ARM template, we defined the mode and batchSize properties to deploy the 20 storage accounts.

Resource Manager will create the storage accounts in serial mode, four at a time. Figure 12-6 highlights the deployment output.

```
DeploymentName             : iFabrikDeployment07-01-2021
ResourceGroupName          : iFabrik
ProvisioningState          : Succeeded
Timestamp                  : 7/1/2021 11:15:56 PM
Mode                       : Incremental
TemplateLink               :
Parameters                 :
                             Name                   Type                         Value
                             ====================   ==========================   ==========
                             storageAccountName     String                       ifabrik
                             itemCount              Int                          20

Outputs                    :
                             Name                Type                         Value
                             ================    ==========================   ==========
                             storageAccounts     Array                        [
                               "https://ifabrik0dev.blob.core.windows.net/",
                               "https://ifabrik1dev.blob.core.windows.net/",
                               "https://ifabrik2dev.blob.core.windows.net/",
                               "https://ifabrik3dev.blob.core.windows.net/",
                               "https://ifabrik4dev.blob.core.windows.net/",
                               "https://ifabrik5dev.blob.core.windows.net/",
                               "https://ifabrik6dev.blob.core.windows.net/",
                               "https://ifabrik7dev.blob.core.windows.net/",
                               "https://ifabrik8dev.blob.core.windows.net/",
                               "https://ifabrik9dev.blob.core.windows.net/",
                               "https://ifabrik10dev.blob.core.windows.net/",
                               "https://ifabrik11dev.blob.core.windows.net/",
                               "https://ifabrik12dev.blob.core.windows.net/",
                               "https://ifabrik13dev.blob.core.windows.net/",
                               "https://ifabrik14dev.blob.core.windows.net/",
                               "https://ifabrik15dev.blob.core.windows.net/",
                               "https://ifabrik16dev.blob.core.windows.net/",
                               "https://ifabrik17dev.blob.core.windows.net/",
                               "https://ifabrik18dev.blob.core.windows.net/",
                               "https://ifabrik19dev.blob.core.windows.net/"
                             ]
```

Figure 12-6. *ARM template output*

Now picture the following scenario: the iFabrik team needs to deploy a specific number of storage accounts per member of the team for testing purposes. They need to be able to deploy multiple storage accounts and specify the name of the member of the team as a prefix.

In the previous ARM template, we defined the parameter itemCount, which refers to an integer value.

For the following example, we will update this parameter. Instead of passing the itemCount, we will pass a parameter called storageAccountNames. This parameter will be an array.

Listing 12-6 shows the `parameters` section of the ARM template.

Listing 12-6. ARM Template, parameters Section

```
"parameters": {
        "storageAccountNames": {
            "type": "array",
            "defaultValue": [
                "bob",
                "stuart",
                "dave"
            ],
            "metadata": {
                "description": "Storage Account Name"
            }
        }
    },
```

Now we will leave the `variables` section as is; then, we will modify the `copy` element and the `name` property as shown in Figure 12-7.

```
"variables": {
    "storageAccountType": "Standard_LRS"
},
"resources": [
    {
        //when creating the name, will use the array position using [copyIndex()]
        "name": "[toLower(concat(parameters('storageAccountNames')[copyIndex()],uniqueString(resourceGroup().id)))]",
        "copy":{
            "name": "storagecopy",
            //get length of the parameter array
            "count": "[length(parameters('storageAccountNames'))]"
        },
        "type": "Microsoft.Storage/storageAccounts",
        "apiVersion": "2019-06-01",
        "tags": {
            "displayName": "storageaccount1"
        },
        "location": "[resourceGroup().location]",
        "kind": "StorageV2",
        "sku": {
            "name": "[variables('storageAccountType')]"
        }
    }
],
```

Figure 12-7. *ARM template, variables and resources sections*

Note that we are only using the name and count properties in the copy element.

Since we are working with an array of elements, we need to modify the name property. We will use the array position and refer to it by using square braces, [ ], and then use copyIndex().

Lastly, we will provide the same copy element as the output to retrieve the storage account endpoints. See Listing 12-7.

Listing 12-7. ARM Template, output Section

```
"outputs": {
  "storageAccounts": {
    "type": "array",
    "copy": {
      "count": "[length(parameters('storageAccountNames'))]",
      "input": "[reference(toLower(concat(parameters('storageAccountNames')
               [copyIndex()],uniqueString(resourceGroup().id)))).
               primaryEndpoints.blob]"
        }
      }
    }
```

If we deploy this ARM template, we will get the output shown in Figure 12-8.

```
DeploymentName       : iFabrikDeployment07-01-2021
ResourceGroupName    : iFabrik
ProvisioningState    : Succeeded
Timestamp            : 7/2/2021 12:20:41 AM
Mode                 : Incremental
TemplateLink         :
Parameters           :
                       Name                      Type                          Value
                       ======================    ==========================    ==========
                       storageAccountNames       Array                         [
                         "bob",
                         "stuart",
                         "dave"
                       ]

Outputs              :
                       Name                      Type                          Value
                       ==================        ==========================    ==========
                       storageAccounts           Array                         [
                         "https://bobdg6hiux6vp3by.blob.core.windows.net/",
                         "https://stuartdg6hiux6vp3by.blob.core.windows.net/",
                         "https://davedg6hiux6vp3by.blob.core.windows.net/"
                       ]
```

Figure 12-8. *ARM template, deployment output*

So far, we have reviewed how to apply loops for a given resource in the ARM template; however, it is also possible to apply loops for the properties of resources.

Resource Dependencies in a Loop

Picture the following example: we have a virtual machine that can have multiple network interfaces or multiple data disks. We can leverage loops to create such properties as well and avoid the definition of each network interface or each data disk.

The ARM template shown in Listing 12-8 highlights the use of loops to create multiple data disks for the same virtual machine.

We will use the template available in the community templates called `101-vm-simple-windows` (https://github.com/Azure/azure-quickstart-templates/tree/master/quickstarts/microsoft.compute/vm-simple-windows).

Then we will add a parameter called `numberOfDataDisks`, as shown in Listing 12-8.

Listing 12-8. ARM Template New Parameter

```
"numberOfDataDisks": {
      "type": "int",
      "metadata": {
        "description": "Number of data disks"
      }
    },
```

Now we are going to modify the properties of the data disk. Listing 12-9 shows the original ARM template definition.

Listing 12-9. ARM Template, Data Disk Definition

```
"dataDisks": [
            {
              "diskSizeGB": 1023,
              "lun": 0,
              "createOption": "Empty"
            }
          ]
```

Now, we are going to modify this and include it inside a copy loop, as shown in Listing 12-10.

Listing 12-10. ARM Template, Copy Loop for Data Disk

```
"copy":[
    {
       "name": "dataDisks",
       "count": "[parameters('numberOfDataDisks')]",
       "input":{
           "name": "[concat('winVM-datadisk', copyIndex('dataDisks'))]",
           "diskSizeGB": 32,
           "lun": "[copyIndex('dataDisks')]",
           "createOption": "Empty"
            }
        }
      ]
```

We will proceed to deploy this ARM template using the Azure portal and pass along the parameters, as shown in Figure 12-9.

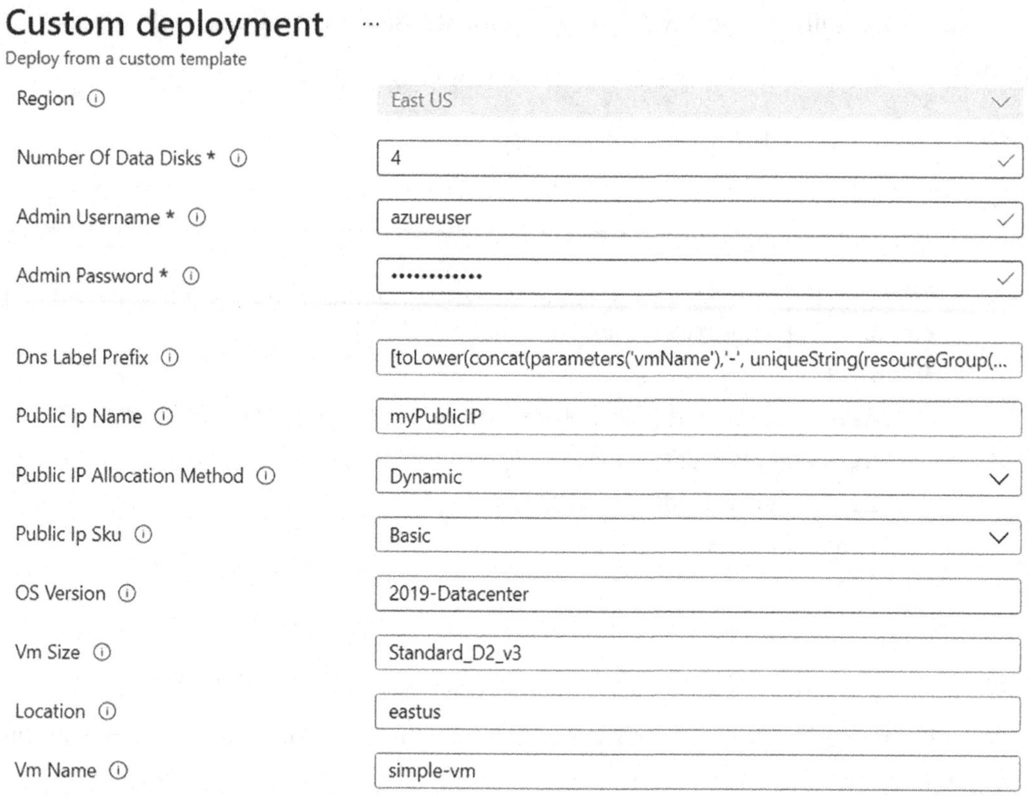

Custom deployment   ...

Deploy from a custom template

Region ⓘ	East US ⌄
Number Of Data Disks * ⓘ	4 ✓
Admin Username * ⓘ	azureuser ✓
Admin Password * ⓘ	••••••••••• ✓
Dns Label Prefix ⓘ	[toLower(concat(parameters('vmName'),'-', uniqueString(resourceGroup(...
Public Ip Name ⓘ	myPublicIP
Public IP Allocation Method ⓘ	Dynamic ⌄
Public Ip Sku ⓘ	Basic ⌄
OS Version ⓘ	2019-Datacenter
Vm Size ⓘ	Standard_D2_v3
Location ⓘ	eastus
Vm Name ⓘ	simple-vm

***Figure 12-9.** Custom deployment*

Once the deployment is complete, you should be able to see the N number of data disks attached to the virtual machine, as shown in Figure 12-10.

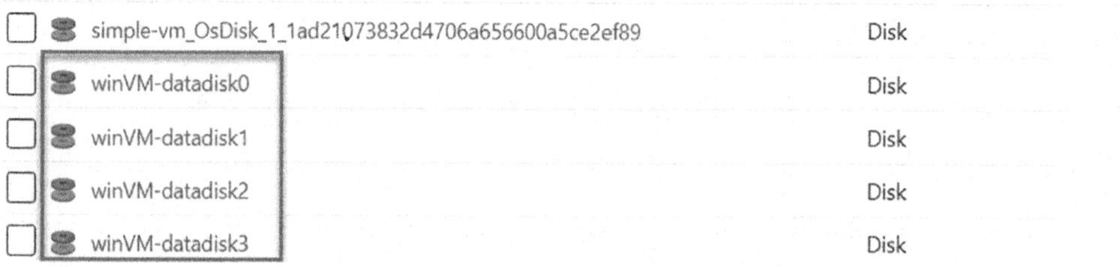

▨ simple-vm_OsDisk_1_1ad21073832d4706a656600a5ce2ef89	Disk
▨ winVM-datadisk0	Disk
▨ winVM-datadisk1	Disk
▨ winVM-datadisk2	Disk
▨ winVM-datadisk3	Disk

***Figure 12-10.** Multiple data disks attached to a virtual machine*

Ideally, with the previous ARM templates, you now understand how you can work with loops in your ARM templates.

The code related to the ARM templates reviewed in this chapter can be found here:

`https://github.com/daveRendon/iac/tree/main/chapter-12`

Summary

In this chapter, we reviewed how to work with loops in ARM templates; we went through various practical examples that demonstrated the use of the `copy` element in ARM templates.

Then, to have more control over our deployment, we reviewed how to set the `mode` property to either serial or parallel mode and showed some a few examples.

Lastly, we reviewed how loops can be applied to the properties of a specific resource in your ARM template.

In the next chapter, we will review how to provide post-deployment configuration and automation tasks on Azure resources.

CHAPTER 13

Understanding Post-Deployment Configurations: Extensions and Deployment Scripts

In the previous chapter, we reviewed how to leverage deployment modes in an ARM template to have more control over our deployments, and we saw that Resource Manager is very flexible when it comes to defining the resources that will be part of our environment.

This leads us to this question: once we define the resources in the ARM template that will serve as the base components for our environment, how can we actually represent a new instantiation of the application or environment in our ARM template that we want to run in Azure?

In this chapter, we will discuss the following:

- Virtual machine extensions

- Deployment scripts

Resource Manager provides various options to configure the last mile of our environment that we want to build in Azure. We will go through some of these options to perform the post-deployment configuration of the resources in Azure in our ARM template.

Sometimes we will need to perform additional configurations on the resources that we have deployed with the ARM template. While there are multiple options to perform additional configurations on resources deployed through the ARM template, it is possible to leverage Resource Manager to perform such post-deployment configurations or automation tasks.

© David Rendón 2022
D. Rendón, *Building Applications with Azure Resource Manager (ARM)*,
https://doi.org/10.1007/978-1-4842-7747-8_13

This chapter will cover two main elements: virtual machine extensions and deployment scripts. Let's start with understanding virtual machine extensions.

Understanding Extensions

When you deploy a virtual machine on Azure, it is possible to add the definition of post-deployment configurations such as virtual machine extensions to perform additional configurations in the virtual machine deployed or install extra utilities in the virtual machine.

A virtual machine extension is essentially a piece of code attached to the virtual machine after deployment. Think of extensions as small applications that can be installed only after the virtual machine has been deployed to add extra features to the virtual machine or any additional configuration on the current resource.

That said, the virtual machine extension that you enable for the Windows or Linux machine will depend on your needs, and it is possible to allow a custom script as an extension.

Extensions are supported for multiple types of resources, including the following:

- Virtual machines

- Virtual machines scale sets

- HDInsight clusters

- SQL databases

- Web

Each of the previous resource types has its own JSON template format. We can add the extensions in the `resource` section of our ARM template as another resource.

Listing 13-1 highlights the JSON template format for a virtual machine extension.

Listing 13-1. Virtual Machine Extension Template Format

```
{
  "name": "string",
  "type": "Microsoft.Compute/virtualMachines/extensions",
  "apiVersion": "2020-12-01",
  "location": "string",
```

```
  "tags": {},
  "properties": {
    "publisher": "string",
    "type": "string",
    "typeHandlerVersion": "string",
    "autoUpgradeMinorVersion": "boolean",
    "enableAutomaticUpgrade": "boolean",
    "settings": {},
    "protectedSettings": {},
    "instanceView": {
      "name": "string",
      "type": "string",
      "typeHandlerVersion": "string",
      "substatuses": [
        {
          "code": "string",
          "level": "string",
          "displayStatus": "string",
          "message": "string",
          "time": "string"
        }
      ],
      "statuses": [
        {
          "code": "string",
          "level": "string",
          "displayStatus": "string",
          "message": "string",
          "time": "string"
        }
      ]
    }
  }
}
```

Now let's see how we can leverage virtual machine extensions in our ARM templates.

In the following ARM template (Figure 13-1), we will define a virtual machine extension that will execute a custom script. We will reuse the ARM template from Chapter 9 that creates a virtual machine with resource dependencies.

If you're using the ARM extension in Visual Studio Code, you will find a snippet that provides the virtual machine extension for Linux and Windows. You can type arm-vm-script, and you will see a pop-up for the custom script for the Linux or Windows machine extension, as shown in Figure 13-1.

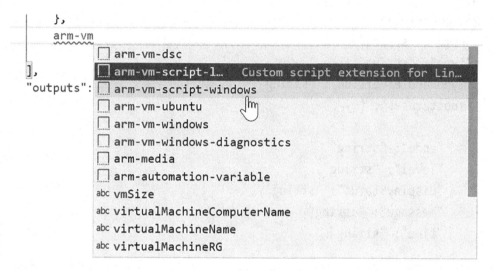

Figure 13-1. *Custom script extension snippet*

The above snippet will add the code shown in Figure 13-2 for the custom script extension in the resources section of the ARM template.

```
{
    "name": "windowsVM1/customScript1",
    "type": "Microsoft.Compute/virtualMachines/extensions",
    "apiVersion": "2019-07-01",
    "location": "[resourceGroup().location]",
    "tags": {
        "displayName": "customScript1 for Windows VM"
    },
    "dependsOn": [
        "[resourceId('Microsoft.Compute/virtualMachines', 'windowsVM1')]"
    ],
    "properties": {
        "publisher": "Microsoft.Compute",
        "type": "CustomScriptExtension",
        "typeHandlerVersion": "1.10",
        "autoUpgradeMinorVersion": true,
        "settings": {
            "fileUris": [
                "[concat('artifactsLocation', '/scripts/customScript.ps1', 'artifactsLocationSasToken')]"
            ]
        },
        "protectedSettings": {
            "commandToExecute": "powershell -ExecutionPolicy Bypass -file customScript.ps1"
        }
    }
}
```

Figure 13-2. *Definition of virtual machine extension in ARM template*

Note that the custom script extension configuration includes properties that specify the script location and the command to be executed.

Now, we will modify the script name for iis-extension.ps1. Listing 13-2 shows the code we will add to the PowerShell script to enable the IIS extension on the virtual machine and define a simple website.

Listing 13-2. PowerShell Script

```
install-windowsfeature -name Web-Server -IncludeManagementTools
Set-Location -Path c:\inetpub\wwwroot
Add-Content iisstart.htm "<!DOCTYPE html><head><meta
charset='utf-8'><title>ARM template - Custom extension</title>
</head><body><H1> Your custom extension works</H1></body></html>"
Invoke-command -ScriptBlock{iisreset}
```

Now, this script can be pulled from an accessible location like from a storage account, from a GitHub repository, from internal servers, or from any other location that can be accessible.

In this case, we will pull the script from a GitHub repository.

It is recommended that you leverage storage accounts to upload your custom scripts and then refer to the location in the ARM template and ensure you enable the proper access to the file location.

Listing 13-3 highlights the use of the IIS extension.

Listing 13-3. ARM Template, Virtual Machine Extension

```
{
  "name": "[concat(parameters('virtualMachineComputerName'),'/',
  variables('vmExtensionName'))]",
      "type": "Microsoft.Compute/virtualMachines/extensions",
          "apiVersion": "2019-07-01",
          "location": "[resourceGroup().location]",
          "tags": {
              "displayName": "custom Script for Windows VM"
          },
          "dependsOn": [
              "[resourceId('Microsoft.Compute/virtualMachines',
              parameters('virtualMachineComputerName'))]"
          ],
          "properties": {
              "publisher": "Microsoft.Compute",
              "type": "CustomScriptExtension",
              "typeHandlerVersion": "1.10",
              "autoUpgradeMinorVersion": true,
              "settings": {
                  "fileUris": [
                      "[concat('https://raw.githubusercontent.com/
                      daveRendon/iac/main/chapter-13/virtual-machine-
                      extension-iis/scripts/iis-extension.ps1?token=AAOY
                      HKQ47A3FS4IUTEWTQVDA4TZTU')]"
                  ]
              },
              "protectedSettings": {
                  "commandToExecute": "powershell -ExecutionPolicy
                  Bypass -file iis-extension.ps1"
              }
          }
      }
```

It is important to define a new network security group (NSG) rule for this specific scenario to allow traffic through port 80.

Figure 13-3 shows the output from the ARM template deployment.

```
DeploymentName           : iFabrikDeployment07-06-2021
ResourceGroupName        : iFabrik
ProvisioningState        : Succeeded
Timestamp                : 7/7/2021 12:20:27 AM
Mode                     : Incremental
TemplateLink             :
Parameters               :
                           Name                          Type                        Value
                           ==========================    ========================    ==========
                           location                      String                      eastus
                           networkInterfaceName          String                      ifabrikNic
                           networkSecurityGroupName      String                      ifabrikNsg
                           networkSecurityGroupRules     Array                       [
                             {
                               "name": "Web",
                               "properties": {
                                 "priority": 310,
                                 "protocol": "TCP",
                                 "access": "Allow",
                                 "direction": "Inbound",
                                 "sourceAddressPrefix": "*",
                                 "sourcePortRange": "*",
                                 "destinationAddressPrefix": "*",
                                 "destinationPortRange": "80"
                               }
                             }
                           ]
                           subnetName                    String                      default
                           virtualNetworkName            String                      ifabrik-vnet
                           addressPrefixes               Array                       [
                             "10.0.0.0/16"
                           ]
                           subnets                       Array                       [
                             {
                               "name": "default",
                               "properties": {
                                 "addressPrefix": "10.0.0.0/24"
                               }
                             }
                           ]
                           publicIpAddressName           String                      ifabrik-pip
                           publicIpAddressType           String                      Static
                           publicIpAddressSku            String                      Standard
                           virtualMachineName            String                      ifabrik-vm
                           virtualMachineComputerName    String                      ifabrik-vm
                           virtualMachineRG              String                      ifabrikRg
                           osDiskType                    String                      StandardSSD_LRS
                           virtualMachineSize            String                      Standard_B4ms
                           adminUsername                 String                      azureuser
                           adminPassword                 SecureString
                           zone                          String                      1
Outputs                  :
DeploymentDebugLogLevel  :
```

Figure 13-3. *ARM template deployment*

The code related to this template is at https://github.com/daveRendon/iac/tree/main/chapter-13/virtual-machine-extension-iis.

Once you deploy this ARM template, you should be able to access the virtual machine IP address using port 80 and see the IIS role and the text "Your custom extension works," as shown in Figure 13-4.

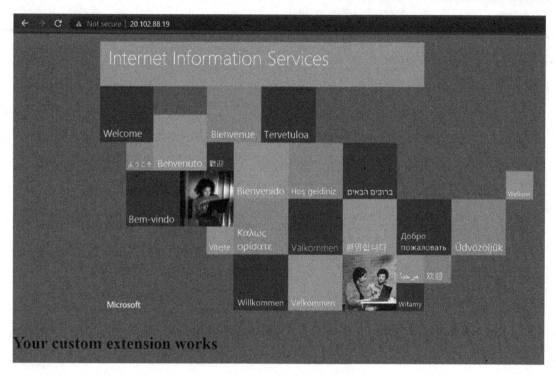

Figure 13-4. *Virtual machine custom script extension*

When working with custom script extensions, it is best to use idempotent scripts; this way, you can minimize errors or changes in the environment that are not desirable.

Custom scripts extensions can be executed only once; however, you can define that you want to run multiple scripts. Another option is to run your custom script extension more than once by referring to the name of the extension and specifying the configuration is updated.

Also, consider minimizing or avoiding dynamic input in your script.

As you can see, custom script extensions become helpful when we need to perform simple post-deployment configurations in our environment.

However, sometimes we can be limited when working with custom script extensions in cases where we need to extend functionality across multiple resources that are part of our environment or perform post-deployment configurations in more than one specific resource in a more dynamic way.

When we need to pass on inputs more dynamically in the custom script extension, we can be somewhat limited, and for those scenarios, we can leverage deployment scripts.

Understanding Deployment Scripts

Deployment scripts are a new way of embedding scripts within our ARM templates. Does this mean that now we will be able to leverage PowerShell or CLI to perform post-deployment configurations from the ARM template? Yes! We can leverage deployment scripts to do the following:

- Work across other systems (even external to Azure)

- Leverage Azure libraries, CLI, or PowerShell

- Perform data plane operations

- Work with resources that might not be available through Resource Manager deployments

Simply put, deployment scripts will help you complete last-mile scenarios using PowerShell and CLI from within your ARM template.

Here are some examples of the post-deployment configurations that we can perform using deployment scripts:

- Creating self-signed certificates

- Performing data plane operations such as copying blobs

- Performing additional configurations like additional setup on network virtual appliances (NVAs)

- Populating databases from non-Azure sources

Now let's understand how deployment scripts work.

How Deployment Scripts Work

Deployment scripts will execute any PowerShell or Bash script as part of your template deployment to complete your last-mile scenario. So, how do deployment scripts work?

From the deployment script resource workflow shown in Figure 13-5, note the following:

- The deployment script resource spins up a Linux-based container using Azure Container Instances and a storage account during the deployment phase.

- When the deployment script completes the execution, then the storage and the Azure Container Instance are immediately cleaned up.

- All outputs are stored in the deployment script resource.

- The deployment script resource is removed after the provided expiration time.

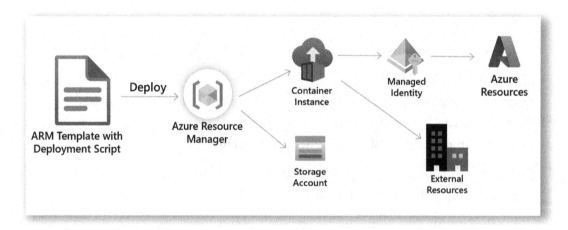

Figure 13-5. *Deployment script resource*

You can also use an existing storage account if you prefer not to leverage a new one. Now let's understand the prerequisites to work with deployment scripts.

Considerations When Working with Deployment Scripts

We have to leverage the `Microsoft.Resources/deploymentScripts` resource provider when working with deployment scripts.

To perform any operation in Azure, the Azure Container Instance needs to have an identity. Therefore, we need to configure a managed identity beforehand with a contributor role to allow access from and to the Azure resources, including the storage account and the Azure Container Instance.

A managed identity solves the challenge of managing credentials. A managed identity in Azure provides an identity for applications to use when working with resources that support Azure Active Directory.

This way, the applications can use a managed identity to access resources like Key Vault and manage secrets.

Lastly, we will need to add the JSON template of the deployment script in the ARM template in the `resources` section of the template and add the parameters as required.

So, what's happening behind the scenes when working with deployment scripts? As noted, a deployment script resource will spin up an Azure Container Instance and a storage account. This means we will be charged for the Azure Container Instance and the storage account while they're up.

The Azure Container Instance will host the PowerShell, CLI, or Azure libraries, and we are going to pass in the script that we want to execute along with any arguments.

Once the deployment script completes the execution, Resource Manager will validate whether the execution was successful and then pull any potential errors and outputs. Then the Azure Container Instance will be stopped.

As mentioned, the use of a managed identities is a must; this identity can be assigned to resources in Azure. We will assign it to the Azure Container Instance to allow access to the resources that the script is going to interact with. This managed identity must exist before we can leverage deployment scripts.

Definition of Deployment Scripts in the ARM Template

The JSON template for deployment scripts resource is reasonably simple and will include the following:

- In the `variables` section, a variable to refer to the deployment script name

- In the `resources` section, the definition of `deploymentScripts` as a resource type

- The managed identity and its properties

- In the `resources` section, the `properties` section to define the actual script or refer to the script and required values

- In the `output` section, optionally, the output of the deployment script

The ARM template shown in Listing 13-4 shows the JSON template for a deployment script.

Listing 13-4. Deployment Script Schema

```
{
  "type": "Microsoft.Resources/deploymentScripts",
  "apiVersion": "2020-10-01",
  "name": "Your-Deployment-Script-Name",
  "location": "[resourceGroup().location]",
  "kind": "AzurePowerShell", // or "AzureCLI"
  "identity": {
    "type": "userAssigned",
    "userAssignedIdentities": {
      "/subscriptions/01234567-89AB-CDEF-0123-456789ABCDEF/
      resourceGroups/myResourceGroup/providers/Microsoft.ManagedIdentity/
      userAssignedIdentities/myID": {}
    }
  },
  "properties": {
    "forceUpdateTag": "1",
    "containerSettings": {
```

```
        "containerGroupName": "Your-ACI"
    },
    "storageAccountSettings": {
        "storageAccountName": "Your-Storage-Account-Name",
        "storageAccountKey": "Your-Storage-Account-Key"
    },
    "azPowerShellVersion": "3.0",  // or "azCliVersion": "2.0.80",
    "arguments": "",
    "environmentVariables": [
        {
            "name": "UserName",
            "value": "jdole"
        },
    ],
    "scriptContent": "Your-Inline-Script-Goes-Here // or
    "primaryScriptUri": "YourDeployment-Script.ps1",
    "supportingScriptUris":[],
    "timeout": "PT30M",
    "cleanupPreference": "OnSuccess",
    "retentionInterval": "P1D"
  }
}
```

As shown in Listing 13-4, we have to define a new resource type. Note that we can use Azure PowerShell or Azure CLI, and we have to pass the managed identity.

Note that we are two types of managed identities: user-assigned identities and system-assigned identities. User-assigned identities can be utilized on multiple resources, while system-assigned identities have their life cycle associated with the resource used.

You can either use an inline script in the ARM template or reference an external resource using `primaryScriptUri`.

Then we can have an `arguments` property to pass at deployment time as well as additional properties such as the `timeout` property to specify when the script should stop.

We also have the `retentionInterval` property that specifies the time that the deployment script will delete itself and the `cleanupPreference` property to dictate when the Azure Container Instance and the storage account should be deleted.

Using Deployment Scripts in Your ARM Template

The ARM template shown in Listing 13-5 will create a new virtual machine and leverage deployment scripts, and it will execute some PowerShell commands. The virtual machine is an NVA; the managed identity will be created beforehand and be referenced in the ARM template.

We will reuse the ARM template from Chapter 10 to create a Windows VM. We will modify it, include the managed identity, include the deployment script, and leverage a different virtual machine image.

Listing 13-5 shows the new definition of the `variables` section of the ARM template.

Listing 13-5. ARM Template, variables Section

```
"variables": {
    "nsgId": "[resourceId(resourceGroup().name, 'Microsoft.Network/
    networkSecurityGroups', parameters('networkSecurityGroupName'))]",
    "vnetId": "[resourceId(resourceGroup().name,'Microsoft.Network/
    virtualNetworks', parameters('virtualNetworkName'))]",
    "subnetRef": "[concat(variables('vnetId'), '/subnets/',
    parameters('subnetName'))]",
    //variables for the Deployment Script
    "storageAccountName": "[toLower( concat( parameters('storageAccountName
    Prefix'), uniqueString(resourceGroup().id) ) )]",
    //variable - blob container name
    "storageBlobContainerName": "config",
    //variable for the Managed Identity Name
    "identityName": "configDeployer",
  //variables for the contributor role for the managed identity
  "roleAssignmentName": "[guid(concat(resourceGroup().id, 'contributor'))]",
  "contributorRoleDefinitionId": "[resourceId('Microsoft.Authorization/
  roleDefinitions', 'b24988ac-6180-42a0-ab88-20f7382dd24c')]",
    "deploymentScriptName": "ConfigScript"
    },
```

The role definition identifier is a static value and can be retrieved using the command `Get-AzRoleDefinition`.

Now, let's see the modifications of the `resources` section. First, we will modify the virtual machine image and its properties, as shown in Listing 13-6.

Listing 13-6. ARM Template, resources Section

```
{
  "name": "[parameters('virtualMachineName')]",
  "type": "Microsoft.Compute/virtualMachines",
  "apiVersion": "2021-03-01",
  "location": "[resourceGroup().location]",
  "dependsOn": [
    "[resourceId('Microsoft.Network/networkInterfaces/',
    parameters('networkInterfaceName'))]"
            ],
      "properties": {
        "hardwareProfile": {
          "vmSize": "[parameters('virtualMachineSize')]"
            },
        "storageProfile": {
            "osDisk": {
            "osType": "Linux",
            "createOption": "fromImage",
            "managedDisk": {
            "storageAccountType": "[parameters('osDiskType')]"
              }
            },
            "imageReference": {
            "publisher": "kemptech",
            "offer": "vlm-azure",
                  "sku": "basic-byol",
                  "version": "7.2.480117992"
                }
            },
          "networkProfile": {
```

```
            "networkInterfaces": [
              {
              "id": "[resourceId('Microsoft.Network/networkInterfaces',
              parameters('networkInterfaceName'))]"
                  }
              ]
            },
        "osProfile": {
        "computerName": "[parameters('virtualMachineComputerName')]",
         "adminUsername": "bal",
         "adminPassword": "[parameters('adminPassword')]",
           "linuxConfiguration": {
              "disablePasswordAuthentication": false,
              "provisionVMAgent": true
                }
            },
          "diagnosticsProfile": {
              "bootDiagnostics": {
                  "enabled": true
                }
            }
        }
      },
    "plan": {
        "name": "basic-byol",
        "publisher": "kemptech",
        "product": "vlm-azure"
    },
    "zones": [
        "[parameters('zone')]"
      ]
    },
```

Now we will add the managed identity and the deployment script, as shown in Listing 13-7.

Listing 13-7. ARM Template, resources Section, Deployment Script Definition

```
//add user-assigned managed identity
 {
   "name": "[variables('identityName')]",
   "type": "Microsoft.ManagedIdentity/userAssignedIdentities",
   "apiVersion": "2018-11-30",
   "location": "[resourceGroup().location]"
 },
//Set the contributor role for the managed identity
 {
 "type": "Microsoft.Authorization/roleAssignments",
 "apiVersion": "2020-04-01-preview",
 "name": "[variables('roleAssignmentName')]",
 "dependsOn": [ "[resourceId('Microsoft.ManagedIdentity/
userAssignedIdentities', variables('identityName'))]" ],
    "properties": {
      "roleDefinitionId": "[variables('contributorRoleDefinitionId')]",
      "principalId": "[reference(resourceId('Microsoft.ManagedIdentity/
      userAssignedIdentities', variables('identityName')),
      '2015-08-31-preview').principalId]",
       "scope": "[resourceGroup().id]",
       "principalType": "ServicePrincipal"
             }
         },
  //Deployment Script definition
  {
    "type": "Microsoft.Resources/deploymentScripts",
    "apiVersion": "2020-10-01",
    "name": "[variables('deploymentScriptName')]",
    "location": "[resourceGroup().location]",
    "kind": "AzurePowerShell", // or "AzureCLI"
        "dependsOn": [
        "[resourceId('Microsoft.Authorization/roleAssignments',
        variables('roleAssignmentName'))]"
            ],
```

```
        "identity": {
          "type": "UserAssigned",
          "userAssignedIdentities": {
            "[resourceId('Microsoft.ManagedIdentity/userAssignedIdentities',
            variables('identityName'))]": {}
                }
            },
```

//define the script
```
        "properties": {
```
//Define PowerShell version
```
    "azPowerShellVersion": "3.0",
```
// can pass an arguement string, double quotes must be escaped
```
        "arguments": "[format(' -lmIp {0} -lmPass {1} ',
        reference(concat('Microsoft.Network/publicIPAddresses/', parameters(
        'publicIpAddressName'))).ipAddress , parameters('adminPassword'))]",
```
//refer to the actual script inline or "primaryScriptUri":
```
    "scriptContent": "
  param(
    [string] [Parameter(Mandatory=$true)] $lmIp,
    [string] [Parameter(Mandatory=$true)] $lmPass
    )
    $PSVersionTable
    Install-Module -Name Kemp.LoadBalancer.Powershell -Force
    Import-Module Kemp.LoadBalancer.PowerShell
    Get-Module Kemp.LoadBalancer.Powershell
Write-Host 'Hello, World!'
    $lmPassword = ConvertTo-SecureString $lmPass -AsPlainText -Force
 $creds = New-Object System.Management.Automation.PSCredential('bal',
$lmPassword)
Enable-SecAPIAccess -LoadBalancer $lmIp -Credential $creds
$lma = Initialize-LmConnectionParameters -Address $lmIp -Credential
$creds -Verbose
$lma | Format-List
",
```
//time until Deployment Script will delete itself

```
    "timeout": "PT30M",
    "cleanupPreference": "OnSuccess",
    "retentionInterval": "P1D"
                }
            }
        ],
```

Note that the previous example will provision the virtual machine of the NVA, and the script will execute an attempt to enable the API on the NVA.

We can validate the inputs and outputs from the deployment script using the Azure portal by looking at the details of the deployment script, as shown in Figure 13-6.

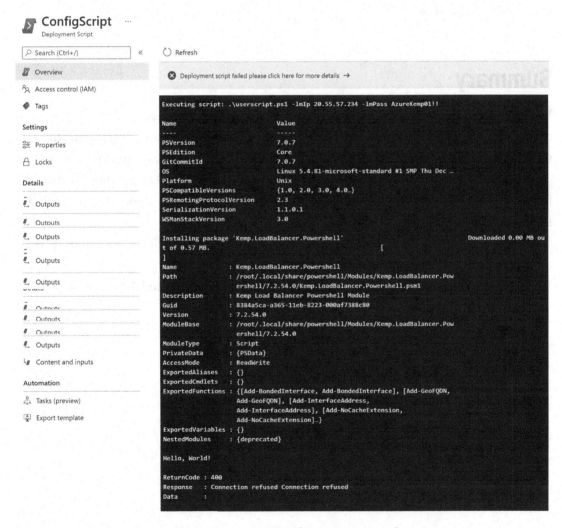

Figure 13-6. *Deployment script output in the Azure portal*

Note that we are installing the Kemp PowerShell module in the script and attempting to enable the NVA API.

In this case, the connection is refused because, by default, the API is accessible only through the virtual machine's web user interface (WUI). We need to enable it in the WUI before performing any additional configuration using the API.

As you can see, we can leverage deployment scripts to complete last-mile scenarios, be more flexible in the way we work with our ARM templates, and pass on external resources to finalize the configuration of the environment in Azure.

You can find the ARM templates related to this chapter here:

```
https://github.com/daveRendon/iac/tree/main/chapter-13/
deployment-script-kemp
```

Summary

In this chapter, we reviewed multiple options to work with post-deployment configurations for your environment in Azure. We examined two key components to work with post-deployment configurations: extensions and deployment scripts.

Then we reviewed that extensions can be leveraged in an ARM template to add extra features to the resources provisioned in Azure, and we covered the benefits of including them in an ARM template.

We also worked with deployment scripts to complete last-mile scenarios and showed a simple example of leveraging deployment scripts.

In the next chapter, we will review how you can work with nested ARM templates.

CHAPTER 14

Working with Larger and More Complex Environments

As we move into creating more extensive solutions using ARM templates, we might face scenarios where we have an extensive ARM template and multiple variables, functions, and resources. Nested ARM templates and linked ARM templates can simplify the way we build larger environments in Azure.

In this chapter, we will go over the following topics:

- Understanding nested templates and linked templates

- Working with variables in linked templates

- Use of template specs

Chapter 13 reviewed how we can add extra functionality and configure last-mile scenarios using extensions and deployment scripts. In this chapter, we will focus on how we can be more efficient when building our environment in Azure using linked and nested templates.

Picture the scenario in which you are part of a larger team in the organization and a few members of the team are working on building an environment in Azure using ARM templates.

We might face some challenges when putting together the complete solution, such as versioning, schemas, scopes, etc.

As we build larger and more complex environments, it might be good to break the solution into multiple pieces in different modules. By leveraging a modularized approach, your team will be able to quickly put together the complete solution.

© David Rendón 2022
D. Rendón, *Building Applications with Azure Resource Manager (ARM)*,
https://doi.org/10.1007/978-1-4842-7747-8_14

The ability to reuse ARM templates is critical in larger and more complex scenarios. Linked templates and nested templates will help you and your team break a solution into multiple modules.

This way, you can even compose solutions from existing modules and minimize the need to author additional ARM templates.

Now let's understand how linked ARM templates work.

Understanding Linked Templates

When we deploy a single website or a storage account in our environment, we probably use a single template with its proper parameter definition. As we move forward into more complex solutions, we might end up having a very large ARM template with multiple references to variables, parameters, and functions.

The idea of having a very large ARM template to deploy a complex solution might not be the right approach. As we have been discussing since Chapter 1, reusability is one of the pillars of the infrastructure-as-code approach.

Instead of having the entire definition of our environment in a single large ARM template, we could break it into smaller ARM templates that contain the definition of specific resources that are the form factor of the complete solution.

Picture the scenario where you have an N-tier application composed of virtual machines, application services, and a SQL database; each resource is in a different resource group.

Figure 14-1 highlights the use of linked templates.

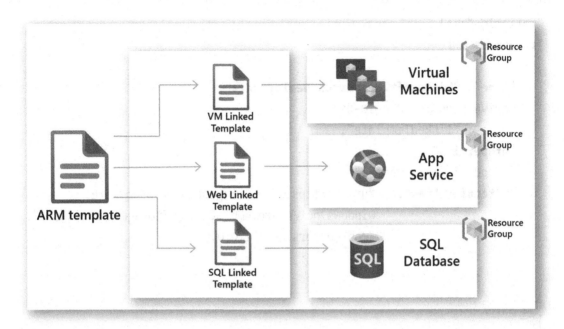

Figure 14-1. *Linked templates*

By leveraging a modularized approach, we can even reuse the same ARM templates to build different solutions.

Through linked templates, you will be able to break your larger ARM template file into smaller ARM templates. We will have separate files for the smaller ARM templates and will reference them in the main or principal ARM template.

We will use *linked templates* to refer to these separate files that will contain a smaller ARM template that will be part of our solution.

In the main template file, we will include a new resource type called `Microsoft` `.Resources/deployments` to reference our linked template.

This resource will contain the properties to reference the linked template.
Listing 14-1 highlights the code to link a template.

Listing 14-1. Code to Link a Template

```
{
  "$schema": "https://schema.management.azure.com/schemas/2019-04-01/
  deploymentTemplate.json#",
  "contentVersion": "1.0.0.0",
  "parameters": {},
```

```
    "variables": {},
    "resources": [
      {
        "type": "Microsoft.Resources/deployments",
        "apiVersion": "2020-10-01",
        "name": "linkedTemplate",
        "properties": {
          "mode": "Incremental",
          "templateLink": { "uri":"https://mystorageaccount.blob.core.
                            windows.net/AzureTemplates/newStorageAccount.json",
                            "contentVersion":"1.0.0.0"
        }
      }
    }
  ],
  "outputs": {
  }
}
```

When we link a template, we have to define the resource type named `Microsoft`
`.Resources/deployments`, and in the properties, we will pass the actual `uri` of the linked
template.

Working with Dynamic Values for Linked Templates

When working with multiple linked templates, it is easier to leverage parameters and
variables to pass on the `uri` of the linked template. This way, we can easily refer multiple
linked templates in our main ARM template.

The `uri` value includes the full value of the referred template; it cannot be a local file
and is preferred to use an `https` downloadable file.

One of the goals when you work with linked templates is the ability to deploy
multiple templates or use them as modules and reference them from a single template.
To achieve this goal, we can organize the linked templates in a location that we can refer
to as *artifacts*.

Listing 14-2 highlights the `uri` value, and instead of hard-coding the location of the
file, we can reference it as a parameter from the artifacts location.

Listing 14-2. uri Referenced from the Artifacts Location

```
"uri": "[concat(parameters('_artifactsLocation'),
'/shared/os-disk-parts-md.json', parameters('_artifactsLocationSasToken'))]"
```

To reference the value of our linked template as a parameter or variable, and as a common pattern, we can use the _artifactsLocation parameter.

This common pattern includes the definition of two values:

- _artifactsLocation: This is the uri value of the linked template. It must be publicly accessible.

- _artifactsLocationSasToken: This is the secret token to securely access the resource.

With these two values, we can generate the complete uri to link our template. It is common to leverage storage accounts or a GitHub repository to refer to linked templates.

Listing 14-3 denotes the use of this common pattern in the ARM template.

Listing 14-3. Parameters Common Pattern for Artifacts

```
{
    "$schema": "https://schema.management.azure.com/schemas/2019-04-01/
    deploymentTemplate.json#",
    "contentVersion": "1.0.0.0",
    "parameters": {
        "_artifactsLocation": {
            "type": "string",
            "metadata": {
                "description": "The base URI"
            },
            "defaultValue": ""
        },
        "_artifactsLocationSasToken": {
            "type": "string",
            "metadata": {
                "description": "The sasToken to access _artifactsLocation"
            },
```

```
                  "defaultValue": ""
        }
    },
    "functions": [],
    "variables": {},
    "resources": [],
    "outputs": {}
}
```

Let's see how this works in a practical example. We will create a solution that includes an app service plan and an app service. We will have the following structure:

- Main ARM template.

- Linked templates folder, where we will store in the linked templates.

    - Linked template #1: This ARM template creates an app service plan.

    - Linked template #2: This ARM template creates an app service.

Figure 14-2 highlights the folder structure for our solution.

Figure 14-2. *Folder structure*

Now let's start by working on the definition of our main ARM template.

Tip   You can leverage the ARM snippet for linked templates as shown in Figure 14-3.

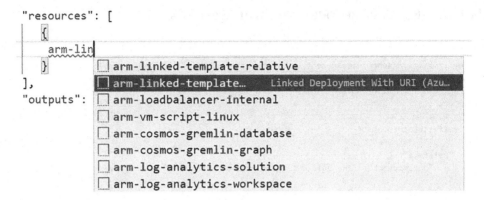

Figure 14-3. *ARM snippet for linked templates*

The snippet will include all the details for the linked template, as shown in Listing 14-4.

Listing 14-4. ARM Snippet, Linked Template

```
"name": "linkedDeployment1",
    "type": "Microsoft.Resources/deployments",
    "apiVersion": "2020-10-01",
    "properties": {
        "mode": "Incremental",
        "templateLink": {
            "uri": "[concat('artifactsLocation',
            '/linkedTemplates/linkedTemplate.json',
            'artifactsLocationSasToken')]", "contentVersion": "1.0.0.0"
        },
        "parameters": {
        }
    }
```

The main ARM template code is shown in Figure 14-4.

```
{
    "$schema": "https://schema.management.azure.com/schemas/2019-04-01/deploymentTemplate.json#",
    "contentVersion": "1.0.0.0",
    Parameter file: "azuredeploy.parameters.json" | Change...
    "parameters": {
        Value: "https://ifabrik.blob.core.windows.net/"
        "_artifactsLocation": {
            "type": "string",
            "metadata": {
                "description": "The base URI where artifacts required by this template are located."
            },
            "defaultValue": "https://ifabrik.blob.core.windows.net/"
        },
        Value: "?sp=racwdyt&st=2021-07-13T21:12:35Z&se=2021-09-30T05:12:35Z&sv=2020-08-04&sr=b&sig=bgCyj!MBuTXEBGEHvbA3ykcfstPAh...
        "_artifactsLocationSasToken": {
            "type": "securestring",
            "metadata": {
                "description": "The sasToken required to access _artifactsLocation"
            },
            "defaultValue": ""
        },
        Value: "ifabrik"
        "webAppName": {
            "type": "string",
            "defaultValue": "[concat('webApp-', uniqueString(resourceGroup().id))]",
            "minLength": 2,
            "metadata": {
                "description": "Web app name."
            }
        },
```

Figure 14-4. *Main ARM template*

We have defined two parameters: _artifactsLocation and
_artifactsLocationSasToken. We use these parameters to make use of the common
pattern to construct the uri for the linked template.

Then in the same main ARM template, we define two variables that will contain the
uri of the linked templates, as shown in Listing 14-5.

Listing 14-5. ARM Template Variables

```
"variables": {
    "appServicePlan-linkedTemplate": "https://gist.githubusercontent.com/
    daveRendon/67a94ea5280f676404da2ac20caef518/raw/9585910a67e29abe268
    dc3394912d24af8aea4c1/armTemplate-appServicePlan.json",
```

```
"appService-linkedTemplate": "[concat(parameters('_artifactsLocation'),
'armtemplates/appService.json', parameters('_artifactsLocationSasToken'))]"

  }
```

In this example, we have two variables:

- appServicePlan-linkedTemplate: This is the linked template that creates an app service plan and is referring to an external resource. Linked templates must be publicly accessible, and we can leverage GitHub or storage accounts to see some examples.

- appService-linkedTemplate: This is the linked template that creates an app service, and we are using the concat() function to construct the uri from the parameter values.

Note that it is possible to use GitHub private repositories, and you will need a manual configuration to get the SaS token. It is preferred to leverage GitHub public endpoints, which should be in raw format, or to utilize storage accounts.

If you prefer to use storage accounts to store your linked templates, ensure you generate the SAS token beforehand.

Then, in the resources section of the main ARM template, we will create two resources related to the deployment type, as shown in Figure 14-5.

```
"resources": [
    {
        "name": "appServicePlan",
        "type": "Microsoft.Resources/deployments",
        "apiVersion": "2020-10-01",
        "properties":{
            "mode": "Incremental",
            Linked template: "https://gist.githubusercontent.com/daveRendon/67a94ea5280f676404da2ac20caef518/raw/9585910a67e29abe268dc3:
            "templateLink": {
                "uri": "[concat(variables('appServicePlan-linkedTemplate'))]",
                "contentVersion": "1.0.0.0"
            }
        }
    },
    {
        "name": "appService",
        "type": "Microsoft.Resources/deployments",
        "apiVersion": "2020-10-01",
        "properties": {
            "mode": "Incremental",
            Linked template: "https://ifabrik.blob.core.windows.net/armtemplates/appService.json?sp=racwdyt&st=2021-07-13T21:12:35Z&se=20..."
            "templateLink": {
                "uri": "[concat(variables('appService-linkedTemplate'))]",
                "contentVersion": "1.0.0.0"
            }
        }
    }
],
```

Figure 14-5. *ARM template, resources section*

In the resources section of the main ARM template, we have defined two deployments: one for the app service plan and one for the app service.

We are defining the incremental mode in both sections. Instead of hard-coding the uri value, we are using the concat() function and passing on the value of the uri from the variables previously defined.

Now that we have our main ARM template, we have to work on the linked templates. We are going to create two linked templates: appService.json and appServicePlan.json.

Listing 14-6 shows the definition of appService.json.

Listing 14-6. appService.json ARM Template

```
{

    "$schema": "https://schema.management.azure.com/schemas/2019-04-01/
    deploymentTemplate.json#",
    "contentVersion": "1.0.0.0",
    "parameters": {
```

```
    "webAppName": {
         "type": "string",
         "defaultValue": "[concat('webApp-',
         uniqueString(resourceGroup().id))]",
         "minLength": 2,
         "metadata": {
             "description": "Web app name."
         }
    },
    "location": {
         "type": "string",
         "defaultValue": "[resourceGroup().location]",
         "metadata": {
             "description": "Location for all resources."
         }
    },
"linuxFxVersion": {
  "type": "string",
  "defaultValue": "DOTNETCORE|3.0",
  "metadata": {
    "description": "The Runtime stack of current web app"
         }
    },
    "repoUrl": {
         "type": "string",
         "defaultValue": " ",
         "metadata": {
             "description": "Optional Git Repo URL"
         }
    },
    "appServicePlanPortalName": {
         "type": "string",
         "defaultValue":"[concat('AppPlan-', parameters('webAppName'))]",
         "metadata": {
```

```
                "description": "description"
            }
        }
    },
    "functions": [],
    "variables": {},
    "resources": [
         {
      "type": "Microsoft.Web/sites",
      "apiVersion": "2020-06-01",
      "name": "[parameters('webAppName')]",
      "location": "[parameters('location')]",

      "properties": {
        "serverFarmId": "[resourceId('Microsoft.Web/serverfarms',
        parameters('appServicePlanPortalName'))]",
        "siteConfig": {
          "linuxFxVersion": "[parameters('linuxFxVersion')]"
        },
        "resources": [
          {
            "condition": "[contains(parameters('repoUrl'),'http')]",
            "type": "sourcecontrols",
            "apiVersion": "2020-06-01",
            "name": "web",
            "location": "[parameters('location')]",
            "dependsOn": [
              "[resourceId('Microsoft.Web/sites', parameters('webAppName'))]"
            ],
            "properties": {
              "repoUrl": "[parameters('repoUrl')]",
              "branch": "master",
              "isManualIntegration": true
            }
          }
```

```
        ]
      }
    }
    ],
    "outputs": {}
}
```

The previous ARM template creates only the app service.

Now let's create the ARM template for the app service plan, as shown in Listing 14-7.

Listing 14-7. appServicePlan.json ARM Template

```
{
    "$schema": "https://schema.management.azure.com/schemas/2019-04-01/
    deploymentTemplate.json#",
    "contentVersion": "1.0.0.0",
    "parameters": {
        "webAppName": {
            "type": "string",
            "defaultValue": "[concat('webApp-',
            uniqueString(resourceGroup().id))]",
            "minLength": 2,
            "metadata": {
                "description": "Web app name."
            }
        },
        "location": {
            "type": "string",
            "defaultValue": "[resourceGroup().location]",
            "metadata": {
                "description": "Location for all resources."
            }
        },
        "appServicePlanPortalName": {
            "type": "string",
            "defaultValue":"[concat('AppPlan-', parameters('webAppName'))]",
```

```
            "metadata": {
                "description": "description"
            }
        }
    },
    "functions": [],
    "variables": {
        "sku": "F1"
    },
    "resources": [
        {
            "type": "Microsoft.Web/serverfarms",
            "apiVersion": "2020-06-01",
            "name": "[parameters('appServicePlanPortalName')]",
            "location": "[parameters('location')]",
            "sku": {
                "name": "[variables('sku')]"
            },
            "kind": "linux",
            "properties": {
                "reserved": true
            }
        }
    ],
    "outputs": {
        "appServicePlanId": {
            "type": "string",
            "value": "[resourceId('Microsoft.Web/serverfarms',
            parameters('appServicePlanPortalName'))]"
        }
    }
}
```

In the previous ARM template, we are defining the app service plan. We can deploy this environment from our main ARM template. Figure 14-6 shows the output from this deployment.

```
DeploymentName          : iFabrikDeployment07-13-2021
ResourceGroupName       : iFabrik
ProvisioningState       : Succeeded
Timestamp               : 7/13/2021 10:23:59 PM
Mode                    : Incremental
TemplateLink            :
Parameters              :
                          Name                          Type                        Value
                          ============================  ==========================  ==========
                          _artifactsLocation            String
                          https://ifabrik.blob.core.windows.net/
                          _artifactsLocationSasToken    SecureString
                          webAppName                    String                      ifabrik
                          location                      String                      eastus
                          linuxFxVersion                String                      DOTNETCORE|3.0
                          appServicePlanPortalName      String                      AppPlan-ifabrik

Outputs                 :
DeploymentDebugLogLevel :
```

Figure 14-6. *Deployment output*

You can see in Figure 14-6 that we have successfully deployed our environment with multiple linked templates that are hosted in different locations that are publicly accessible.

It is possible to verify the deployment from the Azure portal, and you should be able to see the three deployments, one deployment per ARM template, as shown in Figure 14-7.

iFabrik | Deployments
Resource group

◯ Refresh   ⊘ Cancel   ⊤ Redeploy   🗑 **Delete**   ↓ View template

Filter by deployment name or resources in the deployment...

	Deployment name	Status	Last modified
✓	appService	✅ Succeeded	7/13/2021, 5:23:24 PM
✓	appServicePlan	✅ Succeeded	7/13/2021, 5:23:02 PM
✓	iFabrikDeployment07-13-2021	✅ Succeeded	7/13/2021, 5:23:59 PM

Figure 14-7. *ARM template deployment*

You can access the code related to this example at the following URL:

```
https://github.com/daveRendon/iac/tree/main/chapter-14/linked-
template-AppService
```

If needed, parameters can also be passed inline or using an external template URI. In the previous example, we used a local parameters file.

Now let's deep dive into nested templates and understand the core differences between nested and linked templates.

Understanding Nested Templates

Through nested templates, you will be able to break your larger ARM template file into smaller ARM templates. Instead of referring to the ARM templates from an external file, we will embed them in the main or principal ARM template as nested templates.

This is useful when working with different deployment scopes. Picture the following scenario: the iFabrik team needs to deploy an N-tier application that contains app services, app service plans, and databases. Each resource type has to be deployed in a different resource group.

In this case, we could leverage nested templates to define the deployment scope of all the three resource groups and target the subscription scope; then, for all the different resources like the app service, the app service plan, and the databases, we could set the deployment scope to the resource group level.

When working with nested templates, we will have all the resources defined in the same ARM template and include more simple templates within the same ARM template file, as shown in Figure 14-8.

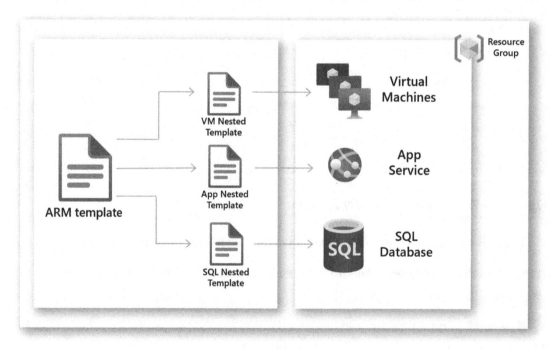

Figure 14-8. *Nested templates*

One of the core differences between linked and nested templates is the ability to determine at what level the expressions will be evaluated in the nested template.

There are two scopes to determine at what level expressions are evaluated in nested templates: inner scope and outer scope.

The outer scope determines that we are going to evaluate parameters and variables outside of the nested template. The inner scope will evaluate only within the nested template level.

Listing 14-8 highlights the JSON template format for nested templates.

Listing 14-8. Nested Template, JSON Format

```
{
"$schema": "https://schema.management.azure.com/schemas/2019-04-01/
deploymentTemplate.json#",
  "contentVersion": "1.0.0.0",
  "parameters": {},
  "variables": {},
  "resources": [
    {
      "type": "Microsoft.Resources/deployments",
      "apiVersion": "2020-10-01",
      "name": "your-nested-template-name",
      "properties": {
        "mode": "Incremental",
        "template": {
          <Your-nested-template>
        }
      }
    }
  ],
  "outputs": {
  }
}
```

Tip   There's a snippet available in the ARM extension in Visual Studio Code for nested templates for outer and inner scopes, as shown in Figure 14-9.

```
        ---
    "resources": [
        {
            arm-ne
        }            arm-nested-template...    Nested (inline) Inner-Scoped De...
    ],               arm-nested-template-outer
    "outputs": {}    arm-nic
```

Figure 14-9. *ARM snippet, nested template*

Note that to define the scope, you can use the property called expressionEvaluationOptions, as shown in Figure 14-10.

```
"name": "nestedDeployment1",
"type": "Microsoft.Resources/deployments",
"apiVersion": "2020-10-01",
"properties": {
    "expressionEvaluationOptions": {
        "scope": "inner"
    },
    "mode": "Incremental",
    "parameters": {
    },
    Nested template with inner scope
    "template": {
        "$schema": "https://schema.management.azure.com/schemas/2019-04-01/deploymentTemplate.json#",
        "contentVersion": "1.0.0.0",
        "parameters": {},
        "variables": {},
        "resources": [],
        "outputs": {}
    }
}
```

Figure 14-10. *ARM snippet, nested template, inner scope*

Now let's create our ARM template that will contain multiple nested templates. In this example, we will create three resource groups at the subscription scope.

To create the three resource groups, we will leverage the copy element to create all the resource groups in the same loop. We will also define the evaluation scope to outer. See Figure 14-11.

```
"resources": [
    //Resource Groups
    {
        "name": "resourceGroups",
        "type": "Microsoft.Resources/deployments",
        "apiVersion": "2020-10-01",
        "location": "[parameters('location')]",
        "properties": {
            "expressionEvaluationOptions": {
                "scope": "inner"
            },
            "mode": "Incremental",
            "parameters": {
            },
            Nested template with inner scope
            "template": {
                "$schema": "https://schema.management.azure.com/schemas/2019-04-01/subscriptionDeploymentTemplate.json#",
                "contentVersion": "1.0.0.0",
                "variables": {
                    "resourceGroupName": "ifabrik-rg-"
                },
                "resources": [
                    {
                        "name": "[concat(variables('resourceGroupName'), copyIndex())]",
                        "type": "Microsoft.Resources/resourceGroups",
                        "apiVersion": "2019-10-01",
                        "location": "eastus",
                        // Copy works here when scope is inner
                        "copy": {
                            "name": "resourcegroupcopy",
                            "count": 3
                        }
                    }
                ],
                "outputs": {
                    "resourceGroupsList": {
                        "type": "array",
                        "copy": {
                            "count": 3,
                            "input": "[concat(variables('resourceGroupName'), copyIndex())]"
                        }
                    }
                }
            }
        }
    },
```

Figure 14-11. *ARM template, nested template with copy element*

In the previous ARM template, we added the nested template in the resources section of the main ARM template; then we defined the prefix of the resource groups and included the copy element.

Note that this nested template targets a subscription level. We have also defined the output in the nested template. The outputs from a nested template can be accessed from a different nested or linked template.

You can access the output value from the main section, as shown in Figure 14-12.

```
          }
        ],
        "outputs": {
            "resourceGroupsList": {          Output from nested template
                "type": "array",
                "copy": {
                    "count": 3,
                    "input": "[concat(variables('resourceGroupName'), copyIndex())]"
                }
            }
          }
        }
      }
    }
  ],
  "outputs": {
    "resourceGroups": {             Output from main template
        "type": "array",
        "copy": {
            "count": 1,
            "input": "[reference('resourceGroups').outputs.resourceGroupsList.value]"
        }
    }
  },
```

Figure 14-12. *Outputs in nested templates*

Now let's add some resources to our environment. The additional nested templates will target the resource group level instead.

The next step is to define a new nested template for each of the resources. We will include the following:

- A nested template for the app service

- A nested template for the app service plan

Figure 14-13 highlights the nested template for the app service.

```
//Nested template: App Service
{
    "name": "appService",
    "type": "Microsoft.Resources/deployments",
    "apiVersion": "2020-10-01",
    "resourceGroup": "[variables('resourceGroupName2')]",
    "dependsOn": [
        "[resourceId('Microsoft.Resources/deployments', 'resourceGroups')]"
    ],
    "properties": {
        "mode": "Incremental",
        "expressionEvaluationOptions": {
            "scope": "outer"
        },
        Nested template with outer scope
        "template": {
            "$schema": "https://schema.management.azure.com/schemas/2019-04-01/deploymentTemplate.json#",
            "contentVersion": "1.0.0.0",

            "resources": [
                {
                    "name": "[parameters('webAppName')]",
                    "type": "Microsoft.Web/sites",
                    "apiVersion": "2018-11-01",
                    "location": "eastus",
                    "properties": {
                        "name": "[concat(parameters('webAppName'))]",
                        "serverFarmdId": "[parameters('appServicePlan_name')]"
                    }
                }
            ],
            "outputs": {}
        }
    }
}
```

Figure 14-13. *Nested template, app service*

Note that we are defining a dependency on the resource groups, leveraging the outer scope. In the resources section of the nested template, we have defined the properties for creating an app service.

Now let's review the nested template for the app service plan.

Figure 14-14 highlights the nested template for the app service plan.

```
//Nested template: App Service Plan
{
    "name": "appServicePlan",
    "type": "Microsoft.Resources/deployments",
    "apiVersion": "2020-10-01",
    "resourceGroup": "[variables('resourceGroupName1')]",
    "dependsOn": [
        "[resourceId('Microsoft.Resources/deployments', 'resourceGroups')]"
    ],
    "properties": {
        "expressionEvaluationOptions": {
            "scope": "outer"
        },
        "mode": "Incremental",
        Nested template with outer scope
        "template": {
            "$schema": "https://schema.management.azure.com/schemas/2019-04-01/deploymentTemplate.json#",
            "contentVersion": "1.0.0.0",
            "resources": [
                {
                    "type": "Microsoft.Web/serverfarms",
                    "apiVersion": "2020-06-01",
                    "name": "[variables('appServicePlanPortalName')]",
                    "location": "[parameters('location')]",
                    "sku": {
                        "name": "[variables('sku')]"
                    },
                    "kind": "linux",
                    "properties": {
                        "reserved": true
                    }
                }
            ],
            "outputs": {
                "appServicePlan": {
                    "type": "string",
                    "value": "[resourceId('Microsoft.Web/serverfarms', variables('appServicePlanPortalName'))]"
                }
            }
        }
    }
},
```

Figure 14-14. *Nested template, app service plan*

In the previous nested template, we have defined our app service plan and included the output value of the app service plan.

You might need to update the Linux app service plan SKU, as the limit is one app service plan per subscription.

Bear in mind that we target to the subscription level using the cmdlet: New-AzDeployment.

You can find these examples at the following URL:

```
https://github.com/daveRendon/iac/tree/main/chapter-14/nested-templates
```

Now that we have seen how linked templates and nested templates work, let's do a quick recap of the core differences:

- Both linked and nested templates will help you modularize your solution and keep track of versioning.

- Linked templates are compounded by separate files, referenced by the main ARM template. You'll have one file that calls multiple separate files.

- With linked templates, you can reference external ARM templates located in an external repository that is publicly accessible, such as GitHub or a storage account.

- To secure your deployment, it is preferred to leverage private storage accounts and use a SAS token.

- Nested templates are smaller ARM templates within or in the same main ARM template. Scope evaluation becomes critical. You'll have one single file that includes all the nested templates.

- Nested templates can help you when you need to target different scope levels such as tenant level, subscription level, and resource group level.

Now that we have created our environment using multiple linked or nested templates, how can we make them available for the rest of our team in the organization? Is there a way to securely share these ARM templates and simplify the deployment from a centralized location? Let's see how template specs can help with these scenarios.

Template Specs

Cloud architects in large enterprises need a way to compose and manage what goes into their Azure subscription, and template specs are one of the key components to solve this challenge.

Template specs will provide you with an easy way to share ARM templates across your organization and deploy them directly or reference them as a module of the environment.

You can think of template specs as an "ARM template private registry" within a tenant that will allow you to store the ARM templates and artifacts in the ARM control plane.

While we could use linked templates, the potential disadvantage is the need to have those templates publicly accessible through GitHub or a storage account.

With templates specs, you will be able to package up the main template, and the child templates are all in one template spec resource.

Any ARM template can be converted into a template spec. This way, any member of your team will be able to deploy the template spec via the Azure portal, PowerShell, CLI, or as a nested deployment.

One of the main benefits of leveraging template specs is keeping track of the version of the environment and managing access through role-based access control instead of SAS tokens.

Figure 14-15 highlights the concept of template specs.

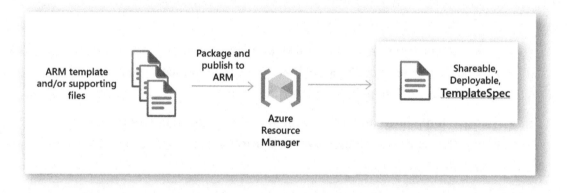

Figure 14-15. *Template specs*

As you can imagine, there is a specific definition for the template specs resource type: `Microsoft.Resources/templateSpecs`.

So how do template specs work? How can this resource type be deployed? We can deploy a template spec as stand-alone or as part of a more complex deployment. Let's dig a bit more into this.

We can leverage the same tools we have been using to deploy ARM templates to provision template specs. You can utilize PowerShell or CLI to deploy a template spec.

Listing 14-9 highlights the PowerShell command to create a template spec.

Listing 14-9. PowerShell Command to Create a Template Spec

```
New-AzTemplateSpec `
-Name storageSpec `
-Version 1.0a `
-ResourceGroupName templateSpecsRg `
-Location westus2 `
-TemplateFile ./mainTemplate.json
```

In Listing 14-9, we utilize the PowerShell command `New-AzTemplateSpec` to define a new template spec. We need to pass some parameters, including for the name, version, resource group, location, and actual template file.

Creating a Simple Template Spec

We previously mentioned that template specs have the same format as the ARM template, so now let's see how we can define our template spec file.

The ARM template shown in Figure 14-16 creates an app service plan.

```
{
    "$schema": "https://schema.management.azure.com/schemas/2019-04-01/deploymentTemplate.json#",
    "contentVersion": "1.0.0.0",

    "parameters": {
        "planName": {
            "type": "string",
            "defaultValue": "[concat('ifabrik-', uniqueString(resourceGroup().id))]",
            "minLength": 2
        },
        "location": {
            "type": "string",
            "defaultValue": "[resourceGroup().location]"
        },
        "sku": {
            "type": "string",
            "defaultValue": "F1"
        }
    },
    "variables": {
        "appServicePlanPortalName": "[concat('AppServicePlan-', parameters('planName'))]"
    },
    "resources": [
        {
            "name": "[variables('appServicePlanPortalName')]",
            "type": "Microsoft.Web/serverfarms",
            "apiVersion": "2018-02-01",
            "location": "[parameters('location')]",
            "sku": {
                "name": "[parameters('sku')]",
                "capacity": 1
            },
            "properties": {
                "name": "[variables('appServicePlanPortalName')]"
            }
        }
    ],
    "outputs": {}
}
```

Figure 14-16. *ARM template that creates an app service plan*

As you can see in Figure 14-16, this is a simple ARM template that creates only an app service plan.

Creating a Template Spec Using PowerShell

Now we will create the template spec with the PowerShell command shown in Listing 14-10.

Listing 14-10. Create a Template Spec Using PowerShell

```
New-AzTemplateSpec -Name appPlanSpec -Version 1.0a -ResourceGroupName
ifabrik -Location westus -TemplateFile ./mainTemplate.json
```

Once we deploy this to Azure, any member of the organization will be able to deploy this template spec.

Figure 14-17 highlights the output from the template spec deployment. Note that through template specs, we will be able to keep versioning our environments.

```
Id                   : /subscriptions/d988cbee-043f-4c46-9a59          /resourceGroups/ifabrik/providers/Microsoft.
                       Resources/templateSpecs/appPlanSpec
Name                 : appPlanSpec
ResourceGroupName    : ifabrik
SubscriptionId       : d988cbee-043f-4c46-9a59
Location             : westus
Versions             : 1.0a
CreationTime(UTC)    : 7/29/2021 11:02:45 PM
LastModifiedTime(UTC) : 7/29/2021 11:02:45 PM
```

Figure 14-17. *Template spec deployment*

We can go to the Azure portal, and in the ifabrik resource group, we will be able to see the template spec that we just deployed, as shown in Figure 14-18.

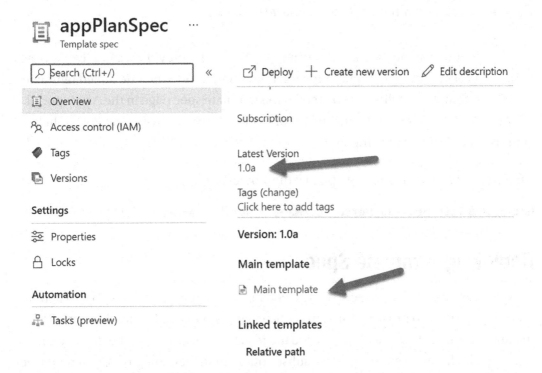

Figure 14-18. *Template spec in the Azure portal*

If we select the "Main template" option, this will show a page with the actual template spec in the Azure portal, as shown in Figure 14-19.

Main template   ✕

```
 1   {
 2       "$schema": "https://schema.management.azure.com/schemas/2019-04-01/deploymentTemplate.json#",
 3       "contentVersion": "1.0.0.0",
 4       "parameters": {
 5           "planName": {
 6               "type": "string",
 7               "defaultValue": "[concat('ifabrik-', uniqueString(resourceGroup().id))]",
 8               "minLength": 2
 9           },
10           "location": {
11               "type": "string",
12               "defaultValue": "[resourceGroup().location]"
13           },
14           "sku": {
15               "type": "string",
16               "defaultValue": "F1"
17           }
18       },
19       "variables": {
20           "appServicePlanPortalName": "[concat('AppServicePlan-', parameters('planName'))]"
21       },
```

Figure 14-19. Main template in template spec page

Note that we can provide a simple template like in the previous example or leverage template specs for more complex and larger environments to include linked templates. The linked templates will also be listed on the template spec page in the Azure portal.

Another option is to verify the details of our template spec using the PowerShell command, as shown in Listing 14-11.

Listing 14-11. Get Template Spec Using PowerShell

```
Get-AzTemplateSpec -ResourceGroupName ifabrik -Name appPlanSpec
```

Deploying Template Spec

Now let's think of the following scenario: Peter is part of our team; he is able to deploy this template spec to provision an app service plan, and instead of passing the URI for the template, he will just need to provide the resource ID and target the deployment to any scope including resource groups, subscription, management group, or tenant level.

Peter only needs to get the resource ID to be able to provision this template spec.

To get the resource ID, we can leverage the previous command and store it in a variable, as shown in Listing 14-12.

Listing 14-12. Store Template Spec ID in PowerShell Variable

```
$templateSpec = Get-AzTemplateSpec -ResourceGroupName ifabrik -Name
appPlanSpec -Version 1.0a
```

Note that the requested version is 1.0a from this template spec. Peter will have more flexibility to build his environment while having control of the version of the template.

Now, to verify the version of the template spec, we can use the command shown in Listing 14-13.

Listing 14-13. Template Spec ID in PowerShell Variable

```
$templateSpec.Versions.Id
```

We will see the output structure shown in Listing 14-14.

Listing 14-14. Template Spec ID

```
/subscriptions/d988cbee-043f-4c46-xxxx-xxxxxx /resourceGroups/ifabrik/
providers/Microsoft.Resources/templateSpecs/appPlanSpec/versions/1.0a
```

Peter can deploy this template spec with the command in Listing 14-15; in this case, we are going to provision the template spec to a resource group called ifabrik2.

Listing 14-15. Deploy Template Spec ID Using PowerShell

```
New-AzResourceGroupDeployment -ResourceGroupName ifabrik2
-TemplateSpecId $templateSpec.Versions.Id
```

Figure 14-20 shows the output from this deployment.

```
DeploymentName          : 74020d93-99ff-4efb-87b7-fd6a7063e054
ResourceGroupName       : ifabrik2
ProvisioningState       : Succeeded
Timestamp               : 7/29/2021 11:35:14 PM
Mode                    : Incremental
TemplateLink            :
                          Uri            :
                          ContentVersion : 1.0.0.0

Parameters              :
                          Name                Type                          Value
                          ================    ==========================    ==========
                          planName            String                        ifabrik-csty7oesmvjce
                          location            String                        eastus
                          sku                 String                        F1

Outputs                 :
DeploymentDebugLogLevel :
```

Figure 14-20. *Template spec deployment*

We can also confirm the deployment of the app service plan in the Azure portal, as shown in Figure 14-21.

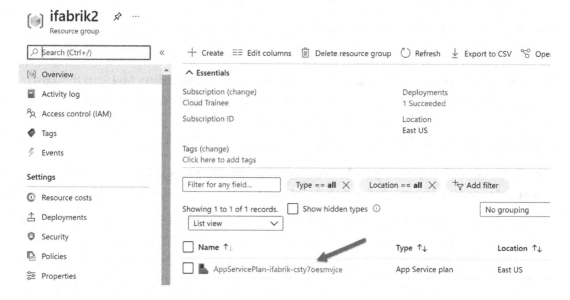

Figure 14-21. *Template spec deployment*

The use of tags and linked templates is also supported in template specs. Here's a summary of the process to define and consume a template spec:

1. Define a new resource type named `Microsoft.Resources/templateSpecs`.

2. Create a JSON file to define your template, which will become the template spec.

3. Convert the JSON file to a template spec using PowerShell.

4. Deploy the template spec to Azure.

5. Deploy the environment defined in the template spec using the template spec ID and version.

Now that we have seen how template specs work, let's review how we can integrate the concept of linked templates and template specs for larger environments.

Template Spec with Linked Templates

For more complex environments, we can have a template spec that references multiple linked templates as artifacts. This approach is similar to linked templates. The only difference is that during the definition, we will pass on the relative path from the template rather than the URL of the linked template.

For example, the iFabrik team defined an environment that includes an app service plan and an app service. Every member of the organization needs to have the ability to deploy its own app service plan and app service. The iFabrik team has to create a template spec to cover this need.

To achieve this, we can create a template spec with two linked templates: one template for the app service and a second template for the app service plan. See Figure 14-22.

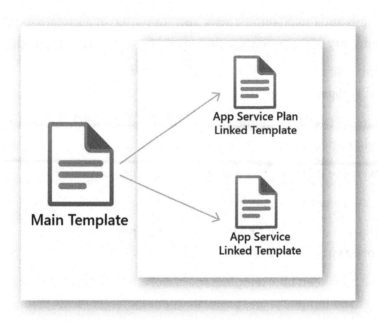

Figure 14-22. *Template spec definition*

The objective is to break the solution into smaller pieces using linked templates, which means we will have a template deploy another template. This way, we can keep smaller files and separate the components of the solution as needed.

We are going to deploy the app service and the app service plan as part of this main template deployment. However, instead of using the URI as we did in the previously linked templates, we will use a relativePath property.

Figure 14-23 highlights the main template spec.

```
{
    "$schema": "https://schema.management.azure.com/schemas/2019-04-01/deploymentTemplate.json#",
    "contentVersion": "1.0.0.0",
    "resources": [
        {
            "name": "appServicePlanDeploy",
            "type": "Microsoft.Resources/deployments",
            "apiVersion": "2020-10-01",
            "properties":{
                "mode": "Incremental",
                Relative linked template: ".\artifacts\appServicePlan.json"
                "templateLink": {
                    //path to child template
                    "relativePath": "./artifacts/appServicePlan.json"
                }
            }
        },
        {
            "name": "appServiceDeploy",
            "type": "Microsoft.Resources/deployments",
            "apiVersion": "2020-10-01",
            "properties": {
                "mode": "Incremental",
                Relative linked template: ".\artifacts\appService.json"
                "templateLink": {
                    //path to child template
                    "relativePath": "./artifacts/appService.json"
                }
            }
        }
    ],
    "outputs": {
        "appServicePlanOutput": {
            "type": "object",
            "value": "[reference('appServicePlanDeploy').outputs]"
        },
        "output1": {
            "type": "object",
            "value": "[reference('appServiceDeploy').outputs]"
        }
    }
}
```

Figure 14-23. *Main template spec*

Note that we are using the property named relativePath to provide the path to the linked templates.

To deploy this template spec, we will use the PowerShell command shown in Listing 14-16.

Listing 14-16. Deploy Template Spec Using PowerShell

```
New-AzTemplateSpec -Name ifabrikApp -ResourceGroupName ifabrik -Location
eastus -Version 0.2 -TemplateFile .\mainTemplate.json
```

Figure 14-24 shows the output from the creation of the template spec.

```
Id                     : /subscriptions/d988cbee-043f-4c46-9a59-dedb2119e48c/resourceGroups/ifabrik/providers/Microsoft
                         Resources/templateSpecs/ifabrikApp
Name                   : ifabrikApp
ResourceGroupName      : ifabrik
SubscriptionId         : d988cbee-043f-4c46-9a59-dedb2119e48c
Location               : eastus
Versions               : 0.2
CreationTime(UTC)      : 8/6/2021 5:44:57 PM
LastModifiedTime(UTC)  : 8/6/2021 5:44:57 PM
```

Figure 14-24. *Template spec deployment output using PowerShell*

We can optionally verify that the template spec is now available using the Azure portal, as shown in Figure 14-25.

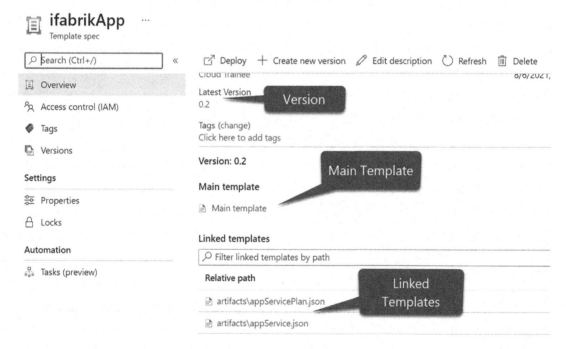

Figure 14-25. *Template spec in the Azure portal*

Now we can have another member of our team deploy this template spec. Again, we would need to have the ID and version from the template spec.

We will consume the previous template spec and deploy the environment into a different resource group called `ifabrik-dev`. See Listing 14-17.

Listing 14-17. Deploy Environment from Template Spec

```
$templateSpec = Get-AzTemplateSpec -ResourceGroupName ifabrik -Name
ifabrikApp -Version 0.2

New-AzResourceGroupDeployment -ResourceGroupName ifabrik-dev -TemplateSpecId
$templateSpec.Versions.Id
```

We can verify that the deployment succeeded, as shown in Figure 14-26.

```
DeploymentName            : 4059d0dd-4b25-4097-b10e-75265a52f2ca
ResourceGroupName         : ifabrik-dev
ProvisioningState         : Succeeded
Timestamp                 : 8/6/2021 7:52:33 PM
Mode                      : Incremental
TemplateLink              :
                            Uri           :
                            ContentVersion : 1.0.0.0

Parameters                :
Outputs                   :
                            Name                    Type                        Value
                            =====================   =========================   ==========
                            appServicePlanOutput    Object                      {
                              "appServicePlanId": {
                                "type": "String",
                                "value": "/subscriptions/d988cbee-043f-4c46-9a59-dedb2119e48c/resourceGroups/ifabrik-dev/providers/Mic
                            rosoft.Web/serverfarms/AppPlan-webApp-ugifoo64xi422"
                              }
                            }
                            output1                 Object                      {}

DeploymentDebugLogLevel :
```

Figure 14-26. *Deployment output*

Another option is the consume the template spec as modules. This way, we can share the template spec with another team of the organization and have them consume that template spec.

Consuming Template Spec as Modules

So, the idea here is that Bob, who is part of the iFabrik team, wants to write his ARM template for his testing environment and include any particular resource such as SQL databases, virtual machines, and so on, and he doesn't want to take care of resources like networking or policies.

In this case, template specs will allow Bob to have someone else from his team provide the templates related to the networking components and policies components, and Bob will consume those templates as modules.

This approach will allow Bob essentially to deploy a template from within another template. .

In this scenario, we will leverage the same nested deployment in the main template and use the property called Id. So, instead of passing the entire URI, we will refer to the ID property of the template spec and the version that Bob wants to deploy.

To achieve this, we can leverage the resourceId() function, as shown in Figure 14-27.

```json
{
    "$schema": "https://schema.management.azure.com/schemas/2019-04-01/deploymentTemplate.json#",
    "contentVersion": "1.0.0.0",
    "resources": [
        {
            "name": "appServicePlanModule",
            "type": "Microsoft.Resources/deployments",
            "apiVersion": "2020-10-01",
            "properties":{
                "mode": "Incremental",

                "templateLink": {
                    //point to Template Spec Id
                    "id": "[resourceId('ifabrik','Microsoft.Resources/templateSpecs/versions', 'ifabrikApp', '0.2')]"
                }
            }
        }
    ]
}
```

Figure 14-27. Consuming template spec as module

We can use the PowerShell command to deploy this template, as shown in Listing 14-18.

Listing 14-18. Deploying the Template

```
New-AzResourceGroupDeployment -ResourceGroupName ifabrik-dev -TemplateFile
.\mainTemplate.json
```

Notice that we are referring in the template to the id property and including all the details needed to consume the template spec as a module, including the resource group where the template spec is deployed, the resource type, the name of the template spec, and the version to utilize for this deployment.

Ideally, this will give you a better understanding of how you can work with larger environments and how to better control the versions of your ARM templates.

So, what's the next step? While template specs are relatively new, the next phase from a lifecycle management standpoint is that Microsoft is working on a feature called *deployment stacks*.

Deployment stacks is a grouping concept that will help you create associations between the resources you can include in your environment and the deployment that can be performed on a defined group.

Think of the scenario where you have a resource group, and then you can provision a deployment stack, which is, in fact, a resource type. The deployment stack will kick off an actual deployment of the resources that you want to include in your environment.

Figure 14-28 highlights the concept of deployment stacks.

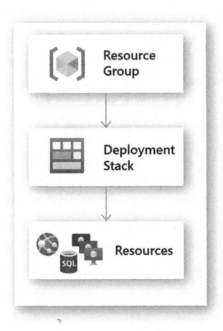

Figure 14-28. *Deployment stacks*

As you can imagine, we will most likely be able to target the scope of a given resource group in a given subscription or target a subscription and multiple resource groups.

Before we reach the end of this chapter, you can find the templates and examples explained at the following URL:

```
https://github.com/daveRendon/iac/tree/main/chapter-14
```

Summary

This chapter reviewed the options to manage our ARM templates better and work with a modularized approach. We also examined the main differences of working with linked and nested templates and showed examples of each approach.

Then we moved into the concept of template specs to improve collaboration across our organization when working with larger environments. We reviewed how to consume template specs as linked templates and as modules.

In the next chapter, we will review how you can work with secrets in your ARM template.

CHAPTER 15

Working with Secrets in Your ARM Template

In the previous chapter, we discussed how you can work with larger and more complex environments by splitting components as modules into multiple ARM templates and how you can share templates and make them accessible to your team members.

This chapter will go over a top security concern when working with ARM templates: how you can work with secret values in ARM templates.

We will review how to retrieve and pass secrets in your ARM template. This chapter also covers the differences when working with static values and dynamic values.

The topics in this chapter include the following:

- Understanding security in ARM templates

- Working with secrets in ARM templates

- Working with static and dynamic values

So far, we have been working with a few string values and hard-coded secure values in our ARM templates; however, in most cases, when we need to deploy resources like virtual machines, where we need to provide the credentials for the resource, it is best to avoid the use of strings or hard-coding the secret or password value.

Understanding Security in ARM Templates

What if you put a secure value like a password of a virtual machine directly in your ARM template or a parameter file, and these files are publicly accessed or leaked?

© David Rendón 2022
D. Rendón, *Building Applications with Azure Resource Manager (ARM)*,
https://doi.org/10.1007/978-1-4842-7747-8_15

How can we make sure that we protect these secrets in the ARM template and parameter files? While it is recommended to use parameters for usernames and passwords, we have to be careful how we handle secrets in our ARM templates.

I can't emphasize enough the importance of securing values in ARM templates, and there's a specific parameter type that we can use for passwords and secrets: secureString.

Using this parameter type will note that the secure string can't be read after deployment.

The parameter types secureString and secureObject should be utilized for all secrets and passwords. There's an important consideration when using this parameter type: the parameter's actual value is not logged or saved to the deployment history.

We reviewed parameters in Chapter 6, but we will recap these parameter types here. Listing 15-1 shows the definition of the parameter type secureString.

Listing 15-1. Secure String Parameter Type

```
"parameters": {
  "secretValue": {
    "type": "securestring"
    }
  }
```

Listing 15-2 shows the definition of the parameter type secureObject.

Listing 15-2. Secure String Parameter Type

```
"parameters": {
  "secretValue": {
    "type": "secureObject"
    }
  }
```

We typically use these parameters on resources like virtual machines. In the template shown in Listing 15-3, we highlight the use of the parameter type secureString.

Listing 15-3. Parameters Definition in ARM Template

```
"parameters": {
    "Password": {
      "type": "securestring"
    },
    "location": {
      "type": "string",
      "defaultValue": "[resourceGroup().location]"
    },
    "username": {
      "type": "string"
    }
  },
```

Listing 15-4 shows the definition of the parameters file and refers to the secure string's actual value at deployment time.

Listing 15-4. Parameters File

```
{
  "$schema": "https://schema.management.azure.com/schemas/2019-04-01/
  deploymentParameters.json#",
  "contentVersion": "1.0.0.0",
  "parameters": {
    "balPassword": {
      "value": "GEN-PASSWORD"
    },
    "username": {
        "value": "GEN-UNIQUE"
    }
  }
}
```

While this is useful for bare deployments, you might think, what if I need to reference a different sensitive value at deployment time? Or how can I refer to a secret value that exists in another place than the resource group we're currently working on?

Working with Secrets in ARM Templates

Passing or referencing secrets in ARM templates is paramount, and Azure provides a service that you can leverage to security pass secrets into your template, called Azure Key Vault.

Think of a scenario where you have to deploy an application that consists of an app service and a SQL database. We would need to set a password for the SQL database and securely reference the password in the ARM template. So, how can we handle this in the ARM template?

We could leverage Azure Key Vault to reference passwords or any other secret in the ARM template to achieve this.

Leveraging Azure Key Vault

Azure Key Vault is a service to help you safeguard and maintain control of keys and other secrets like passwords or certificates and enforces the encryption of data in transit using the Transport Layer Security protocol.

Once Azure Key Vault is provisioned in your Azure subscription, you will be able to pass and retrieve secrets as parameters from the ARM template, as shown in Figure 15-1.

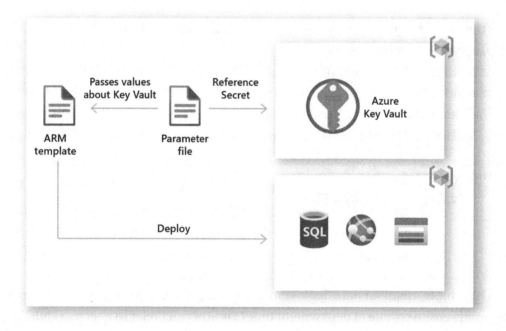

Figure 15-1. *Azure Key Vault workflow*

Note that Key Vault admits two types of permission model: vault permission and role-based access control (RBAC) permission model.

The vault permission model is an authorization system built in to Key Vault that provides access to keys, certificates, and secrets.

The RBAC permission model provides you with more granular access management of resources. You have to create role assignments if you plan to use this permission model.

This role is outside the scope of the built-in owner or contributor roles since this is considered as a data-tier access.

We will use a managed identity for our following example and enable the RBAC permission model for the Key Vault.

Creating an Instance of Azure Key Vault

The ARM template shown in Listing 15-5 created an instance of an Azure Key Vault, a secret value, and a secret name.

Remember that you will need to create a security principal or managed identity beforehand and get the object ID from the managed identity.

Listing 15-5 shows the `parameters` section of the ARM template.

Listing 15-5. parameters Section, ARM Template

```
"parameters": {
    "keyVaultName": {
        "type": "string"
    },
    "location": {
        "type": "string",
        "defaultValue": "[resourceGroup().location]"
    },
    "enabledForDeployment": {
        "type": "bool",
        "defaultValue": true,
        "allowedValues": [
            true,
            false
        ]
```

```
        },
        "enableRbacAuthorization": {
            "type": "bool",
            "defaultValue": true,
            "allowedValues": [
                true,
                false
            ]
        },
        "enabledForDiskEncryption": {
            "type": "bool",
            "defaultValue": false,
            "allowedValues": [
                true,
                false
            ]
        },
        "enabledForTemplateDeployment": {
            "type": "bool",
            "defaultValue": true,
            "allowedValues": [
                true,
                false
            ]
        },
        "tenantId": {
            "type": "string",
            "defaultValue": "[subscription().tenantId]"
        },
        "objectId": {
            "type": "secureString"
        },
        "keysPermissions": {
            "type": "array",
            "defaultValue": [
```

```
                "list"
        ]
    },
    "secretsPermissions": {
        "type": "array",
        "defaultValue": [
            "all"
        ]
    },
    "skuName": {
        "type": "string",
        "defaultValue": "Standard",
        "allowedValues": [
            "Standard",
            "Premium"
        ]
    },
    "secretName": {
        "type": "string"
    },
    "secretValue": {
        "type": "securestring"
    }
},
```

Figure 15-2 shows the resources section of the ARM template.

```
"resources": [
    {
        1 child: ${secretName} (secrets)
        "type": "Microsoft.KeyVault/vaults",
        "apiVersion": "2019-09-01",
        "name": "[parameters('keyVaultName')]",
        "location": "[parameters('location')]",
        "properties": {
            "enabledForDeployment": "[parameters('enabledForDeployment')]",
            "enabledForDiskEncryption": "[parameters('enabledForDiskEncryption')]",
            "enabledForTemplateDeployment": "[parameters('enabledForTemplateDeployment')]",
            "enableRbacAuthorization": "[parameters('enableRbacAuthorization')]",
            "tenantId": "[parameters('tenantId')]",
            "accessPolicies": [
                {
                    "objectId": "[parameters('objectId')]",
                    "tenantId": "[parameters('tenantId')]",
                    "permissions": {
                        "keys": "[parameters('keysPermissions')]",
                        "secrets": "[parameters('secretsPermissions')]"
                    }
                }
            ],
            "sku": {
                "name": "[parameters('skuName')]",
                "family": "A"
            },
            "networkAcls": {
                "defaultAction": "Allow",
                "bypass": "AzureServices"
            }
        }
    },
    {
        Parent: ${keyVaultName} (vaults)
        "type": "Microsoft.KeyVault/vaults/secrets",
        "apiVersion": "2019-09-01",
        "name": "[concat(parameters('keyVaultName'), '/', parameters('secretName'))]",
        "location": "[parameters('location')]",
        "dependsOn": [
            "[resourceId('Microsoft.KeyVault/vaults', parameters('keyVaultName'))]"
        ],
        "properties": {
            "value": "[parameters('secretValue')]"
        }
    }
]
```

Figure 15-2. Resources section, ARM template

The latest API version of the previous Key Vault and secrets is 2021-06-01. I recommend you take a look at the most recent versions in the documentation. Also note that the Key Vault name should be globally unique.

To deploy this ARM template, will use the commands shown in Listing 15-6.

Listing 15-6. Deploying ARM Template Using PowerShell

```
$date = Get-Date -Format "MM-dd-yyyy"
$deploymentName = "iFabrikDeployment"+"$date"
New-AzResourceGroupDeployment -Name $deploymentName -ResourceGroupName
iFabrik -TemplateFile .\azuredeploy.json -TemplateParameterFile
.\azuredeploy.parameters.json
```

Figure 15-3 shows the output from the deployment.

```
DeploymentName        : iFabrikDeployment08-07-2021
ResourceGroupName     : iFabrik
ProvisioningState     : Succeeded
Timestamp             : 8/8/2021 12:40:20 AM
Mode                  : Incremental
TemplateLink          :
Parameters            :
                        Name                          Type                        Value
                        ============================  ==========================  ==========
                        keyVaultName                  String                      ifabrikKeyVault
                        location                      String                      eastus
                        enabledForDeployment          Bool                        True
                        enableRbacAuthorization       Bool                        True
                        enabledForDiskEncryption      Bool                        False
                        enabledForTemplateDeployment  Bool                        True
                        tenantId                      String
                        objectId                      SecureString
                        keysPermissions               Array                       [
                          "list"
                        ]
                        secretsPermissions            Array                       [
                          "all"
                        ]
                        skuName                       String                      Standard
                        secretName                    String                      mySecretName
                        secretValue                   SecureString
```

Figure 15-3. *Deployment output*

Note that both the `objectId` from the managed identity and the `secretValue` are secrets referenced as `secureObject` and `secureString` in the parameters and are never visible in the deployment history nor stored in the logs.

The next step is to work with the secrets in the ARM template. We can now reference or retrieve any secrets from our Azure Key Vault.

Working with Static and Dynamic Values

To reference a secret value on the ARM template, we can leverage a parameter that references the Key Vault and provide the name of the secret, not the secret value, as shown in Figure 15-4.

In the previous example, we pass the secret `secretName` created in the Key Vault. As you can see firsthand, we will have to provide the `id` of the Key Vault and include the subscription `id`, the resource group name, and the name of the Key Vault.

```
{
  "$schema": "https://schema.management.azure.com/schemas/2019-04-01/deploymentParameters.json#",
  "contentVersion": "1.0.0.0",
  "parameters": {
    "adminPassword": {
      "reference": {
        "keyVault": {
          "id": "/subscriptions/<subscription-id>/resourceGroups/<rg-name>/providers/Microsoft.KeyVault/vaults/<vault-name>"
        },
        "secretName": "vmPassword"
      }
    }
  }
}
```

Figure 15-4. *Referencing Key Vault secret*

We can utilize the command in Listing 15-7 to get the Key Vault ID.

Listing 15-7. Get Key Vault ID Using PowerShell

```
$KvName = "Name-Of-Your-Key-Vault"
Get-AzKeyVault -VaultName $KvName | Select-Object -ExpandProperty
ResourceId
```

Listing 15-8 shows the output from the previous command.

Listing 15-8. Output, Key Vault ID

```
/subscriptions/d988cbee-043f-4c46-9a59x-XXXXXXXX/resourceGroups/
iFabrik/providers/Microsoft.KeyVault/vaults/ifabrikKeyVault
```

The previous Key Vault ID string is the value we will use to reference secrets in the ARM template.

While we are leveraging mostly PowerShell to configure Key Vault, bear in mind that it is possible to use Azure CLI, and if you want to retrieve secrets, you can use the Azure Portal, .NET, and Node.js.

The next step is to reference secrets in the ARM template. The first prerequisite is to be able to have access to the secrets in the Key Vault. So make sure that the user-related has access to the secrets or grant access to the secrets.

In our previous ARM template where we created the Key Vault, we also defined a section called accessPolicies to grant access to the secrets, as shown in Figure 15-5.

```
"accessPolicies": [
    {
        "objectId": "[parameters('objectId')]",
        "tenantId": "[parameters('tenantId')]",
        "permissions": {
            "keys": "[parameters('keysPermissions')]",
            "secrets": "[parameters('secretsPermissions')]"
        }
    }
],
```

Figure 15-5. *Output, Key Vault ID*

Once you have the proper access to the secrets, we can reference any secrets in a parameter file, not in the actual ARM template. This approach is mainly known as referencing secrets with static IDs.

Reference Secrets with Static ID

When working with static IDs, we will reference the Key Vault in our parameters file instead of referencing secrets in the actual ARM template.

Figure 15-6 highlights the workflow of referencing secrets with static IDs.

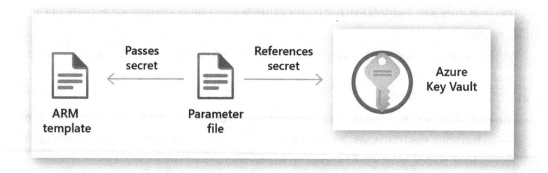

Figure 15-6. *Referencing secrets with static ID*

This approach looks simple and is helpful for scenarios where you can reference secrets in a separate parameters file.

For example, when you deploy a virtual machine and need to provide the admin user's password. In this case, we can reference the Key Vault in the parameter file and not in the ARM template.

Example: Reference Secrets with Static ID

In this example, we will deploy a Windows-based virtual machine and leverage Key Vault. We will reference the Key Vault from a parameter file.

Prerequisites

Here are the prerequisites to be able to deploy this template:

- We have created a new secret in the Key Vault called `azVmPassword` that contains the password for the admin user of the virtual machine.

- We have created a new resource group called `ifabrik-vm` in the EastUS region.

We are going to leverage the quickstart template that provisions a Windows VM. You can find this template at the following URL `https://raw.githubusercontent.com/Azure/azure-quickstart-templates/master/quickstarts/microsoft.compute/vm-simple-windows/azuredeploy.json`.

Now, let's start with the definition of the `parameters` section in the ARM template. Figure 15-7 shows the `parameters` section of the ARM template.

```
"parameters": {
  Value: "ifabrikUser"
  "adminUsername": {
    "type": "string",
    "metadata": {
      "description": "Username for the Virtual Machine."
    }
  },
  Value: (KeyVault reference)
  "adminPassword": {
    "type": "secureString",
    "minLength": 12,
    "metadata": {
      "description": "Password for the Virtual Machine."
    }
  },
  Value: "ifabrik"
  "dnsLabelPrefix": {
    "type": "string",
    "defaultValue": "[toLower(format('{0}-{1}', parameters('vmName'), uniqueString(resourceGroup().id, parameters('vmName'))))]",
    "metadata": {
      "description": "Unique DNS Name for the Public IP used to access the Virtual Machine."
    }
  },
        Value: "myPublicIP"
        "publicIpName": {
          "type": "string",
          "defaultValue": "myPublicIP",
          "metadata": {
            "description": "Name for the Public IP used to access the Virtual Machine."
          }
        },
        Value: "Dynamic"
        "publicIPAllocationMethod": {
          "type": "string",
          "defaultValue": "Dynamic",
          "allowedValues": [
            "Dynamic",
            "Static"
          ],
          "metadata": {
            "description": "Allocation method for the Public IP used to access the Virtual Machine."
          }
        },
        Value: "Basic"
        "publicIpSku": {
          "type": "string",
          "defaultValue": "Basic",
          "allowedValues": [
            "Basic",
            "Standard"
          ],
          "metadata": {
            "description": "SKU for the Public IP used to access the Virtual Machine."
          }
        },
        Value: "2019-Datacenter"
        "OSVersion": {
          "type": "string",
          "defaultValue": "2019-Datacenter",
          "metadata": {
            "description": "The Windows version for the VM."
          }
        },
        Value: "Standard_D2_v3"
        "vmSize": {
          "type": "string",
          "defaultValue": "Standard_D2_v3",
          "metadata": {
            "description": "Size of the virtual machine."
          }
        },
        Value: "eastus"
        "location": {
          "type": "string",
          "defaultValue": "[resourceGroup().location]",
          "metadata": {
            "description": "Location for all resources."
          }
        },
        Value: "ifabrik-vm"
        "vmName": {
          "type": "string",
          "defaultValue": "simple-vm",
          "metadata": {
            "description": "Name of the virtual machine."
          }
        }
      },
```

Figure 15-7. Parameters section, ARM template

In Figure 15-7, which shows the `parameters` section of the ARM template, we have defined the following parameters:

- adminUsername

- adminPassword

- dnsLabelPrefix

- publicIpName

- publicIPAllocationMethod

- publicIpSku

- OSVersion

- vmSize

- location

- vmName

The parameter called `adminPassword` will refer to the secret in the Key Vault.

Now let's review the `functions` and `variables` section of the ARM template, as shown Figure 15-8.

```
"functions": [],
"variables": {
  "storageAccountName": "[format('bootdiags{0}', uniqueString(resourceGroup().id))]",
  "nicName": "myVMNic",
  "addressPrefix": "10.0.0.0/16",
  "subnetName": "Subnet",
  "subnetPrefix": "10.0.0.0/24",
  "virtualNetworkName": "MyVNET",
  "networkSecurityGroupName": "default-NSG"
},
```

Figure 15-8. *Functions and variables section, ARM template*

In the `variables` section, we have defined the variables needed for the storage, networking, and security group configuration. Now we will describe the actual resources.

Figure 15-9 highlights the `resources` section of the ARM template.

```
"resources": [
  {
    "type": "Microsoft.Storage/storageAccounts",
    "apiVersion": "2021-04-01",
    "name": "[variables('storageAccountName')]",
    "location": "[parameters('location')]",
    "sku": { ⋯
    },
    "kind": "Storage"
  },
  {
    "type": "Microsoft.Network/publicIPAddresses",
    "apiVersion": "2021-02-01",
    "name": "[parameters('publicIpName')]",
    "location": "[parameters('location')]",
    "sku": { ⋯
    },
    "properties": { ⋯
    }
  },
  {
    "type": "Microsoft.Network/networkSecurityGroups",
    "apiVersion": "2021-02-01",
    "name": "[variables('networkSecurityGroupName')]",
    "location": "[parameters('location')]",
    "properties": { ⋯
    }
  },
  {
    "type": "Microsoft.Network/virtualNetworks",
    "apiVersion": "2021-02-01",
    "name": "[variables('virtualNetworkName')]",
    "location": "[parameters('location')]",
    "properties": { ⋯
    }
  },
  {
    "type": "Microsoft.Network/virtualNetworks/subnets",
    "apiVersion": "2021-02-01",
    "name": "[format('{0}/{1}', variables('virtualNetworkName'), variables('subnetName'))]",
    "properties": { ⋯
    },
    "dependsOn": [
      "[resourceId('Microsoft.Network/networkSecurityGroups', variables('networkSecurityGroupName'))]",
      "[resourceId('Microsoft.Network/virtualNetworks', variables('virtualNetworkName'))]"
    ]
  },
  {
    "type": "Microsoft.Network/networkInterfaces",
    "apiVersion": "2021-02-01",
    "name": "[variables('nicName')]",
    "location": "[parameters('location')]",
    "properties": { ⋯
    },
    "dependsOn": [
      "[resourceId('Microsoft.Network/publicIPAddresses', parameters('publicIpName'))]",
      "[resourceId('Microsoft.Network/virtualNetworks/subnets', variables('virtualNetworkName'), variables('subnetName'))]"
    ]
  },
  {
    "type": "Microsoft.Compute/virtualMachines",
    "apiVersion": "2021-03-01",
    "name": "[parameters('vmName')]",
    "location": "[parameters('location')]",
    "properties": { ⋯
    },
    "dependsOn": [
      "[resourceId('Microsoft.Network/networkInterfaces', variables('nicName'))]",
      "[resourceId('Microsoft.Storage/storageAccounts', variables('storageAccountName'))]"
    ]
  }
],
```

Figure 15-9.   *Resources section, ARM template*

In the previous section of the ARM template, we have defined the following resources:

- Storage account

- Public IP address

- Network security groups

- Virtual network

- Subnet

- Network interfaces

- Virtual machine

Then, in the `outputs` section of the ARM template, we include the FQDN of the virtual machine, as shown in Figure 15-10.

```
"outputs": {
  "hostname": {
    "type": "string",
    "value": "[reference(resourceId('Microsoft.Network/publicIPAddresses', parameters('publicIpName'))).dnsSettings.fqdn]"
  }
}
```

Figure 15-10. *Outputs section, ARM template*

Now let's move forward with the parameters file. In the parameters file, we will reference the secret from the Key Vault.

Figure 15-11 shows the definition of the parameters file. Note that, in the parameter called `vmPassword`, we provide the ID of the Key Vault, and we are only passing the secret's name, not the actual password.

```
{
    "$schema": "https://schema.management.azure.com/schemas/2019-04-01/deploymentParameters.json#",
    "contentVersion": "1.0.0.0",
    "parameters": {
        "adminUsername": {
            "value": "ifabrikUser"
        },
        "adminPassword": {
            "reference": {                          Key Vault ID
                "keyVault": {
                    "id": "/subscriptions/d988cbee-043f-4c46-          /resourceGroups/iFabrik/providers/Microsoft.KeyVault/vaults/ifabrikKeyVault"
                },
                "secretName": "azVmPassword"          Secret Name
            }
        },
        "dnsLabelPrefix": {
            "value": "ifabrik"
        },
        "publicIpName": {
            "value": "myPublicIP"
        },
        "publicIPAllocationMethod": {
            "value": "Dynamic"
        },
        "publicIpSku": {
            "value": "Basic"
        },
        "OSVersion": {
            "value": "2019-Datacenter"
        },
        "vmSize": {
            "value": "Standard_D2_v3"
        },
        "location": {
            "value": "eastus"
        },
        "vmName": {
            "value": "ifabrik-vm"
        }
    }
}
```

Figure 15-11. *Parameters file*

Note that in the parameters file, we are leveraging a parameter value called
adminPassword. Within it, we provide the reference object to the Key Vault.

The properties on this "reference" object include the Key Vault ID and the
secret name.

At deployment time, the parameter file will be passed, along with the secret's name.
This way, we will not expose the actual password and keep the password of the virtual
machine secure.

Now let's deploy this ARM template; see Listing 15-9. We will use the PowerShell
command shown in Listing 15-9 to deploy this ARM template in the resource group
called ifabrik-vm.

Listing 15-9. ARM Template Deployment Using PowerShell

```
New-AzResourceGroupDeployment -Name $deploymentName -ResourceGroupName
ifabrik-vm -TemplateFile .\azuredeploy.json -TemplateParameterFile
.\azuredeploy.parameters.json
```

Figure 15-12 shows the output from this deployment.

```
DeploymentName           :  iFabrikDeployment08-09-2021
ResourceGroupName        :  ifabrik-vm
ProvisioningState        :  Succeeded
Timestamp                :  8/9/2021 4:51:17 PM
Mode                     :  Incremental
TemplateLink             :
Parameters               :
                            Name                          Type                          Value
                            ===========================   ===========================   ==========
                            adminUsername                 String                        ifabrikUser
                            adminPassword                 SecureString
                            dnsLabelPrefix                String                        ifabrik
                            publicIpName                  String                        myPublicIP
                            publicIPAllocationMethod       String                        Dynamic
                            publicIpSku                   String                        Basic
                            osVersion                     String                        2019-Datacenter
                            vmSize                        String                        Standard_D2_v3
                            location                      String                        eastus
                            vmName                        String                        ifabrik-vm

Outputs                  :
                            Name              Type                          Value
                            ===============   ===========================   ==========
                            hostname          String                        ifabrik.eastus.cloudapp.azure.com
```

Figure 15-12. *Deployment output*

As you can see, referencing secrets with static IDs in the ARM template is a straightforward process.

Note that in this example, we hard-coded the value of the Key Vault ID.

This leads us to the following scenario: how would you reference a secret that depends on the deployment context?

Let's say we don't have the Key Vault ID available, and we can't hard-code it. How can we dynamically get the Key Vault ID? Good for us; we can reference secrets with Dynamic IDs.

Reference Secrets with Dynamic ID

We will leverage the dynamic ID approach when we need to modify the secret reference or dynamically get the Key Vault ID from the ARM template.

For example, we can have a Key Vault with two secrets: a secret that references a password of a virtual machine and a secret that references a password of a database.

While we can hard-code the Key Vault ID, we might need to update the secret name depending on the resource we work with in the ARM template. And what if you had two Key Vaults with two secrets each?

For this use case, we can leverage nested templates or linked templates.

Example: Reference Secrets with Dynamic ID

In the following example, we will create a SQL Server instance and reference the Key Vault ID in a nested template. For this example, we have created a new secret for the password of the SQL server instance and a new resource group called `ifabrik-sql`.

In the ARM template, we will pass two parameters: one parameter for the name of the Key Vault and another parameter for the secret's name.

Remember that we will still have to use the Key Vault ID; therefore, we will define a parameter definition for the subscription ID and another parameter for the resource group name.

That said, the ARM template will contain four parameters related to the Key Vault.

- Key Vault name

- Secret name

- Subscription ID

- Resource group name

Figure 15-13 shows the `parameters` section of the ARM template.

```
"parameters": {
      Using default value
    "location": {
        "type": "string",
        "defaultValue": "[resourceGroup().location]",
        "metadata": {
            "description": "The location where the resources will be deployed."
        }
    },
      Value: "ifabrikKeyVault"
    "vaultName": {
        "type": "string",
        "metadata": {
            "description": "The name of the keyvault that contains the secret."
        }
    },
      Value: "sqlPassword"
    "secretName": {
        "type": "string",
        "metadata": {
            "description": "The name of the secret."
        }
    },
      Value: "iFabrik"
    "vaultRgName": {
        "type": "string",
        "metadata": {
            "description": "The name of the resource group that contains the keyvault."
        }
    },
      Using default value
    "vaultSubscription": {
        "type": "string",
        ".defaultValue": "[subscription().subscriptionId]",
        "metadata": {
            "description": "The name of the subscription that contains the keyvault."
        }
    }
},
```

Figure 15-13. *ARM template, parameters section*

Now we are going to create a nested template. In this nested template, we will define top-level parameters passed onto the nested template, as shown in Figure 15-14.

```
"resources": [
    {
        "type": "Microsoft.Resources/deployments",
        "apiVersion": "2020-10-01",
        "name": "dynamicSecret",
        "properties": {
            "mode": "Incremental",
            "expressionEvaluationOptions": {
                "scope": "inner"
            },
            "parameters": {
                "location": {
                    "value": "[parameters('location')]"
                },
                "adminLogin": {
                    "value": "ifabrikAdminUser"
                },
                "adminPassword": {
                    "reference": {
                        "keyVault": {
                            "id": "[resourceId(parameters('vaultSubscription'), parameters('vaultRgName'), 'Microsoft.KeyVault/vaults', parameters('vaultName'))]"
                        },
                        "secretName": "[parameters('secretName')]"
                    }
                }
            },
            Nested template with inner scope
            "template": {
                "$schema": "https://schema.management.azure.com/schemas/2019-04-01/deploymentTemplate.json#",
                "contentVersion": "1.0.0.0",
                "parameters": {
                    Value: "ifabrikAdminUser"
                    "adminLogin": {
                        "type": "string"
                    },
                    Value: (KeyVault reference)
                    "adminPassword": {
                        "type": "securestring"
                    },
                    Value: "[parameters('location')]"
                    "location": {
                        "type": "string"
                    }
                },
                "variables": {
                    "sqlServerName": "[concat('sql-', uniqueString(resourceGroup().id, 'sql'))]"
                },
                "resources": [
                    {
                        "type": "Microsoft.Sql/servers",
                        "apiVersion": "2018-06-01-preview",
                        "name": "[variables('sqlServerName')]",
                        "location": "[parameters('location')]",
                        "properties": {
                            "administratorLogin": "[parameters('adminLogin')]",
                            "administratorLoginPassword": "[parameters('adminPassword')]"
                        }
                    }
                ],
                "outputs": {
                    "sqlFQDN": {
                        "type": "string",
                        "value": "[reference(variables('sqlServerName')).fullyQualifiedDomainName]"
                    }
                }
            }
        }
    }
],
```

Callouts: Key Vault reference, secret name, password referenced from Key Vault, referenced from parameters in nested template

Figure 15-14. *ARM template, resources section*

We will deploy the previous template using the PowerShell command shown in Listing 15-10.

Listing 15-10. ARM Template Deployment Using PowerShell

```
$date = Get-Date -Format "MM-dd-yyyy"
$deploymentName = "iFabrikDeployment"+"$date"
New-AzResourceGroupDeployment -Name $deploymentName -ResourceGroupName
ifabrik-sql -TemplateFile .\azuredeploy.json -TemplateParameterFile
.\azuredeploy.parameters.json
```

Figure 15-15 shows the output from this deployment.

```
DeploymentName          : iFabrikDeployment08-09-2021
ResourceGroupName       : ifabrik-sql
ProvisioningState       : Succeeded
Timestamp               : 8/10/2021 12:31:36 AM
Mode                    : Incremental
TemplateLink            :
Parameters              :
                          Name                  Type                         Value
                          ===================   ==========================   ==========
                          location              String                       eastus
                          vaultName             String                       ifabrikKeyVault
                          secretName            String                       sqlPassword
                          vaultRgName           String                       iFabrik
                          vaultSubscription     String                       d988cbee-043f-4c46-9a59

Outputs                 :
DeploymentDebugLogLevel :
```

Figure 15-15. *ARM template, deployment output*

Note that in the output, we can see the name of the Key Vault and the secret name dynamically referenced in the ARM template.

Figure 15-16 summarizes the workflow for referencing secrets for dynamic IDs.

- The parameter file passes values about the Key Vault, such as the Key Vault name, the secret name, and the resource group where the Key Vault is located.

- The ARM template will include the definition of the parameters mentioned earlier and will dynamically create the Key Vault ID needed to reference the secret.

- The nested deployment can contain a nested template or a linked template.

- The nested or linked template will have inline parameters and will pass the secret name. The inline parameter will reference the secret from Key Vault.

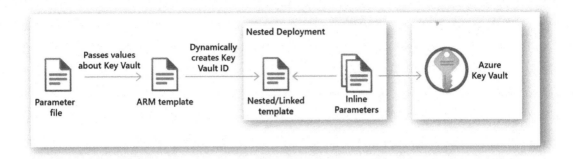

Figure 15-16. *Referencing secrets with dynamic ID, workflow*

The code related to the examples demonstrated along this chapter is at the following URL:

```
https://github.com/daveRendon/iac/tree/main/chapter-15
```

Summary

This chapter reviewed the importance of securing values in ARM templates and how you can leverage some components available in Resource Manager to reference your secrets in your deployments.

We analyzed the options available and best practices to reference secrets such as passwords using Key Vault. We went through some practical examples on how to reference static and dynamic IDs.

Now that we have gone through the fundamentals of ARM templates, we will look at more advanced features to help you validate your ARM templates. In the next chapter, we will review how to debug ARM templates.

CHAPTER 16

Validating Your ARM Template

In the previous chapter, we discussed the importance of securing values in ARM templates and how you can leverage some components available in Resource Manager to reference your secrets in your deployments.

When authoring ARM templates, it is inevitable to have potential errors; we are humans, and it's OK to have errors, whether it's a syntax error or a logical error. This chapter will review some tools to help you succeed and minimize potential errors in your ARM templates.

This chapter will provide you with the tooling needed to validate the ARM templates that are part of your environment and show examples of leveraging these tools.

The topics in this chapter include the following:

- Why you should debug and validate ARM templates

- The ARM template test toolkit

- Working with What-IF to validate your deployment

The process of validating and fixing potential errors in ARM templates might be time-consuming. It can become an overwhelming task to perform before we can successfully deploy our environment in Azure.

Whether there's an error on a parameter value, function, the definition of the properties of a specific resource in the ARM template, or a logical error, we have to ensure our ARM templates are always ready to be deployed.

Let's understand why the debug and validation is critical when working with ARM templates.

© David Rendón 2022
D. Rendón, *Building Applications with Azure Resource Manager (ARM)*,
https://doi.org/10.1007/978-1-4842-7747-8_16

Why You Should Debug and Validate ARM Templates

As with every other programming language, the code that we throw in our ARM templates should always be validated before committing any deployment.

The more complex environment we define in our ARM templates, the more time we might need to validate it before successfully deploying it. The validation and debugging process might be overwhelming if we don't have the fundamentals of ARM templates, and it can become frustrating if we don't have the proper tooling.

Moreover, Azure Resource Manager is constantly under updates, and we have to be aware of the impact of those updates. Keeping up-to-date with the latest schema versions, policies, and best practices can sometimes be a personal challenge.

There are some tools we can leverage to validate and debug our ARM templates in a simple manner.

While there are various third-party solutions to validate code, we will narrow our scope to two tools that are primarily focused on validating ARM templates: the ARM template test toolkit and the What-IF capability.

Before we deep dive into these tools, let's understand the two main error categories

The preflight errors we can fall into when authoring ARM templates: preflight and inflight.

refer to those that occur at deployment time when Resource Manager is interpreting your ARM template. Preflight errors are mainly related to the syntax of the definition of a resource, property, or missing parameter.

For example, when creating a storage account, a preflight error can be the storage type property value missing in the definition.

Resource Manager can detect a potential error in the preflight error types before reaching out to the Resource Provider.

The inflight errors we can fall into when authoring ARM templates: preflight and inflight.

are those in which Resource Manager must reach out to the Resource Provider before seeing an error in the output.

Remember that each resource has its own Resource Provider; when deploying an ARM template, Resource Manager will first interpret your ARM template and, if it's valid (preflight errors), reach out to the Resource Provider before deploying your resources defined in the ARM template (inflight errors).

An example of an inflight error could be having the wrong SKU of an app service plan.

290

Errors are shown up in the console or the Azure portal.

Microsoft provides a reference of error codes that you can find at the following URL:

```
https://docs.microsoft.com/en-us/azure/azure-resource-manager/templates/
common-deployment-errors
```

This list of error codes includes potential mitigation as well as more information per error code. Let's review the simple example shown in Listing 16-1. We have a new ARM template and have defined a storage account.

Listing 16-1. ARM Template That Creates a Storage Account with an Inflight Error

```
{
 "$schema": "https://schema.management.azure.com/schemas/2019-04-01/
 deploymentTemplate.json#",
    "contentVersion": "1.0.0.0",
    "resources": [
        {
            "name": "ifabrikstorage!",
            "type": "Microsoft.Storage/storageAccounts",
            "apiVersion": "2019-06-01",
            "location": "[resourceGroup().location]",
            "kind": "StorageV2",
            "sku": {
                "name": "Premium_LRS",
                "tier": "Premium"
            }
        }
    ],
    "outputs": {}
}
```

In the previous code, in the resources section, we intentionally provided the name of the storage account that includes the prohibited character ! . These are inflight errors as Resource Manager will evaluate this only after communicating with the Resource Provider.

Figure 16-1 shows the error output from this ARM template.

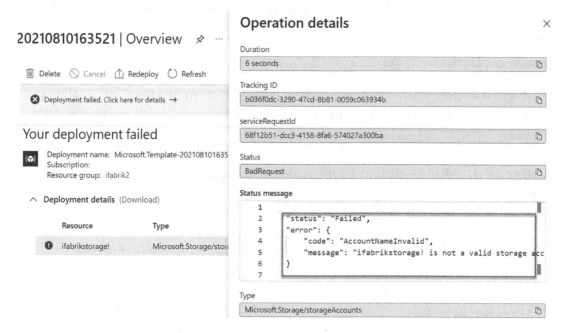

Figure 16-1. *Operation details, output in the Azure portal*

Now, let's reuse the same ARM template for the following example, and in the location property note, we are using a function to get the location. We will modify it to [resourceGrou().location] and intentionally misspell the name of the function, as shown in Listing 16-2.

Listing 16-2. ARM Template That Creates a Storage Account with a Preflight Error

```
{
  "$schema": "https://schema.management.azure.com/schemas/2019-04-01/
  deploymentTemplate.json#",
    "contentVersion": "1.0.0.0",
    "resources": [
        {
            "name": "ifabrikstorage",
            "type": "Microsoft.Storage/storageAccounts",
            "apiVersion": "2019-06-01",
            "location": "[resourceGrou().location]",
```

```
        "kind": "StorageV2",
        "sku": {
            "name": "Premium_LRS",
            "tier": "Premium"
        }
    }
  ],
  "outputs": {}
}
```

If we try to deploy the previous ARM template, we will get the error shown in Listing 16-3.

Listing 16-3. Deployment Output

```
{
  "code": "InvalidTemplate",
  "message": "Deployment template validation failed: 'The template resource
  'ifabrikstorage' at line '12' and column '9' is not valid: The template
  function 'resourceGrou' is not valid. Please see https://aka.ms/arm-
  template-expressions for usage details.. Please see https://aka.ms/arm-
  template-expressions for usage details.'."
}
```

Validating these errors can be tricky, and it can be pretty frustrating when working with more complex environments.

To help you validate and debug your ARM templates, we can leverage the ARM template test toolkit and the What-IF capabilities.

Let's take a look at the ARM template test toolkit.

The ARM Template Test Toolkit

Authoring ARM templates involves defining the resources you want to include in your environment and considering the best practices to ensure your ARM templates are always ready for deployment.

Instead of going through all your ARM templates and manually validating the values, syntax, and logic, you can leverage the ARM template test toolkit (ARM-TTK).

What Is the Toolkit?

ARM-TTK is a PowerShell module containing a suite of tests that you can leverage to ensure that ARM templates in your environment follow the best practices and help you correct any potential problems before deployment.

Given that the ARM-TTK is a PowerShell module, you can download it to the machine where you're working with the ARM templates and import the module to start working with it.

ARM-TTK will run a suite of tests and validate that the ARM template is compliant with the best practices.

It is essential to highlight that ARM-TTK is not intended to rerun the same tests or validations provided by Resource Manager.

The suite of tests included in the ARM-TTK module will help you to quickly check that you're using the parameters or variables defined in the ARM template along with the environment you described. It will also validate security best practices and adhere to ARM template coding best practices like the proper use of functions.

The ARM-TTK can be cloned from the following GitHub repository:

```
git clone https://github.com/Azure/arm-ttk.git
```

You can also download it directly from your browser using the following URL:

```
https://github.com/Azure/arm-ttk/archive/master.zip
```

Once you download the PowerShell module, extract the files, and then import the module with the command shown in Listing 16-4.

Listing 16-4. Import Module

```
Import-Module C:\Users\Your-Username\Downloads\arm-ttk-master\arm-ttk
```

Note   You might have to set the policy to `Unrestricted` using the command `Set-ExecutionPolicy Unrestricted` or `Set-ExecutionPolicy Bypass`.

Running a Test Using ARM-TTK

Once the import process of the PowerShell module is complete, we can start working with ARM-TTK. We can go tho the directory where the ARM templates are located and then use the command shown in Listing 16-5 to start a test run.

Listing 16-5. Test ARM-TTK

```
Test-AzTemplate -TemplatePath $TemplateFileOrFolder
```

With the previous command, the ARM-TTK will start the testing process of the ARM template and will provide you with a list of changes that have to be taken into consideration before deploying the ARM template.

The list of considerations is preceded by the notation shown here:

- [-]: Means this is a failed test

- [+]: Means this is a passed test

At the end of the results, you will see the total number of tests, the passed tests, and the number of failed tests.

The good thing about ARM-TTK is the compatibility with Windows and Linux. To run the tests on Linux, you will need to install PowerShell Core. For macOS, you will also need to have PowerShell Core and Coreutils.

In the following example, we will run a test using the ARM template in Listing 16-6 that creates a storage account.

Listing 16-6. ARM Template That Creates a Storage Account

```
{
    "$schema": "https://schema.management.azure.com/schemas/2019-04-01/
    deploymentTemplate.json#",
    "contentVersion": "1.0.0.0",
    "parameters": {},
    "functions": [],
    "variables": {},
```

```
    "resources": [
        {
            "name": "ifabrikstorage",
            "type": "Microsoft.Storage/storageAccounts",
            "apiVersion": "2021-06-01",
            "location": "[resourceGroup().location]",
            "kind": "StorageV2",
            "sku": {
                "name": "Premium_LRS",
                "tier": "Premium"
            }
        }
    ],
    "outputs": {}
}
```

We hard-coded the name of the storage account, and we're passing the location from the resource group using the function resourceGroup().location.

Now we will run a test using ARM-TTK with the command shown in Listing 16-7.

Listing 16-7. Test-AzTemplate Command

```
Test-AzTemplate -TemplatePath azuredeploy.json
```

If you want to test only a single ARM template, you can pass on the parameter -File and the name of the ARM template, as shown in Listing 16-8.

Listing 16-8. Test-AzTemplate -File Parameter

```
Test-AzTemplate -TemplatePath $TemplateFolder -File your-template.json
```

Figure 16-2 shows the results from the test.

```
Validating error-types\azuredeploy.json
  AllFiles
    [+] JSONFiles Should Be Valid (2 ms)
  deploymentTemplate
    [+] adminUsername Should Not Be A Literal (2 ms)
    [+] apiVersions Should Be Recent In Reference Functions (2 ms)
    [+] apiVersions Should Be Recent (3 ms)
    [+] artifacts parameter (1 ms)
    [+] CommandToExecute Must Use ProtectedSettings For Secrets (3 ms)
    [+] DependsOn Best Practices (2 ms)
    [+] Deployment Resources Must Not Be Debug (2 ms)
    [+] DeploymentTemplate Must Not Contain Hardcoded Uri (1 ms)
    [+] DeploymentTemplate Schema Is Correct (1 ms)
    [+] Dynamic Variable References Should Not Use Concat (1 ms)
    [+] IDs Should Be Derived From ResourceIDs (2 ms)
    [-] Location Should Not Be Hardcoded (1 ms)
        azuredeploy.json must use the location parameter, not resourceGroup().location or deployment().location
(except when used as a default value in the main template)

    [+] ManagedIdentityExtension must not be used (1 ms)
    [+] Min And Max Value Are Numbers (1 ms)
    [+] Outputs Must Not Contain Secrets (2 ms)
    [+] Parameters Must Be Referenced (1 ms)
    [+] providers apiVersions Is Not Permitted (1 ms)
    [+] ResourceIds should not contain (1 ms)
    [+] Resources Should Have Location (1 ms)
    [+] Resources Should Not Be Ambiguous (3 ms)
    [+] Secure Params In Nested Deployments (2 ms)
    [+] Secure String Parameters Cannot Have Default (1 ms)
    [+] Template Should Not Contain Blanks (1 ms)
    [+] Variables Must Be Referenced (1 ms)
    [+] Virtual Machines Should Not Be Preview (3 ms)
    [+] VM Images Should Use Latest Version (1 ms)
    [+] VM Size Should Be A Parameter (2 ms)
Validating error-types\azuredeploy.parameters.json
  deploymentParameters
    [+] DeploymentParameters Should Have ContentVersion (2 ms)
    [+] DeploymentParameters Should Have Parameters (2 ms)
    [+] DeploymentParameters Should Have Schema (1 ms)
    [+] DeploymentParameters Should Have Value (1 ms)
Total : 32
Pass  : 31
Fail  : 1
```

Figure 16-2. *Output test, ARM-TTK*

The test results show how many tests were successful and which ones failed. In the previous example, we can see that there's a recommendation related to the location. This property shouldn't be hard-coded. Let's go and fix this.

Fixing Your ARM Template

We will now modify the ARM template and update the location property. We will create a parameter for the location and pass it in the property of the storage account, as shown in Figure 16-3.

```
{
    "$schema": "https://schema.management.azure.com/schemas/2019-04-01/deploymentTemplate.json#".
    "contentVersion": "1.0.0.0",
    Parameter file: "azuredeploy.parameters.json" | Change...
    "parameters": {
        Value: "eastus"
        "location": {
            "type": "string"
        }
    },
    "resources": [
        {
            "name": "ifabrikstorage",
            "type": "Microsoft.Storage/storageAccounts",
            "apiVersion": "2021-06-01",
            "location": "[parameters('location')]",
            "kind": "StorageV2",
            "sku": {
                "name": "Premium_LRS",
                "tier": "Premium"
            }
        }
    ],
    "outputs": {}
}
```

Figure 16-3. *ARM template*

We will also create a parameters file and pass the location value. Listing 16-9 shows the parameters file.

Listing 16-9. ARM Template

```
{
    "$schema": "https://schema.management.azure.com/schemas/2019-04-01/
    deploymentParameters.json#",
    "contentVersion": "1.0.0.0",
    "parameters": {
        "location": {
            "value": "eastus"
        }
    }
}
```

Now we will rerun the test using the command in Listing 16-10.

Listing 16-10. Test-AzTemplate Command

Test-AzTemplate -TemplatePath azuredeploy.json

Figure 16-4 shows the results from the second test.

```
Validating error-types\azuredeploy.json
  AllFiles
    [+] JSONFiles Should Be Valid (2 ms)
  deploymentTemplate
    [+] adminUsername Should Not Be A Literal (2 ms)
    [+] apiVersions Should Be Recent In Reference Functions (2 ms)
    [+] apiVersions Should Be Recent (4 ms)
    [+] artifacts parameter (1 ms)
    [+] CommandToExecute Must Use ProtectedSettings For Secrets (3 ms)
    [+] DependsOn Best Practices (2 ms)
    [+] Deployment Resources Must Not Be Debug (2 ms)
    [+] DeploymentTemplate Must Not Contain Hardcoded Uri (1 ms)
    [+] DeploymentTemplate Schema Is Correct (1 ms)
    [+] Dynamic Variable References Should Not Use Concat (1 ms)
    [+] IDs Should Be Derived From ResourceIDs (4 ms)
    [+] Location Should Not Be Hardcoded (4 ms)
    [+] ManagedIdentityExtension must not be used (1 ms)
    [+] Min And Max Value Are Numbers (2 ms)
    [+] Outputs Must Not Contain Secrets (2 ms)
    [+] Parameters Must Be Referenced (32 ms)
    [+] providers apiVersions Is Not Permitted (1 ms)
    [+] ResourceIds should not contain (2 ms)
    [+] Resources Should Have Location (1 ms)
    [+] Resources Should Not Be Ambiguous (1 ms)
    [+] Secure Params In Nested Deployments (3 ms)
    [+] Secure String Parameters Cannot Have Default (1 ms)
    [+] Template Should Not Contain Blanks (2 ms)
    [+] Variables Must Be Referenced (1 ms)
    [+] Virtual Machines Should Not Be Preview (3 ms)
    [+] VM Images Should Use Latest Version (1 ms)
    [+] VM Size Should Be A Parameter (2 ms)
Validating error-types\azuredeploy.parameters.json
  deploymentParameters
    [+] DeploymentParameters Should Have ContentVersion (1 ms)
    [+] DeploymentParameters Should Have Parameters (1 ms)
    [+] DeploymentParameters Should Have Schema (1 ms)
    [+] DeploymentParameters Should Have Value (2 ms)
Total : 32
Pass  : 32
Fail  : 0
```

Figure 16-4. ARM-TTK test output

Now all the tests have passed. As shown in Figure 16-4, we can benefit from the ARM-TTK by simplifying the testing and validation process of the ARM templates that will be part of our environment.

Running Your Own Tests

While ARM-TTK provides you with a default suite of tests that you can try, it is also possible to run only a specific test depending on your use case. The test suites are located in /arm-ttk/testcases/deploymentTemplate, as shown in Figure 16-5.

```
    Directory: C:\Users\dave\Downloads\arm-ttk\arm-ttk\testcases

Mode                 LastWriteTime         Length Name
----                 -------------         ------ ----
d----        8/10/2021    5:11 PM                 AllFiles
d----        8/10/2021    5:11 PM                 CreateUIDefinition
d----        8/10/2021    5:11 PM                 deploymentParameters
d----        8/10/2021    5:11 PM                 deploymentTemplate
```

Figure 16-5. *ARM-TTK test cases*

You can specify that you want to run only a single test using the parameter -Test and the test name: Location-Should-Not-Be-Hardcoded. Listing 16-11 shows how you run an individual test.

Listing 16-11. Test-AzTemplate Command

```
Test-AzTemplate -TemplatePath $TemplateFolder -Test "Location-Should-Not-
Be-Hardcoded"
```

We will use the command in Listing 16-12 to validate that our ARM template doesn't have the parameter location hard-coded.

Listing 16-12. Test-AzTemplate Single Test

```
Test-AzTemplate -TemplatePath .\azuredeploy.json -Test "Location-Should-
Not-Be-Hardcoded"
```

The previous command will run only one test. Figure 16-6 shows the output from this test.

```
Validating error-types\azuredeploy.json
   deploymentTemplate
      [+] Location Should Not Be Hardcoded (2 ms)
```

Figure 16-6. *ARM-TTK test output*

To author your own test, you can create a file in this directory: /arm-ttk/testcases/ deploymentTemplate. Once the file is created, you can customize it in PowerShell and then run the file.

You could create a new test to detect if the API version is older, enforce a standard, and use the Find-JsonContent cmdlet to search for attributes within the resource definition, including the apiVersion.

While we can leverage ARM-TTK and the entire suite of tests included in the PowerShell module, we haven't addressed scenarios when you update your ARM template; how can you validate the impact on the existing environment in Azure before deploying your updated ARM templates?

While we could keep track of the versions of the ARM templates, it doesn't mean we will be able to see the immediate impact on the updated resources that we previously deployed.

In the past, when working with ARM templates, you had to deploy the ARM template to see the impact and changes on your resources in Azure. This approach is quite frustrating as you had to perform manual tests.

A recent capability was published and allows you to quickly verify and validate the impact on existing resources in Azure before you perform the actual deployment of the updated ARM template. This feature is called What-IF.

Working with What-IF to Validate Your Deployment

To reduce the frustrating process of manually verifying the impact on existing resources in Azure when you update ARM templates, What-IF will help you preview the deployment before doing the actual deployment process of the newer ARM templates.

Think of this feature as a preflight validation: you can have a virtual machine in Azure with the size Standard_A4. You update the ARM template, and the new size of the virtual machine has been updated to Standard_B2s.

Instead of deploying the ARM template and potentially impacting the environment, we can use What-IF to preview the impact of these changes in the ARM template.

This way, we can validate all the changes in the newer version of the ARM template and minimize potential failures on the environment already running in Azure.

What-IF is part of the PowerShell Az module, Azure CLI, and REST API operations.

How Does What-IF Work?

What-IF includes a series of commands available in the PowerShell module, CLI, and RESTful API. For the scope of the following examples, we will use PowerShell.

What-IF will look at our ARM template and compare it to the existing resources you have in Azure. Then, What-IF will show a preview of all the properties of the resources that will be impacted.

This means that we will see if a resource will be created or deleted or if any properties of the existing resources will be updated.

With this validation, we can minimize potential failures on the deployment and better understand the resources that will be updated before performing the actual deployment.

Let's start by working on a few examples. The only prerequisite for the following examples is to deploy a Windows-based virtual machine. We will use the following ARM template to deploy the virtual machine.

Figure 16-7 shows the `parameters` section.

```
"parameters": {
        Value: "azureuser"
    "adminUsername": {
        "type": "string"
    },
        Value: "AzVmPassword"
    "adminPassword": {
        "type": "secureString",
        "minLength": 12
    },
        Value: "ifabrik"
    "dnsLabelPrefix": {
        "type": "string",
        "defaultValue": "[toLower(format('{0}-{1}', parameters('vmName'), uniqueString(resourceGroup().id, parameters('vmName'))))]"
    },
        Value: "ifabrikpip"
    "publicIpName": {
        "type": "string",
        "defaultValue": "myPublicIP"
    },
        Value: "Dynamic"
    "publicIPAllocationMethod": {
        "type": "string",
        "defaultValue": "Dynamic",
        "allowedValues": [
            "Dynamic",
            "Static"
        ]
    },
        Value: "Basic"
    "publicIpSku": {
        "type": "string",
        "defaultValue": "Basic",
        "allowedValues": [
            "Basic",
            "Standard"
        ]
    },
        Value: "2019-Datacenter"
    "OSVersion": {
        "type": "string",
        "defaultValue": "2019-Datacenter"
    },
        Value: "Standard_D2_v3"
    "vmSize": {
        "type": "string",
        "defaultValue": "Standard_D2_v3"
    },
        Value: "eastus"
    "location": {
        "type": "string",
        "defaultValue": "[resourceGroup().location]"
    },
        Value: "simple-vm"
    "vmName": {
        "type": "string",
        "defaultValue": "simple-vm"
    }
},
```

Figure 16-7. ARM template that deploys a virtual machine, parameters section

Figure 16-8 shows the `variables` section.

```
"variables": {
    "storageAccountName": "[format('bootdiags{0}', uniqueString(resourceGroup().id))]",
    "nicName": "myVMNic",
    "addressPrefix": "10.0.0.0/16",
    "subnetName": "Subnet",
    "subnetPrefix": "10.0.0.0/24",
    "virtualNetworkName": "MyVNET",
    "networkSecurityGroupName": "default-NSG"
},
```

Figure 16-8. *ARM template that deploys a virtual machine, variables section*

Figure 16-9 shows the `resources` section.

```json
"resources": [
    {
        "type": "Microsoft.Storage/storageAccounts",
        "apiVersion": "2021-04-01",
        "name": "[variables('storageAccountName')]",
        "location": "[parameters('location')]",
        "sku": { ...
        },
        "kind": "Storage"
    },
    {
        "type": "Microsoft.Network/publicIPAddresses",
        "apiVersion": "2021-02-01",
        "name": "[parameters('publicIpName')]",
        "location": "[parameters('location')]",
        "sku": { ...
        },
        "properties": { ...
        }
    },
    {
        "type": "Microsoft.Network/networkSecurityGroups",
        "apiVersion": "2021-02-01",
        "name": "[variables('networkSecurityGroupName')]",
        "location": "[parameters('location')]",
        "properties": {
            "securityRules": [ ...
            ]
        }
    },
    {
        "type": "Microsoft.Network/virtualNetworks",
        "apiVersion": "2021-02-01",
        "name": "[variables('virtualNetworkName')]",
        "location": "[parameters('location')]",
        "properties": { ...
        }
    },
    {
        "type": "Microsoft.Network/virtualNetworks/subnets",
        "apiVersion": "2021-02-01",
        "name": "[format('{0}/{1}', variables('virtualNetworkName'), variables('subnetName'))]",
        "properties": { ...
        },
        "dependsOn": [ ...
        ]
    },
    {
        "type": "Microsoft.Network/networkInterfaces",
        "apiVersion": "2021-02-01",
        "name": "[variables('nicName')]",
        "location": "[parameters('location')]",
        "properties": { ...
        },
        "dependsOn": [ ...
        ]
    },
    {
        "type": "Microsoft.Compute/virtualMachines",
        "apiVersion": "2021-03-01",
        "name": "[parameters('vmName')]",
        "location": "[parameters('location')]",
        "properties": { ...
        },
        "dependsOn": [ ...
        ]
    }
],
```

Figure 16-9. ARM template that deploys a virtual machine, resources section

Once you deploy this ARM template, it is time to try What-IF. Figure 16-10 shows the output from the deployment.

```
DeploymentName            : iFabrikDeployment08-11-2021
ResourceGroupName         : ifabrik2
ProvisioningState         : Succeeded
Timestamp                 : 8/11/2021 6:32:19 PM
Mode                      : Incremental
TemplateLink              :
Parameters                :
                            Name                           Type                          Value
                            ==========================     =========================     ==========
                            adminUsername                  String                        azureuser
                            adminPassword                  SecureString
                            dnsLabelPrefix                 String                        ifabrik
                            publicIpName                   String                        ifabrikpip
                            publicIPAllocationMethod       String                        Dynamic
                            publicIpSku                    String                        Basic
                            osVersion                      String                        2019-Datacenter
                            vmSize                         String                        Standard_D2_v3
                            location                       String                        eastus
                            vmName                         String                        simple-vm

Outputs                   :
                            Name              Type                          Value
                            ==============    =========================     ==========
                            hostname          String                        ifabrik.eastus.cloudapp.azure.com
```

Figure 16-10. *ARM template deployment output*

We will now modify the parameters file. We will do a quick test and change the size of the virtual machine to Standard_B4ms, as shown in Listing 16-13.

Listing 16-13. Parameters File

```
{
    "$schema": "https://schema.management.azure.com/schemas/2019-04-01/
    deploymentParameters.json#",
    "contentVersion": "1.0.0.0",
    "parameters": {
        "adminUsername": {
            "value": "azureuser"
        },
        "adminPassword": {
            "value": "YourAdminUserPass"
        },
        "dnsLabelPrefix": {
            "value": "ifabrik"
        },
```

```
    "publicIpName": {
        "value": "ifabrikpip"
    },
    "publicIPAllocationMethod": {
        "value": "Dynamic"
    },
    "publicIpSku": {
        "value": "Basic"
    },
    "OSVersion": {
        "value": "2019-Datacenter"
    },
    "vmSize": {
        "value": "Standard_B4ms"
    },
    "location": {
        "value": "eastus"
    },
    "vmName": {
        "value": "simple-vm"
    }
  }
}
```

The next step is to use the What-IF command, as shown in Listing 16-14. We will validate the changes before we resize the virtual machine.

Listing 16-14. What-IF command

```
New-AzResourceGroupDeployment -Name $deploymentName -ResourceGroupName
ifabrik2 -TemplateFile .\azuredeploy.json -TemplateParameterFile
.\azuredeploy.parameters.json -Whatif
```

Note that the previous command targets the resource group. It is also possible to target to a subscription level using the command New-AzDeployment -Whatif.

There are six types of changes that you will see in the validation with What-IF:

- *Create*: This refers to the creation of a new resource.

- *Delete*: The deletion process will work only when using the complete mode for deployment.

- *Ignore*: This means we have an existing resource in Azure, but it is not defined in the ARM template; therefore, it will not be touched.

- *NoChange*: This means we have an existing resource in Azure that is defined in the ARM template, and it will be redeployed with no impact on the properties.

- *Modify*: This is the same as NoChange, but the properties will be updated.

- *Deploy*: We have an existing resource in Azure that is defined in the ARM template, and the properties of the resource might or might not change.

Figure 16-11 shows the output from this validation.

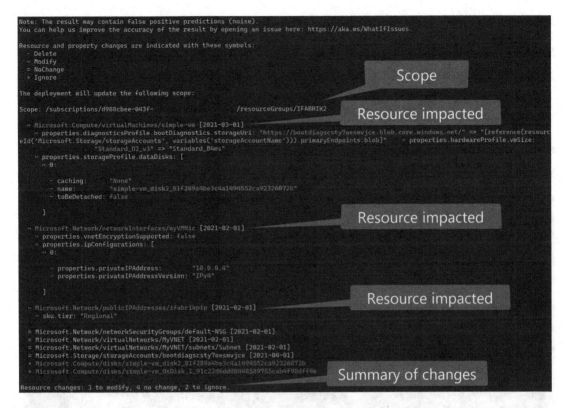

Figure 16-11. *Output from What-IF command*

The output from a command will throw a JSON response with the impact on resources and properties.

There are four main notations:

- *Green*: Means additions

- *Orange*: Means deletions and updates

- *Equal symbol*: Means no changes

- *Asterisk*: Means ignore

The previous command will not perform the deployment of the ARM template. We can use another flag to confirm the deployment once the ARM template is valid.

We will use the command in Listing 16-15 with the -Confirm flag.

Listing 16-15. Flag -Confirm

New-AzResourceGroupDeployment -**Name** $deploymentName -**ResourceGroupName**
ifabrik2 -**TemplateFile** .\azuredeploy.json -**TemplateParameterFile**
.\azuredeploy.parameters.json -**Confirm**

The previous command will perform the validation process of the ARM template and summarize the changes on the existing resources. It will give you the option to confirm if you want to perform the deployment operation, as shown in Figure 16-12.

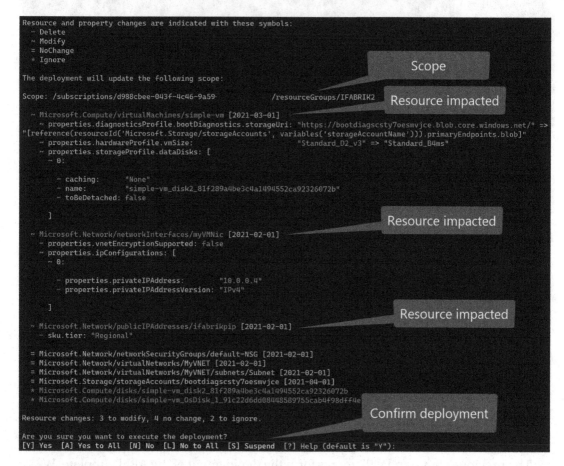

Figure 16-12. *Output using -Confirm flag*

The -Confirm flag can help you quickly validate changes in the ARM template and impact the existing resources. Think of this flag as the preflight validation.

As previously demonstrated, the validation and debugging process for your ARM templates become relevant. The larger the environment is, the more time we will invest in validating the ARM templates.

By leveraging ARM-TTK and What-IF, we will be able to adopt best practices and validate our ARM templates before impacting the existing environment in Azure.

The ARM templates and examples shown in this chapter are available here:

```
https://github.com/daveRendon/iac/tree/main/chapter-16
```

Summary

This chapter reviewed the importance of validating ARM templates and how you can leverage tools like ARM-TTK and What-IF to quickly validate your environment and adopt best practices in your code.

We went through some practical examples of how to test ARM templates using the ARM-TTK and validate your environment before performing the deployment operation.

At this stage, you should better understand how you can author ARM templates and manage the lifecycle of resources defined in the templates that are part of your environment.

In the next chapter, we will extend beyond ARM templates and see how you can work with ARM templates and Azure DevOps.

## CHAPTER 17

Building Your Environment with Azure DevOps and ARM Templates

One of the main benefits of the infrastructure-as-code approach is the ability to modularize components and enable the reuse of existing templates.

This chapter will focus on how you can utilize Azure DevOps. This platform can be consumed as a service or on-premises to effectively collaborate across teams in your organization and improve how you build and deploy your environment in Azure.

This chapter will provide you with a better understanding of how you can use Azure DevOps and integrate your ARM templates in Azure Pipelines.

These are the topics that we will cover in this chapter:

- The fundamentals of Azure DevOps

- Integrating your ARM templates in Azure Pipelines

- Examples of how you can configure a build pipeline and a release pipeline

In Chapter 14, we reviewed the options and features applicable in ARM templates to split our environment into multiple ARM templates, consume them as modules, and share the definition of the environment with other members of our organization.

313

© David Rendón 2022
D. Rendón, *Building Applications with Azure Resource Manager (ARM)*,
https://doi.org/10.1007/978-1-4842-7747-8_17

Then in Chapter 17, we learned that the more complex the environment we build, the more time we need to spend validating templates before deploying them into our environment in Azure.

Effective collaboration means seamlessly working with other members of your team and achieving goals faster. We are not talking about tools; we are referring to the ability to adopt a culture in which each member of the organization plays an essential role in each phase to some extent.

While we will not go through a deep dive into DevOps terminology, it is crucial to understand that collaboration and productivity are vital components to achieve goals in our organizations.

A DevOps culture becomes relevant when working toward the same goals and adopting the practices to improve how we build applications, products, or environments for our customers.

Microsoft defines DevOps as "the union of people, process, and products to enable continuous delivery of value to our end users." DevOps represents the convergence between people, processes, and technology to add value to stakeholders continuously.

With this context in mind, we can think of infrastructure as code as one of the practices that should be considered in a DevOps culture.

Azure DevOps will bring value to our organizations to better plan, develop, deliver, and help us maintain and troubleshoot applications in production environments.

In this chapter, we will create and configure a practice of testing each of our ARM template modules with continuous integration and deployment pipelines in Azure DevOps.

The goal is to help you better understand how to utilize Azure DevOps to integrate ARM templates in a modularized approach and learn how to configure pipelines in Azure DevOps. Then, we will create a build pipeline and a release pipeline to build our environment in Azure.

The Fundamentals of Azure DevOps

The Azure DevOps platform provides you with a set of different features from the planning phase down to maintenance and troubleshooting. Azure DevOps will provide you with the tools to assist you in the planning, maintenance, collaboration, and delivery phases of your applications.

There are some key concepts and terminology we need to be familiar with before moving forward.

In addition, it is necessary to download and install Git SCM, or a similar Git client.

Azure DevOps Components

Azure provides a set of features in Azure DevOps that you can use as stand-alone services or can integrate them in the lifecycle of your delivery process. They include the following:

- *Azure Repos*: You can integrate a source control from multiple sources like GitHub, local repositories, or Team Foundation Version Control.

- *Azure Pipelines*: This enables you to configure pipelines to build and release services and help you set up continuous integration and delivery of your environments.

- *Azure Boards*: This will help you plan and track your team's work. It includes Kanban and Scrum methods.

- *Azure Test Plans*: This feature will provide you with the tools to take care of the quality of your system.

- *Azure Artifacts*: You will be able to share extensions like packages from public and private sources into your pipelines.

The following URL will send you directly to Azure DevOps to get started:

`https://dev.azure.com/`

Now we will review how you can integrate your ARM templates, and before doing that, we will need to get you started with the project and validate we have the proper access from Azure DevOps to our Azure subscription to be able to deploy our ARM templates from Azure DevOps.

Azure DevOps Initial Setup

First, we are going to head to `https.//dev.azure.com` and create a new organization; you can sign in with your Microsoft account, as shown in Figure 17-1.

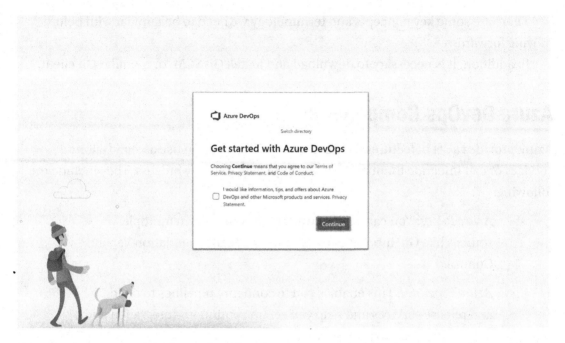

Figure 17-1. *Azure DevOps initial setup*

Once you're in, the following steps are to create a new organization in Azure DevOps and select the region where you want to host your projects. In this example, we will provide the name `ifabrik` and select the region Central US. See Figure 17-2.

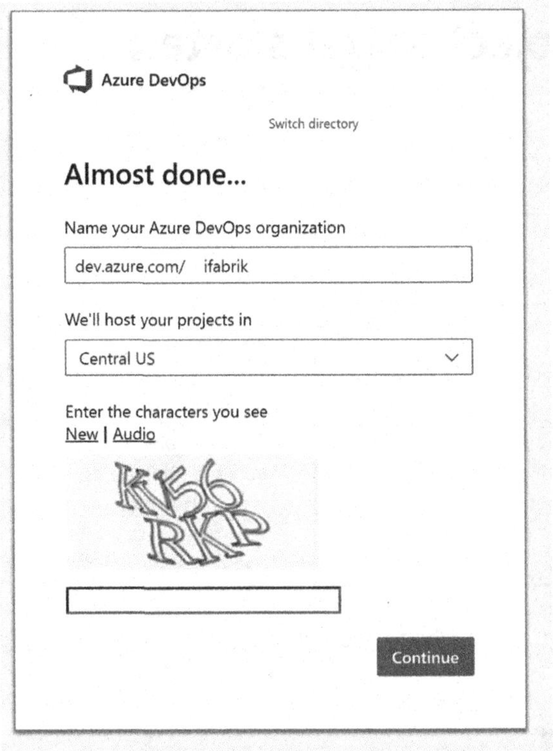

Figure 17-2. *Azure DevOps organization setup*

Now Azure DevOps will walk you through the process of creating a new project.

A project in Azure DevOps provides a repository for your source code and the configuration for the users in the organization to plan, track their progress, and collaborate on the solution.

Think of a project as a container where all the data related to it is stored. When you create a new project, a team is created using the same name. You can have multiple repositories under one project.

We will provide the name of the project called ifabrikApp and then set the visibility to Public, as shown in Figure 17-3.

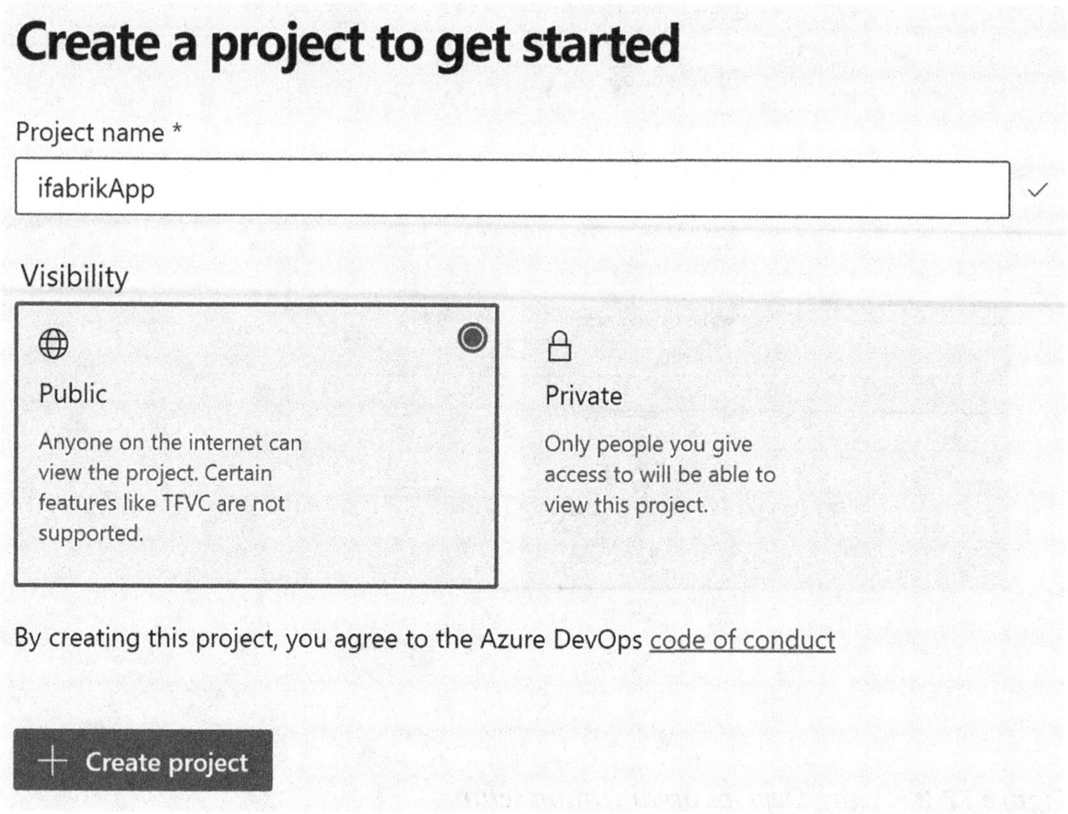

Create a project to get started

Project name *

ifabrikApp ✓

Visibility

⊕ ◉   🔒

Public   Private

Anyone on the internet can view the project. Certain features like TFVC are not supported.   Only people you give access to will be able to view this project.

By creating this project, you agree to the Azure DevOps code of conduct

+ Create project

Figure 17-3. *Azure DevOps project setup*

Then we will create our project. Click the "Create project" button, and then you will see the initial dashboard of your project, as shown in Figure 17-4.

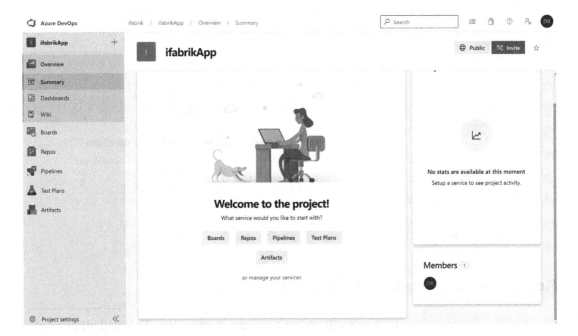

Figure 17-4. *Azure DevOps initial dashboard*

Now you have your Azure DevOps project ready!

The next step is to configure the access from Azure DevOps to your Azure subscription. How can we grant access?

We will use a managed identity. We can reuse the managed identity created in Chapter 15 when we worked with Key Vault.

In this example, the managed identity we are going to use is named `configDeployer`.

In the Azure DevOps initial screen, we will go to the bottom-left corner and select the Project Settings option. This will take you to the settings page of your project. Then in the left menu, go to the Pipelines section and select the "Service connections" option, as shown in Figure 17-5.

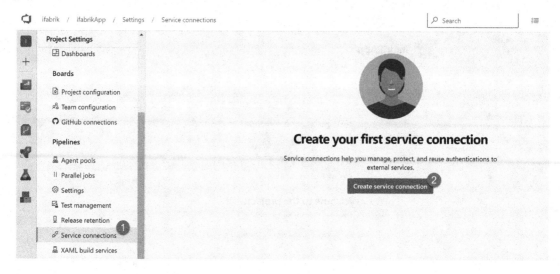

Figure 17-5. *Azure pipelines service connection*

Once you select this option, we will create a service connection. This will allow you to connect Azure DevOps to your Azure subscription using a managed identity.

Then select the option Azure Resource Manager from the options listed, as shown in Figure 17-6.

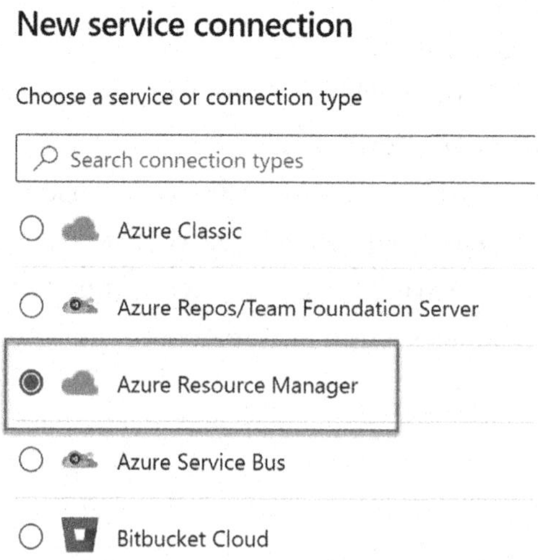

New service connection

Choose a service or connection type

🔍 Search connection types

○ 🌥 Azure Classic

○ 🖥 Azure Repos/Team Foundation Server

◉ 🌥 Azure Resource Manager

○ 🖥 Azure Service Bus

○ 🪣 Bitbucket Cloud

Figure 17-6. *Azure service connection configuration*

In the next step, we have to configure the authentication for the service connection. In this case, we will select the "Managed identity" option, as shown in Figure 17-7.

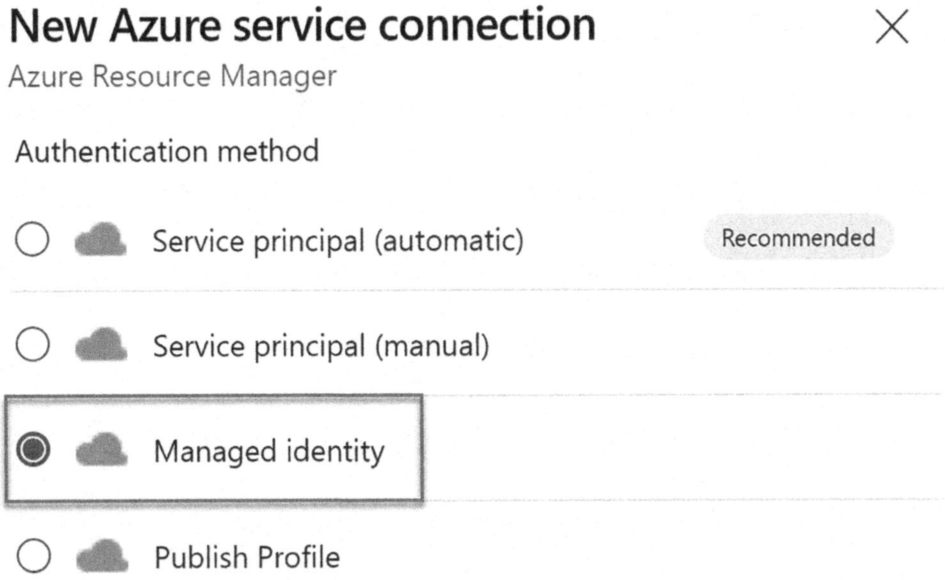

New Azure service connection   ✕
Azure Resource Manager

Authentication method

○ ☁ Service principal (automatic)   Recommended

○ ☁ Service principal (manual)

◉ ☁ Managed identity

○ ☁ Publish Profile

Figure 17-7. *Azure service connection, authentication method*

Now we will provide the parameters for the connection. We have to pass on the subscription ID, subscription name, tenant ID, and connection name. Don't forget to enable the checkbox to grant permission to all pipelines. We will name this connection ifabrikAzureDevOpsConnection. See Figure 17-8.

New Azure service connection   ✕

Azure Resource Manager using managed identity

Environment

| Azure Cloud   ⌄ |

Scope Level

◉ Subscription
○ Management Group
○ Machine Learning Workspace

Subscription Id

| |

Subscription Id from the publish settings file

Subscription Name

| |

Subscription Name from the publish settings file

Authentication

Tenant Id

| |

Tenant Id of the subscription for which the MSI VM has access to

Details

Service connection name

| |

Description (optional)

| |
| |

Security

☑ Grant access permission to all pipelines

Learn more
Troubleshoot   **Back**   Save

Figure 17-8. *Azure service connection, managed identity*

You can get the information needed for the previous configuration from the Azure portal in the subscription and Azure AD pages.

At this point, we have configured the organization, created a new project, and created a service connection from Azure DevOps to the Azure subscription using a managed identity.

The next step is to prepare the code we will use in our pipelines. We can leverage Azure Repos to store the ARM templates in Azure DevOps.

Configuring Azure Repos

One of the features included in Azure DevOps is Azure Repos, which provides you with a set of tools for version control. Instead of using any external repositories like GitHub, you can have all the necessary tools to manage your code from Azure Repos.

In the following example, we will review how you can leverage Azure Repos to create a repository for your source code. We will use Azure Repos to host the ARM templates that will be part of our environment.

Creating Azure Repo

In Azure DevOps in the left menu, we will select the Repos option, as shown in Figure 17-9.

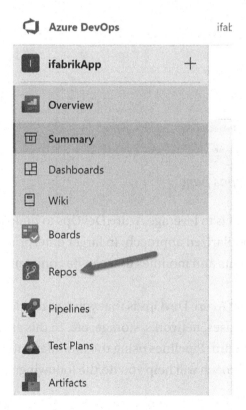

Figure 17-9. *Azure Repos*

Once you select Azure Repos, you will see a page with multiple options to configure your source code.

In the left menu, under Azure Repos, we will see a drop-down menu that includes Files, Commits, Pushes, Branches, Tags, and Pull Requests.

On the right side, you will see the options to move your code from an external source to Azure Repos, as shown in Figure 17-10.

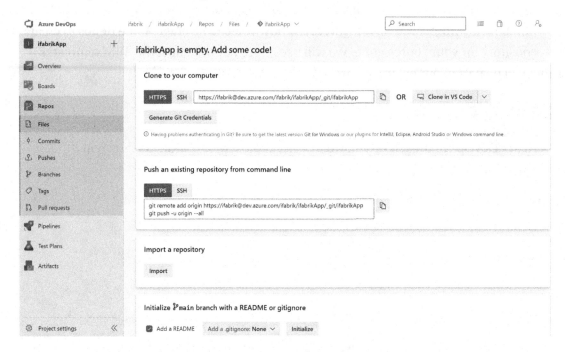

Figure 17-10. *Azure Repos page*

As mentioned, the goal is to leverage Azure DevOps to build and deploy our environment using a modularized approach. In larger enterprises, it is common to see automation components and modules that can be consumed depending on the environment type.

A huge benefit of using Azure DevOps is that you can divide automation assets into logical parts such as databases, networks, storage, etc. In this example, we will deploy ARM templates through Azure Pipelines using the modularization of the ARM templates.

This modularized approach will help you do the following:

- Reuse components

- Manage and maintain your code

- Subdivide work and responsibilities across teams

- Troubleshoot more quickly

Before breaking a solution into multiple modules, it is recommended to identify what Azure resources have dependencies and create the appropriate ARM templates based on those dependencies.

Keeping a folder structure that facilitates the management of your environment is also a best practice.

The environment that we will review includes three tiers all under the same repository:

- *Tier 3*: Contains the application itself and all the related code

- *Tier 2*: Contains the application management components like the virtual machines, disks, and load balancers

- *Tier 1*: Contains the platform components such as the virtual network, the SQL Server, storage accounts, and an automation account

As mentioned, we will have three tiers, with one tier per folder, and each tier will contain different resources. We will have an ARM template per resource:

- *Tier 1*: ARM templates for a virtual network, storage account, SQL database, automation account

- *Tier 2*: Contains the ARM templates for a load balancer and virtual machine

- *Tier 3*: Includes the actual code of the application

We will use the open source code from the Parts Unlimited repository as a baseline. The code related to this specific example is at the following URL:

```
https://github.com/daveRendon/iac/tree/main/chapter-17
```

The next step is to download the code to your local machine. Once you have downloaded the code, let's push it to the Azure Repos.

Pushing an Existing Repository from the Command Line

Remember, we installed Git at the beginning of this chapter. You can install Git from the following URL:

```
https://www.git-scm.com/downloads
```

Once you have the source code in your local machine, head to the folder where the code is located and then initialize Git using the Git console or the PowerShell console with the command in Listing 17-1.

Listing 17-1. git init Command Line

```
git init
```

You should see the output shown in Listing 17-2.

Listing 17-2. git init Output

```
Initialized empty Git repository in C:/Users/Username/azure-repos/.git/
```

Before we push the code to Azure Repos, we will add the remote origin using the command in Listing 17-3.

Listing 17-3. Push an Existing Repository from Command Line

```
git remote add origin https://ORGNAME@dev.azure.com/ORGNAME/ifabrikApp/_git/
ifabrikApp
```

Once you initialized the repo and added the remote origin, use the command `git add .` in your bash to add all the files to the given folder. You can use the command `git status` to review the files to be staged to the first commit, as shown in Figure 17-11.

```
On branch master

No commits yet

Changes to be committed:
  (use "git rm --cached <file>..." to unstage)
        new file:   Tier1/AutomationAccount/azuredeploy.json
        new file:   Tier1/AzureSQLServerwithDatabase/azuredeploy.json
        new file:   Tier1/StorageAccount/azuredeploy.json
        new file:   Tier1/Vnet/azuredeploy.json
        new file:   Tier2/LB/azuredeploy.json
        new file:   Tier2/Vm/azuredeploy.json
        new file:   Tier3/Tier3.zip
```

Figure 17-11. *Files to be staged to the first commit*

Figure 17-11 shows the files that will be uploaded to Azure Repos.

Then, we have to set the account identity with the commands in Listing 17-4.

Listing 17-4. Set Account Identity

```
git config --global user.email "you@example.com"
git config --global user.name "Your Name"
```

As an example, Listing 17-5 shows the command.

Listing 17-5. Set Account Identity

```
git config --global user.email "dave.rendon@outlook.com"
git config --global user.name "Dave"
```

Now, let's use the following command to commit the files staged in the local repository: `git commit -m 'your message'`. Figure 17-12 shows the output from the previous command.

```
[master (root-commit) c6726ec] first commit
 7 files changed, 645 insertions(+)
 create mode 100644 Tier1/AutomationAccount/azuredeploy.json
 create mode 100644 Tier1/AzureSQLServerwithDatabase/azuredeploy.json
 create mode 100644 Tier1/StorageAccount/azuredeploy.json
 create mode 100644 Tier1/Vnet/azuredeploy.json
 create mode 100644 Tier2/LB/azuredeploy.json
 create mode 100644 Tier2/Vm/azuredeploy.json
 create mode 100644 Tier3/Tier3.zip
```

Figure 17-12. *Files to be staged to the first commit*

Now we will push the code to Azure Repos using the command in Listing 17-6.

Listing 17-6. Push an Existing Repository from Command Line

```
git push -u origin --all
```

Figure 17-13 shows the output from the previous command.

```
Enumerating objects: 18, done.
Counting objects: 100% (18/18), done.
Delta compression using up to 8 threads
Compressing objects: 100% (11/11), done.
Writing objects: 100% (18/18), 11.18 MiB | 17.51 MiB/s, done.
Total 18 (delta 3), reused 0 (delta 0), pack-reused 0
remote: Analyzing objects... (18/18) (257 ms)
remote: Storing packfile... done (505 ms)
remote: Storing index... done (44 ms)
To https://dev.azure.com/ifabrik/ifabrikApp/_git/ifabrikApp
 * [new branch]      master -> master
Branch 'master' set up to track remote branch 'master' from 'origin'.
```

Figure 17-13. *Files pushed to Azure Repos*

Now we can go back to Azure DevOps and select Azure Repos; you should see the files already present in the repository, as shown in Figure 17-14.

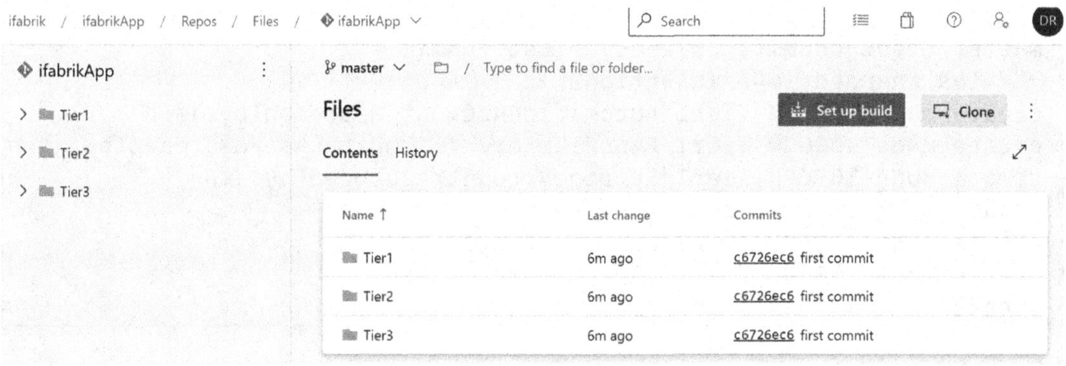

Figure 17-14. *Files present in Azure Repos*

Now, this completes the setup of the Azure repository. The next step is to create the build pipeline and the release pipeline.

Configuring a Build Pipeline in Azure DevOps

Remember, Tier 1 contains the ARM templates for the storage account, the automation account, the virtual network, and SQL Server.

In this section, we will build a pipeline in Azure Pipelines to achieve continuous integration, reduce the build time of our environment, and automate the testing process if there are changes in the code of the ARM templates.

In Azure DevOps, go to Pipelines and click Create Pipeline, as shown in Figure 17-15.

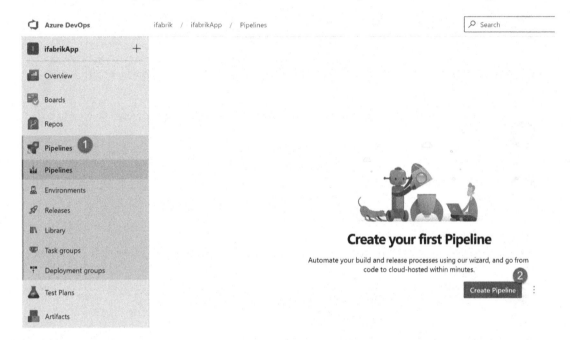

Figure 17-15. *Creating a pipeline*

Now on the Connect tab, select the classic editor to create a build pipeline using the ARM templates, as shown in Figure 17-16.

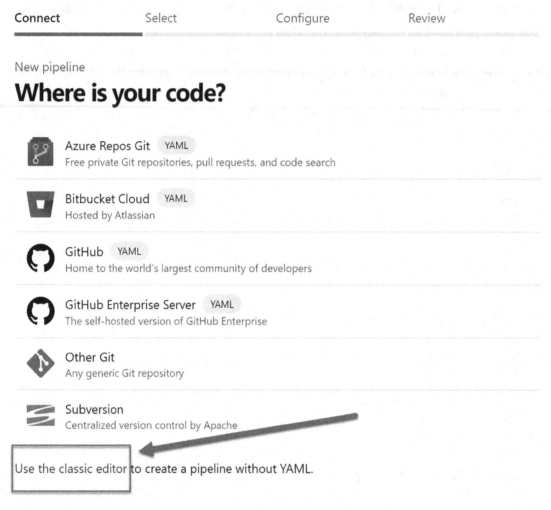

Connect   Select   Configure   Review

New pipeline

Where is your code?

Azure Repos Git   YAML
Free private Git repositories, pull requests, and code search

Bitbucket Cloud   YAML
Hosted by Atlassian

GitHub   YAML
Home to the world's largest community of developers

GitHub Enterprise Server   YAML
The self-hosted version of GitHub Enterprise

Other Git
Any generic Git repository

Subversion
Centralized version control by Apache

Use the classic editor to create a pipeline without YAML.

Figure 17-16. *Creating a pipeline, Connect tab*

In the next step, select your repository and master branch and then click the Continue option. See Figure 17-17.

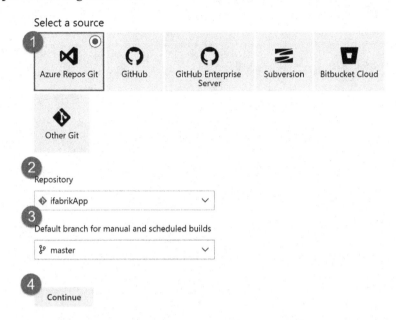

Figure 17-17. *Creating a pipeline, selecting a source*

On the "Select a template" page, select "Empty job." See Figure 17-18.

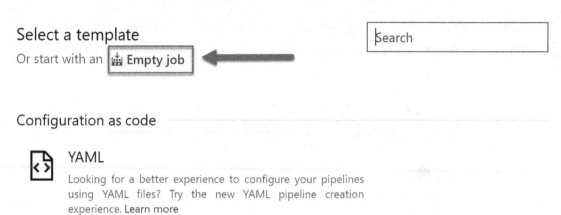

Figure 17-18. *Selecting a template page*

Then we will provide the configuration for the pipeline. Provide a name to this pipeline. We will name it ifabrikApp-CI. See Figure 17-19.

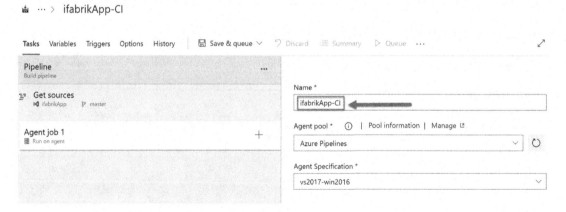

Figure 17-19. *Providing the name of the pipeline*

Then we will go to the left pane where it says Agent Job 1. Select this option and then click the plus icon (+) to add a task to Agent Job 1. See Figure 17-20.

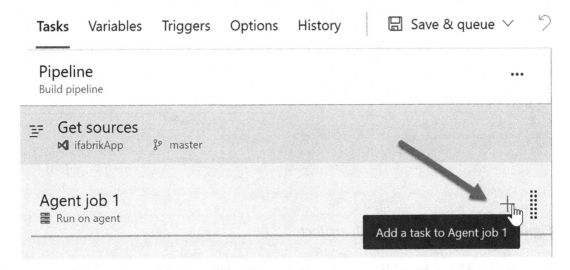

Figure 17-20. *Add a task to agent job 1*

Then in the search box, type **Publish Build Artifact** and add it, as shown in Figure 17-21.

Figure 17-21. *Adding publish build artifacts*

Now in the task called "Publish Artifact: drop," change the display name, for example, to Tier1-CI-AutomationAccount. See Figure 17-22.

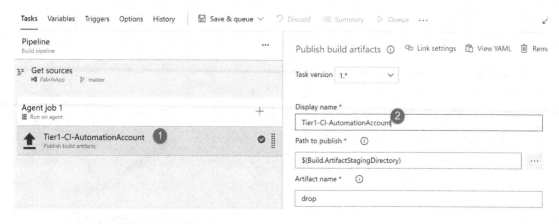

Figure 17-22. *Name of publish artifact*

Now in the "Path to publish" field, click the three-dot icon, as shown in Figure 17-23.

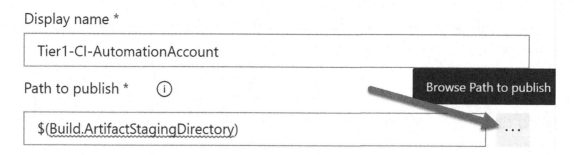

Figure 17-23. *Browsing the path to publish*

Now look for the folder of the Azure resource. Expand the repository folder, then look for the folder called Automation Account, and finally click OK. See Figure 17-24.

Select path

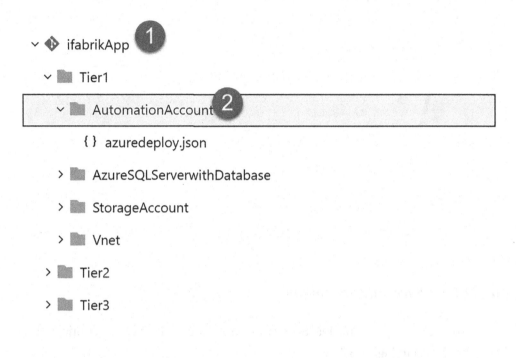

Figure 17-24. Path to automation account

Let's kick off a build manually to ensure that we have a working build pipeline. Click the "Save & queue" option. See Figure 17-25.

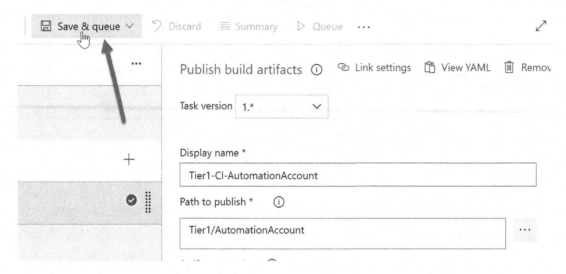

Figure 17-25. *"Save & queue" option*

Now provide a comment under "Save comment" and then select the option "Save and run," as shown in Figure 17-26.

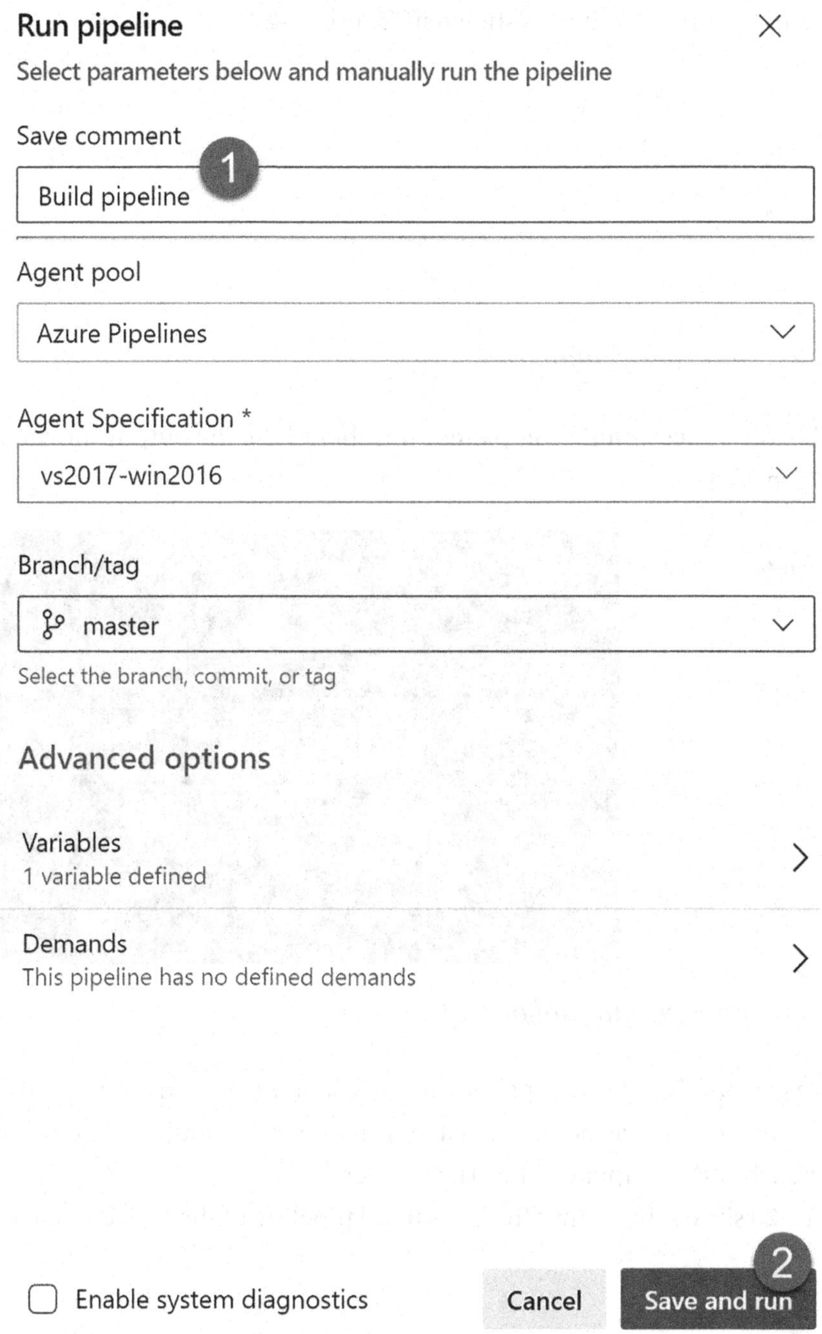

Run pipeline   ✕

Select parameters below and manually run the pipeline

Save comment

Build pipeline

Agent pool

Azure Pipelines   ∨

Agent Specification *

vs2017-win2016   ∨

Branch/tag

⌥ master   ∨

Select the branch, commit, or tag

Advanced options

Variables   >
1 variable defined

Demands   >
This pipeline has no defined demands

⬚ Enable system diagnostics   Cancel   Save and run

Figure 17-26. *Saving and running*

This will trigger the pipeline, as shown in Figure 17-27.

Figure 17-27. *Pipeline manual run*

Once the job is successfully completed, you should see the output shown in
Figure 17-28 in your job.

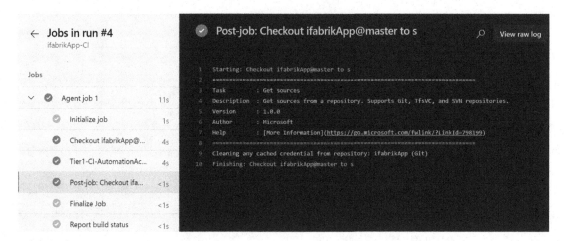

Figure 17-28. *Pipeline manual output*

Next, we will build an Azure pipeline for the rest of the Azure resources. We will
perform the same process as before per each resource. You should have one "build"
pipeline for each ARM template in the Tier1 folder.

Figure 17-29 shows the output from the build pipeline of the SQL database.

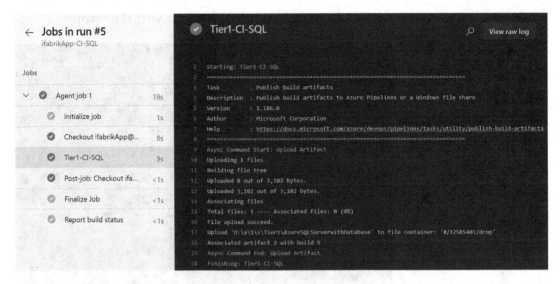

Figure 17-29. *Pipeline manual output, SQL server and database*

Figure 17-30 shows the output from the build pipeline of the storage account.

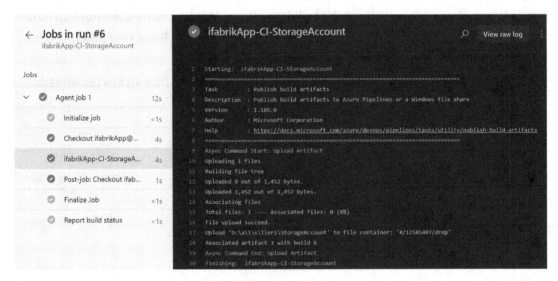

Figure 17-30. *Pipeline manual output, storage account*

Figure 17-31 shows the output from the build pipeline of the virtual network.

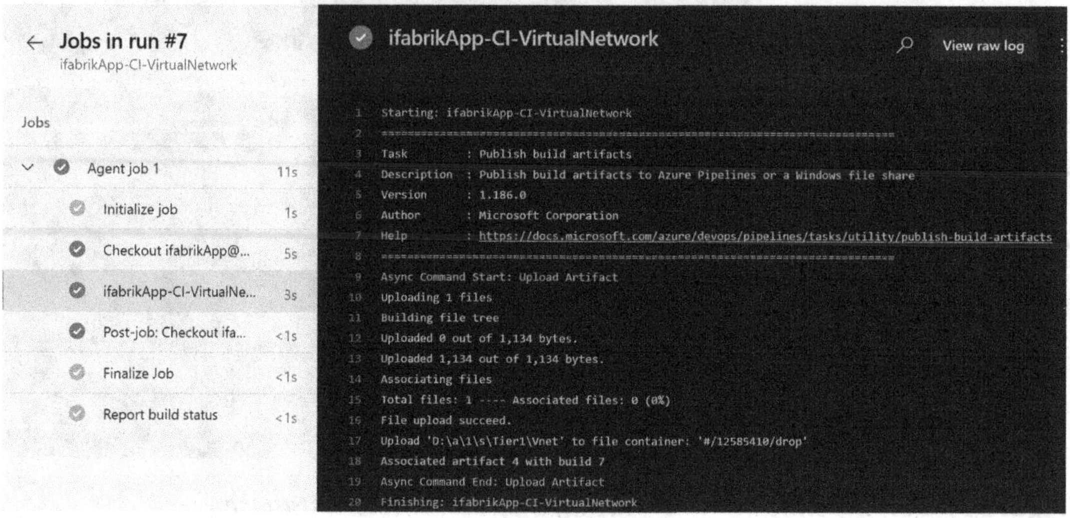

Figure 17-31. *Pipeline manual output, virtual network*

This completes the creation of the build pipelines. At this moment, we have an Azure repository with the files of our environment and four build pipelines, one pipeline per resource included in the Tier 1 folder of the repository.

Figure 17-32 shows the recently run pipelines. There is one pipeline per resource.

Figure 17-32. *Pipeline manual output, virtual network*

We can enable continuous integration on the build pipeline on the Triggers tab of the pipeline. See Figure 17-33.

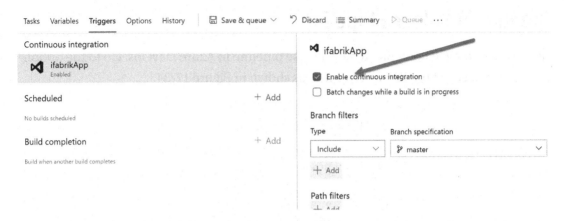

Figure 17-33. *Enabling continuous integration*

This option will help us automate our build process; this process is usually referred to as *continuous integration*. If there's any change in the code, a new job will be triggered with the latest version of the code.

Note   Every time you run a pipeline, you will receive a notification in your mail.

Now it is time to build the release pipeline and automate the release process of the resources that will be part of our environment in Azure. We can achieve this through continuous delivery and creating release pipelines in Azure DevOps.

Configuring a Release Pipeline in Azure DevOps

To create a release pipeline, you must specify the artifacts that make up the application and the release pipeline.

An *artifact* is a term that refers to a deployable component or extension that will be part of your application. It is typically produced through a continuous integration or a build pipeline like we previously created.

The release pipeline is defined through stages; for example, you can have a stage called Development, another stage called Production, and another stage called QA.

You will be able to restrict deployments into or out of a stage using manual or automated approvals. You can define the automation per stage using jobs and tasks.

Creating a Release Pipeline

Now we are going to configure a new release pipeline in Azure DevOps. Go to the option Pipelines and select the Releases option, as shown in Figure 17-34.

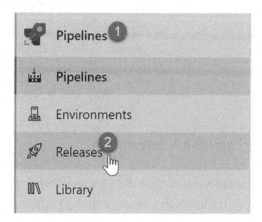

Figure 17-34. *Releases option*

Now we will create a new pipeline and select the option "Empty job," as shown in Figure 17-35.

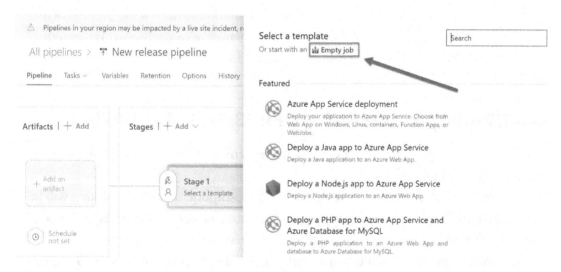

Figure 17-35. *New release pipeline, empty job*

Now we will name this stage Dev and modify the name of the release pipeline, as shown in Figure 17-36.

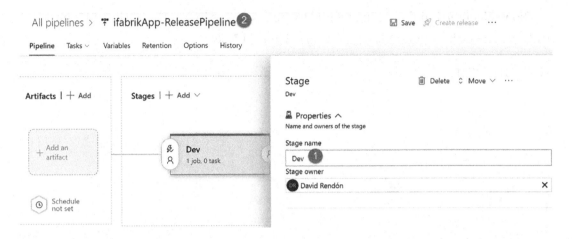

Figure 17-36. *New release pipeline*

At this point, we have created a new release pipeline with a new stage. The next step is to add the artifacts.

The artifacts will be the ARM templates: the virtual network, the automation account, the storage account, and the SQL Server.

Now, close the stage tab and select the option "Add an artifact." See Figure 17-37.

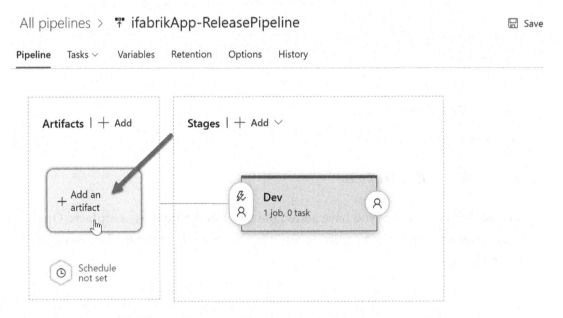

Figure 17-37. *Adding artifacts*

Now select the build pipeline related to the resources in Tier1. We will add four artifacts, one artifact per build pipeline. See Figure 17-38.

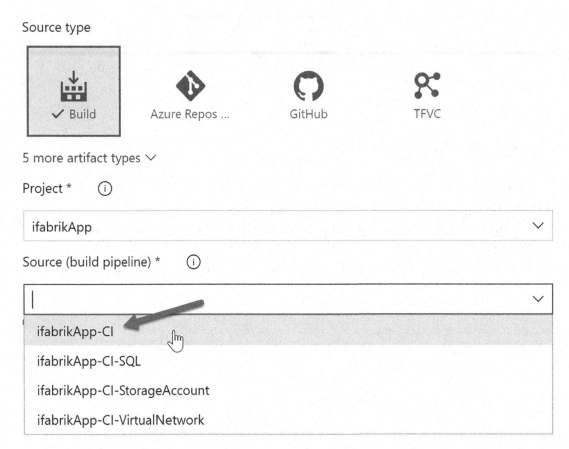

Figure 17-38. *Adding artifacts*

Repeat the process until you have added the four build pipelines as artifacts. Once you added the four pipelines as artifacts, you should see them in the Artifacts section, as shown in Figure 17-39.

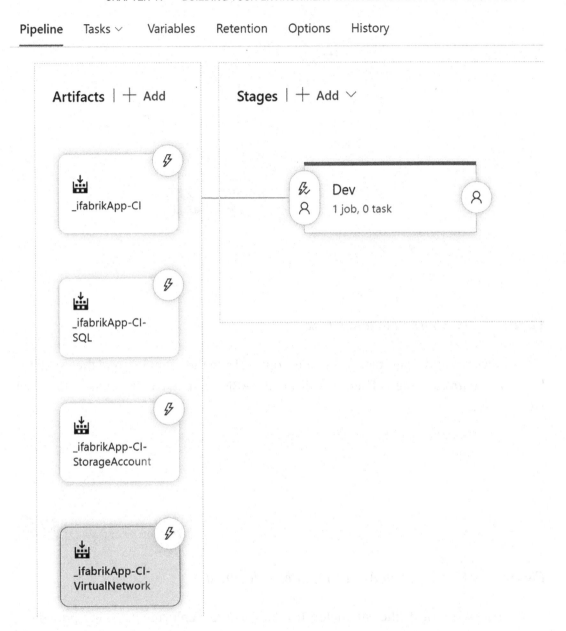

Figure 17-39. Four artifacts

The next step is to add a new task in the Dev stage. You can select the shortcut in the Dev stage, as shown in Figure 17-40.

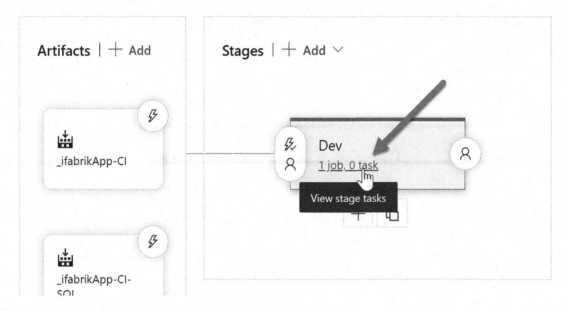

Figure 17-40. *Shortcut to add a task*

Now we will add a new task, select the + option from the agent job, and then search for *azure resource manager*. Then we will add the ARM template deployment option. See Figure 17-41.

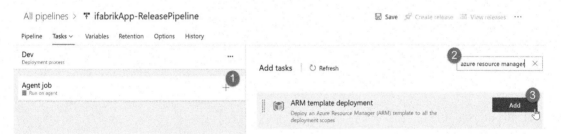

Figure 17-41. *Adding an ARM template deployment*

Now we will provide the parameters to configure this deployment. We will provide the Azure Resource Manager connection, select the subscription, and provide the resource group and the location. See Figure 17-42.

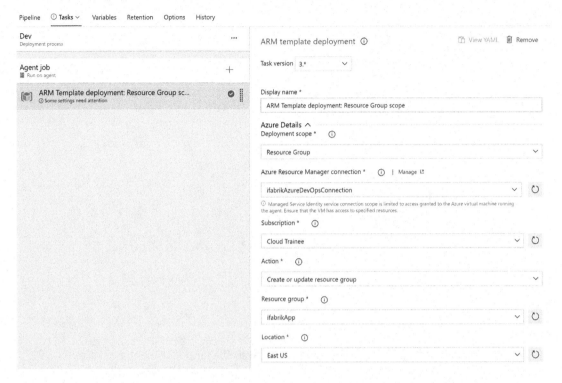

Figure 17-42. *Parameters for the deployment*

Note that you should have previously created the service connection. The other
option is to select the subscription, and Azure DevOps will configure the connection for
you for this pipeline.

Then we will do a quick test, and in the template section select the file of the ARM
template. In this case, we are going to start with the virtual network, as shown in
Figure 17-43.

Select a file or folder

×

▲ ▦ Linked artifacts
   ▶ ▦ _ifabrikApp-CI (Build)
   ▶ ▦ _ifabrikApp-CI-SQL (Build)
   ▶ ▦ _ifabrikApp-CI-StorageAccount (Build)
   ▲ ▦ _ifabrikApp-CI-VirtualNetwork (Build)
      ▲ ▦ drop
          🗋 azuredeploy.json

The artifacts published by each version will be available for deployment in release pipelines. The last successful version of **_ifabrikApp-CI-VirtualNetwork (Build)** published the following artifacts: ***drop***.

Location _ifabrikApp-CI-VirtualNetwork/drop/azuredeploy.json

OK   Cancel

Figure 17-43. *ARM template selection*

You can optionally override the template parameters, as shown in Figure 17-44.

Override template parameters

Name	Value
VnetName	ifabrikVnet
SubnetName	frontendSubnet

Figure 17-44. *Overriding template parameters*

Now save and click "Create release," as shown in Figure 17-45.

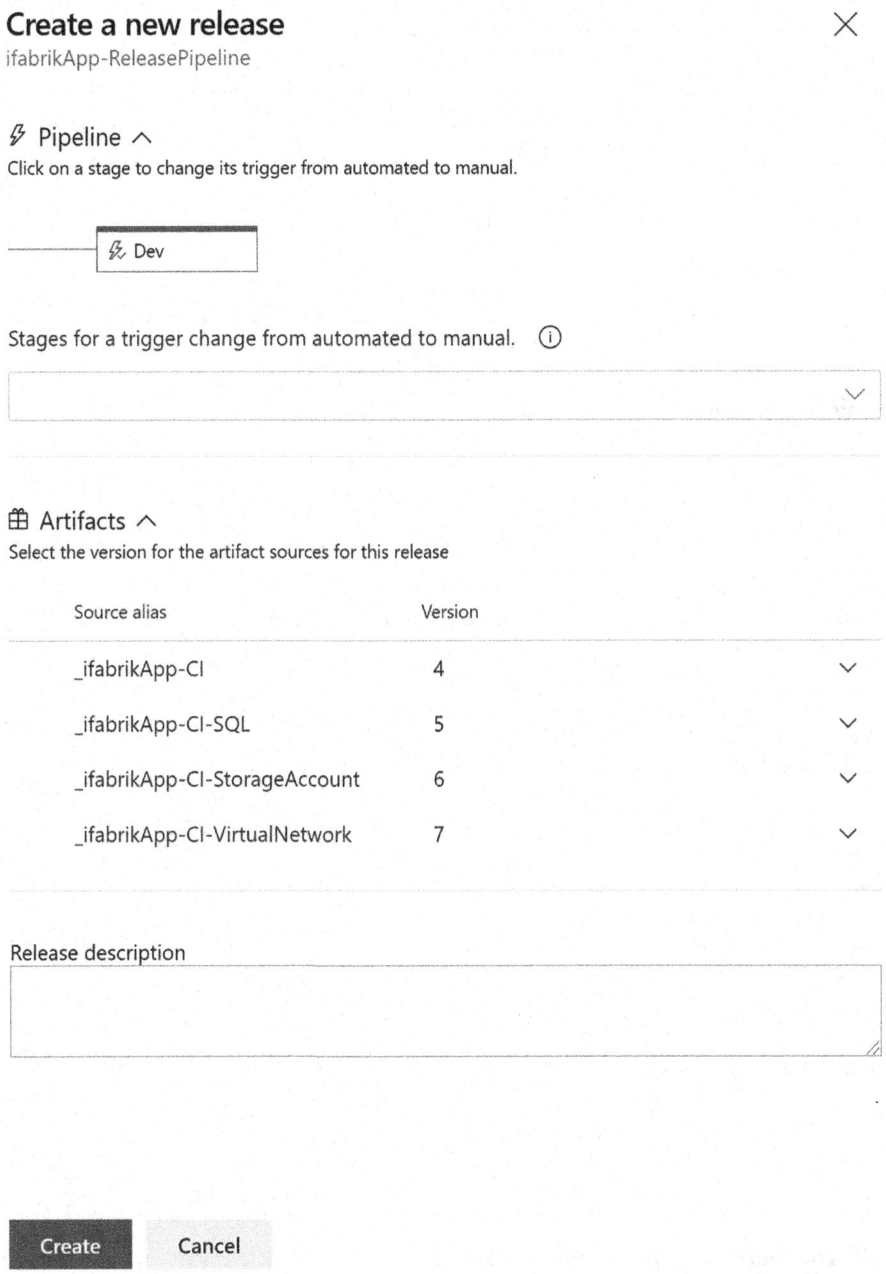

Create a new release

ifabrikApp-ReleasePipeline

⚡ Pipeline ∧

Click on a stage to change its trigger from automated to manual.

⚡ Dev

Stages for a trigger change from automated to manual.   ⓘ

⊞ Artifacts ∧

Select the version for the artifact sources for this release

Source alias	Version	
_ifabrikApp-CI	4	∨
_ifabrikApp-CI-SQL	5	∨
_ifabrikApp-CI-StorageAccount	6	∨
_ifabrikApp-CI-VirtualNetwork	7	∨

Release description

Create   Cancel

Figure 17-45. *Release pipeline*

Click Create, and you will see the release pipeline progress, as shown in Figure 17-46.

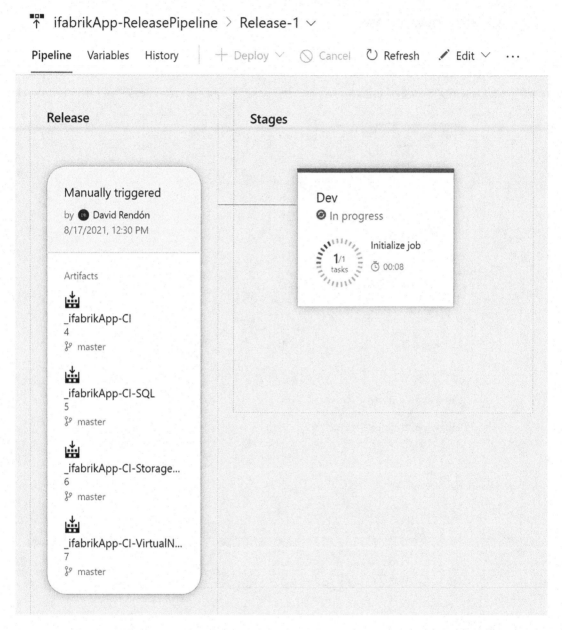

Figure 17-46. *Release pipeline in progress*

After a few seconds, you should see the job completed, as shown in Figure 17-47.

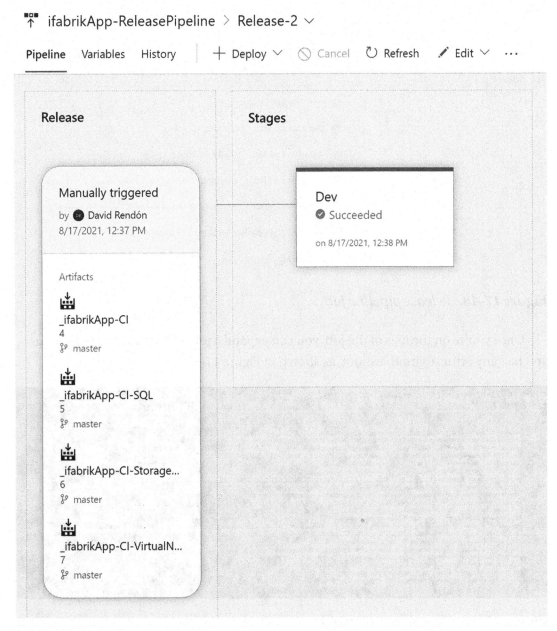

Figure 17-47. *Release pipeline complete*

You can also check on the logs and see the complete job and its details, as shown in Figure 17-48.

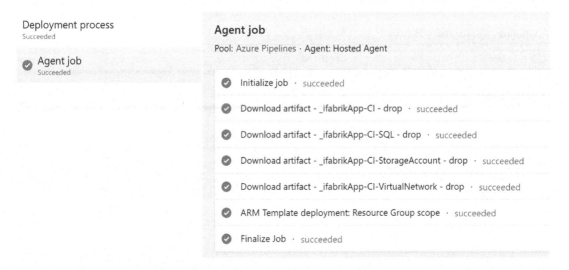

Figure 17-48. *Release pipeline job*

Once you're on the logs of the job, you can expand a job and see the details in case you had any errors to troubleshoot, as shown in Figure 17-49.

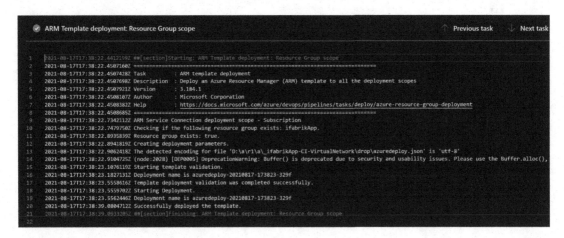

Figure 17-49. *Release pipeline logs*

Now we have our virtual network provisioned in the ifabrikApp resource group; we could proceed and create the necessary resources for our environment. Figure 17-50 shows the virtual network created from this release pipeline.

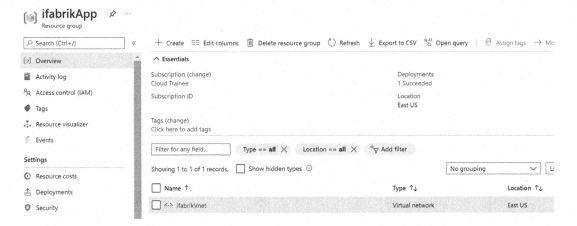

Figure 17-50. *Virtual network created from the release pipeline*

Ideally, this gives you an idea of what we can achieve when using ARM templates in a modularized approach with Azure DevOps.

Summary

This chapter provided you with an overview of Azure DevOps and the importance of leveraging a modularized approach with ARM templates.

We reviewed the core concepts of Azure DevOps and how you can build multiple pipelines. Then we created a few build pipelines and a release pipeline.

At the end of the chapter, we reviewed the output from the release pipeline and confirmed that the resource was created in the resource group.

In the next chapter, we will go over the deployment of ARM templates using GitHub actions.

## CHAPTER 18

Deploy ARM Templates Using GitHub Actions

The previous chapter provided you with an overview of Azure DevOps and the importance of leveraging a modularized approach with ARM templates. We went through the core concepts of Azure DevOps and how you can build a continuous integration/continuous deployment pipeline in Azure DevOps.

This chapter will focus on integrating GitHub actions to implement a continuous integration/continuous deployment to publish your environment in Azure.

Along with this chapter, we will review the following topics:

- The fundamentals of GitHub actions

- How to build a GitHub action

- Working with GitHub actions to deploy ARM templates

GitHub has become one of the most popular platforms for shipping applications and securing open source code at scale. One of the benefits of using GitHub is automating software workflows using a CI/CD strategy.

This way, you can host your code in GitHub and build, test, and deploy your application directly from GitHub.

What we are talking about here is the ability to have workflows within GitHub to perform the creation of a new release. If you want to deploy a web application in GitHub, you could use GitHub actions.

© David Rendón 2022
D. Rendón, *Building Applications with Azure Resource Manager (ARM)*,
https://doi.org/10.1007/978-1-4842-7747-8_18

The Fundamentals of GitHub Actions

A GitHub action is an event-driven job that will help you automate various workflows and enable continuous integration/continuous deployment in GitHub. Think of GitHub actions as software testing scripts.

A GitHub action will define an event that will trigger a workflow with a set of jobs.

Inside these jobs, you will define the steps to control the order you want to run specific actions. These actions are commands to automate your pipeline.

While Azure DevOps Pipelines and GitHub Actions share some similarities in terms of configuration, GitHub Actions will leverage YAML files to define workflows, and you will find that there's no graphical interface to edit pipelines.

Note GitHub Actions requires explicit configuration, and you will be able to separate stages through multiple YAML workflow files.

Figure 18-1 shows the components of GitHub actions.

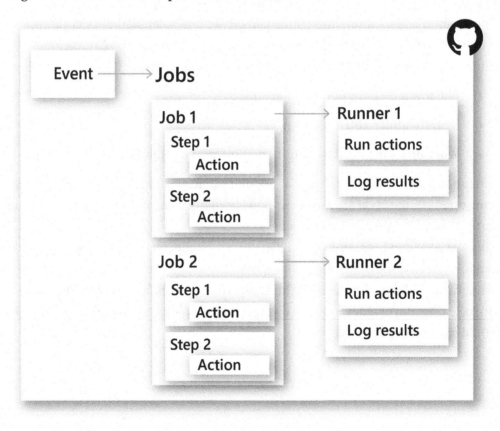

Figure 18-1. *Components of GitHub Actions.*

To better understand GitHub actions, let's simplify the core concepts of the components of GitHub actions:

- *Workflows*: A workflow is an automation process that you add to the GitHub repository, usually in the `.github\workflows` directory. A workflow can contain a set of jobs. A workflow will help you build, test, or deploy an application.

- *Events*: An event triggers a workflow. This represents an activity such as a commit or a push.

- *Jobs*: A job represents a set of steps to be executed, and those are related to the same runner. Your workflow can contain multiple jobs and run them in parallel or in sequence.

- *Steps*: This is an individual task defined inside a job. A step is usually a shell command or an action.

- *Actions*: An action is a command and works in conjunction with steps to create a job.

- *Runners*: Think of a runner as a server that hosts a specific application. You can host runners, but GitHub usually hosts these. This is a virtual machine hosted by GitHub with the GitHub actions runner application installed. It can be Linux, Windows, or macOS-based.

So, how can we create workflows? How do GitHub actions work?

Defining GitHub Actions

GitHub actions are based on YAML files, and we have to store them in our GitHub repository in the `.github/workflows` directory.

Each GitHub action is a file, and you can create any number of GitHub actions. At a minimum, we have to include three properties in a GitHub action: `name`, `on`, and `jobs`.

Listing 18-1 shows the basic definition of a GitHub action.

Listing 18-1. Definition of a GitHub Action

```
name: hello-world
on: [push]
jobs:
  write-to-console:
    runs-on: ubuntu-latest
    steps:
      - run: echo 'Hello world!'
```

Example: GitHub Action "Hello World"

In this example, we will create our first GitHub action. As a prerequisite, you need to have a GitHub account.

Let's go to `https://github.com` and create a new repository. We will name this repository `github-actions`.

Now we will work on the definition of the GitHub action.

In your GitHub repository, go to the Actions tab, as shown in Figure 18-2.

Figure 18-2. *GitHub repository, actions*

Then select the option "Skip this and set up a workflow yourself."

We will create a new YAML file and include the code in Listing 18-2.

Listing 18-2. GitHub Action Definition

```
# This is a basic workflow to help you get started with Actions
name: iFabrikCI
# Controls when the workflow will run
on:
```

```
  # Triggers the workflow on push or pull request events but only for the
main branch
  push:
    branches: [ main ]
  pull_request:
    branches: [ main ]
# Allows you to run this workflow manually from the Actions tab
  workflow_dispatch:
# A workflow run is made up of one or more jobs that can run sequentially
or in parallel
jobs:
  # This workflow contains a single job called "build"
  build:
    # The type of runner that the job will run on
    runs-on: ubuntu-latest
    # Steps represent a sequence of tasks that will be executed as part
of the job
    steps:
      # Checks-out your repository under $GITHUB_WORKSPACE, so your job can
access it
      - uses: actions/checkout@v2
      # Runs a single command using the runners shell
      - name: Run a one-line script
        run: echo Hello, world!
      # Runs a set of commands using the runners shell
      - name: Run a multi-line script
        run: |
          echo Add other actions to build,
          echo test, and deploy your project.
```

Figure 18-3 shows the code of the `main.yml` file in GitHub.

Figure 18-3. Definition of main.yml file

Now click "Start commit" and provide a comment for the initial commit, as shown in Figure 18-4.

Figure 18-4. Commit of the main.yml file

Once you trigger this commit, you will see in the Actions tab that the workflow has started, as shown in Figure 18-5.

Figure 18-5. Workflows

As shown in Figure 18-5, in the left pane, you will see the current workflows in your repository, and on the right side, you will see the recent runs of a workflow.

You can select the details of the workflow, and you will see a page that shows the details of the execution of the job, as shown in Figure 18-6.

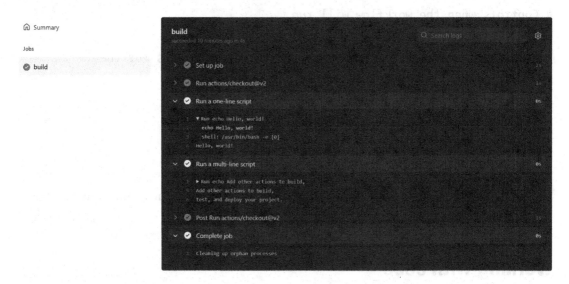

Figure 18-6. Job details

So, what just happened? We created a new workflow called `ifabrik-CI` that contains a job called `build`.

This job runs on a Linux-based virtual machine hosted by GitHub.

Then, in the Steps section, we defined an action called checkout@v2 to check out our code and included two "runs": one run for a single shell command and another that runs a multiline script.

To provide you with a better understanding of how GitHub actions work, let's take the previous example and analyze each component of the GitHub action we utilized. Let's start with the events component.

Working with Events

Remember that an event triggers a workflow. This represents an activity such as a commit or a push.

The event type can be defined in the YAML file. In the previous example, we included the event on push and pull_request, as shown in Listing 18-3.

Listing 18-3. GitHub Actions, Events

```
# This is a basic workflow to help you get started with Actions
name: iFabrik-CI

# Controls when the workflow will run
on:
  # Triggers the workflow on push or pull request events for the
    main branch
  push:
    branches: [ main ]
  pull_request:
    branches: [ main ]
```

Note that we can define the branch that we want to target at the event. Now let's take a look at the following component: jobs.

Working with Jobs

A job can include a set of steps to be executed. Your workflow can contain multiple jobs and run them in parallel or in sequence.

In the previous example, the workflow contained a single job called build and ran on a Linux-based virtual machine. See Listing 18-4.

Listing 18-4. GitHub Actions, jobs

```
jobs:
  # This workflow contains a single job called "build"
  build:
    # The type of runner that the job will run on
    runs-on: ubuntu-latest
```

Jobs can be executed on Windows, Linux, or macOS hosts. Now that we have defined our jobs, let's take a look at the steps.

Working with Steps

In each job, you should define the series of steps to determine what to run in each job, as shown in Listing 18-5.

Listing 18-5. GitHub Actions, Steps

```
# Steps represent a sequence of tasks that will be executed as part
of the job
    steps:
      # Checks-out your repository under $GITHUB_WORKSPACE, so your job can
        access it
      - uses: actions/checkout@v2

      # Runs a single command using the runners shell
      - name: Run a one-line script
        run: echo Hello, world!

      # Runs a set of commands using the runners shell
      - name: Run a multi-line script
        run: |
          echo Add other actions to build,
          echo test, and deploy your project.
```

In the previous listing, we use the property called uses that lets you leverage GitHub actions created by the community. You can find a list of GitHub actions at the GitHub Marketplace:

```
https://github.com/marketplace?type=actions
```

Note that we're using the action called check-out to check out the Git repository under $GITHUB_WORKSPACE so that it can be accessible to our workflow.

Now that we understand GitHub actions better, we will use a GitHub action to deploy an ARM template in the following example.

Example: Deploy ARM Template Using GitHub Actions

We can use GitHub actions to build our environment and enable a CI/CD strategy, and the first step is to create the infrastructure where the application will run.

That said, we will start by including the ARM templates in the GitHub repository.

There are some prerequisites that we need to validate before working with GitHub actions to deploy ARM templates, including the following:

- A GitHub account

- An active Azure subscription

- A service principal

- Your code in GitHub

Once you have these prerequisites, let's start building our GitHub action to deploy the ARM templates.

For the following example, we will use an ARM template that deploys a WordPress web app on Azure App Service with MySQL in App.

The code of this ARM template can be found in the following URL:

```
https://github.com/daveRendon/github-actions/blob/main/azuredeploy.json
```

Configure the Service Principal

Before deploying our ARM templates, we must configure the GitHub secrets and associate them with the service principal. Remember to create a resource group beforehand. We have created the resource group called ifabrikApp.

You can use Azure CLI to create a service principal with the command shown in Listing 18-6.

Listing 18-6. Creating a Service Principal

```
az ad sp create-for-rbac --name ifabrikApp --role contributor --scopes
/subscriptions/{subscription-id}/resourceGroups/ifabrikApp --sdk-auth
```

If you run the previous command to create the service principal, you should see output like Figure 18-7.

```
{
  "clientId": "c16f5e80-0a63-4c53-8114-be58d052cf7c",
  "clientSecret": "ihTBKflAA-hPStZYaAX.7cZxdi3Ke6Jfya",
  "subscriptionId": "d988cbee-043f-4c46-9a59-dedb2119e48c",
  "tenantId": "f6d82f6e-3b62-4cd2-a876-4b37092058ce",
  "activeDirectoryEndpointUrl": "https://login.microsoftonline.com",
  "resourceManagerEndpointUrl": "https://management.azure.com/",
  "activeDirectoryGraphResourceId": "https://graph.windows.net/",
  "sqlManagementEndpointUrl": "https://management.core.windows.net:8443/",
  "galleryEndpointUrl": "https://gallery.azure.com/",
  "managementEndpointUrl": "https://management.core.windows.net/"
}
```

Figure 18-7. *Creation of service principal*

Now copy the clientId, clientSecret, subscriptionId, and tenantId values.

Configure GitHub Secrets

Now that we have our service principal, the next step is to integrate the service principal into our GitHub repository.

Go to your GitHub repository and go to Settings ➤ Secrets ➤ New repository secret. See Figure 18-8.

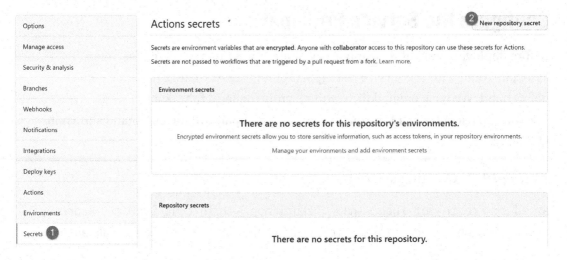

Figure 18-8. *Creating a new secret*

Then we will place the JSON output from the Azure CLI command in the secret's value field and name it **AZURE_CREDENTIALS**, as shown in Figure 18-9.

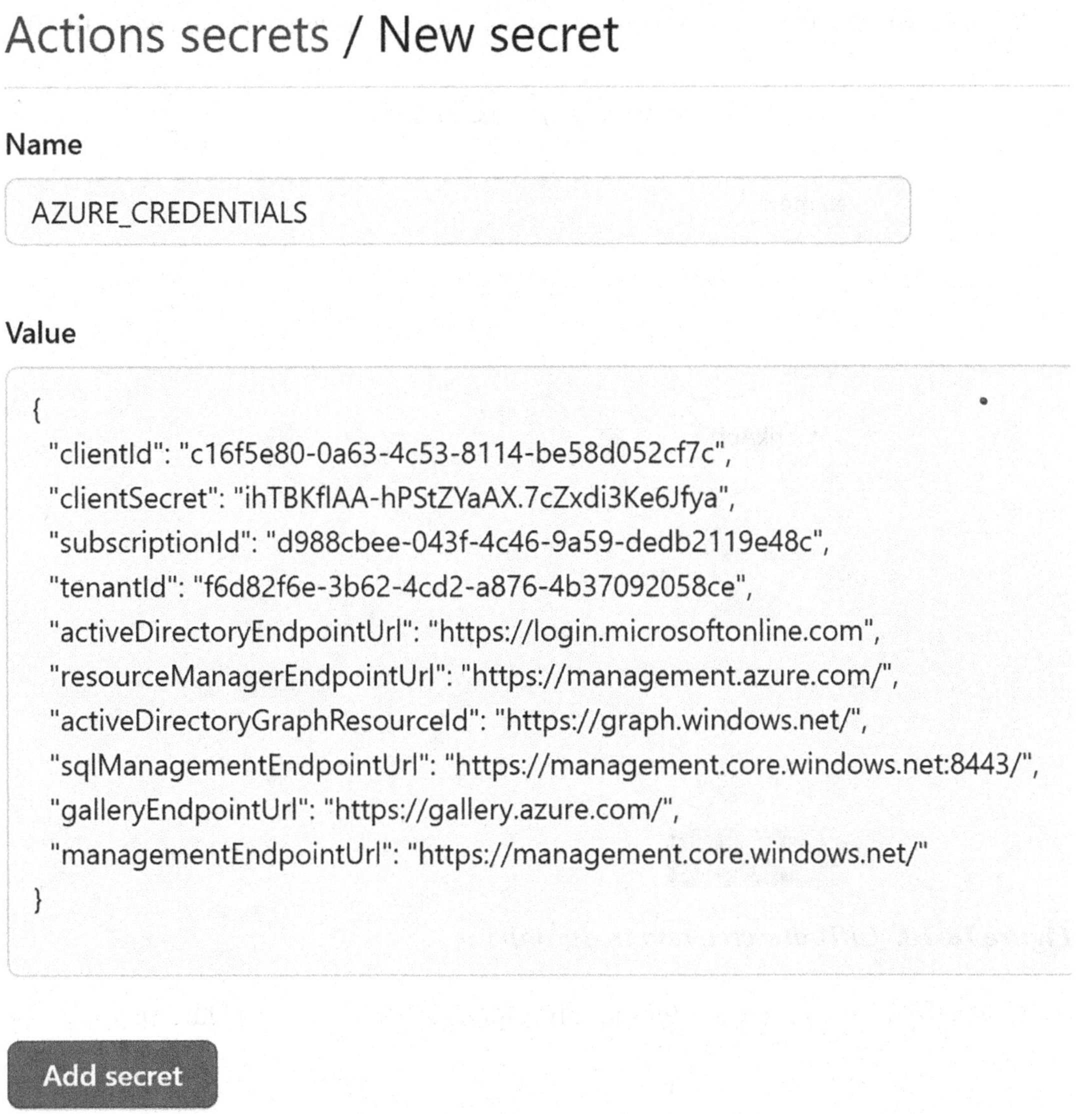

Actions secrets / New secret

Name

AZURE_CREDENTIALS

Value

```
{
  "clientId": "c16f5e80-0a63-4c53-8114-be58d052cf7c",
  "clientSecret": "ihTBKflAA-hPStZYaAX.7cZxdi3Ke6Jfya",
  "subscriptionId": "d988cbee-043f-4c46-9a59-dedb2119e48c",
  "tenantId": "f6d82f6e-3b62-4cd2-a876-4b37092058ce",
  "activeDirectoryEndpointUrl": "https://login.microsoftonline.com",
  "resourceManagerEndpointUrl": "https://management.azure.com/",
  "activeDirectoryGraphResourceId": "https://graph.windows.net/",
  "sqlManagementEndpointUrl": "https://management.core.windows.net:8443/",
  "galleryEndpointUrl": "https://gallery.azure.com/",
  "managementEndpointUrl": "https://management.core.windows.net/"
}
```

Add secret

Figure 18-9. *New secret, Azure credentials*

Then we will create another secret for our resource group, as shown in Figure 18-10.

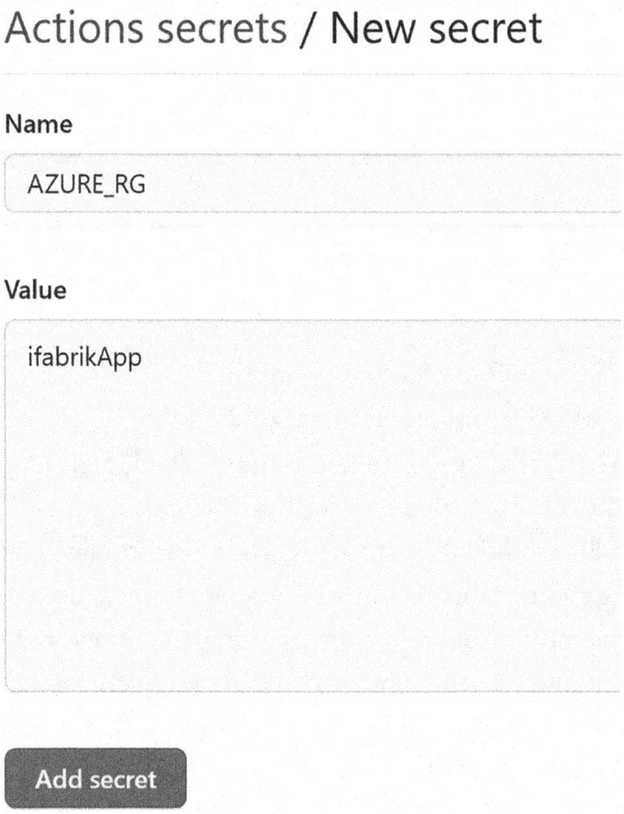

Actions secrets / New secret

Name

AZURE_RG

Value

ifabrikApp

Add secret

Figure 18-10. GitHub secret, resource group

Lastly, we will create a secret for the subscription ID, as shown in Figure 18-11.

Actions secrets / New secret

Name

AZURE_SUBSCRIPTION

Value

d988cbee-XXXX-XXXX-XXXX-XXXXXXXXXX

Add secret

Figure 18-11. *GitHub secret, subscription ID*

Now you should see three secrets listed in your GitHub repository, as shown in Figure 18-12.

Repository secrets			
🔒 AZURE_CREDENTIALS	Updated 3 minutes ago	Update	Remove
🔒 AZURE_RG	Updated 1 minute ago	Update	Remove
🔒 AZURE_SUBSCRIPTION	Updated now	Update	Remove

Figure 18-12. *GitHub secrets*

Create GitHub Action to Deploy the ARM Template

To deploy the ARM templates from our repository, we will use two GitHub actions:

- Actions/Checkout@master: This will check out the repository so that the workflow can access the ARM templates.

- Actions/arm-deploy@v1: This will deploy the ARM template.

Listing 18-7 shows an example of the definition of the GitHub action to deploy an ARM template.

Listing 18-7. GitHub Action, Deploying an ARM Template

```
# This is a workflow to deploy ARM templates with Actions
name: deployARMTemplate
# Controls when the workflow will run
on:
  # Triggers the workflow on push or pull request events for the
main branch
  push:
    branches: [ main ]
  pull_request:
    branches: [ main ]

jobs:
# This workflow contains a single job called "build-and-deploy"
  build-and-deploy:
    runs-on: ubuntu-latest
# Steps represent a sequence of tasks that will be executed as part
of the job
    steps:
# Checks-out your repository under $GITHUB_WORKSPACE, so your job can
access it
    - uses: actions/checkout@master
    - uses: azure/login@v1
      with:
        creds: ${{ secrets.AZURE_CREDENTIALS }}
```

```
# Deploy ARM template
- name: Run ARM deploy
  uses: azure/arm-deploy@v1
  with:
    subscriptionId: ${{ secrets.AZURE_SUBSCRIPTION }}
    resourceGroupName: ${{ secrets.AZURE_RG }}
    template: ./azuredeploy.json
    # parameters: your-parameters-values-here

    # output appName variable from ARM template
- run: echo ${{ steps.deploy.outputs.hostingPlanName }}
```

In Listing 18-7, we are using the service principal to log in to the Azure subscription, and we have provided the secret of the resource group. Ensure you create the resource group before running this GitHub action.

Then, we pass on the ARM template, and you can also provide the parameters file.

Lastly, we included an output; this is referenced from the variable defined in the ARM template.

Run Workflow

The last step is to upload your YAML file into the workflows directory and commit a change in the ARM template. You can rename the YAML file as needed.

When there's any change in the ARM template, the workflow will be executed, and you will see the updated resources in the resource group.

Figure 18-13 shows the workflow that deploys the running ARM template.

Figure 18-13. *Workflow in progress*

We can go and verify the details of the job, as shown in Figure 18-14.

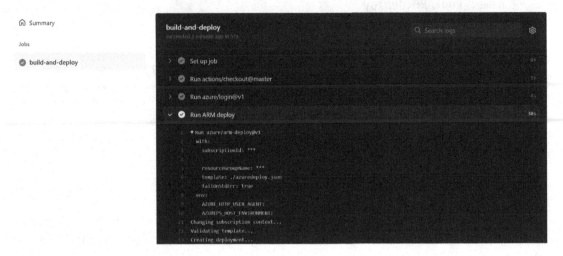

Figure 18-14. *Job details*

We can also verify that the ARM template has been successfully deployed using the Azure portal, as shown in Figure 18-15.

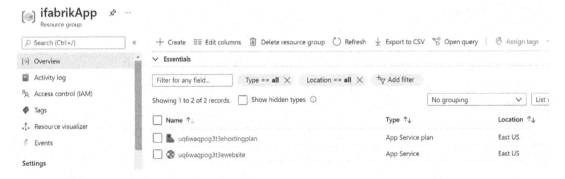

Figure 18-15. *ifabrikApp deployment*

Since the ARM template deployed a WordPress application, we can verify that the WordPress instance is running. See Figure 18-16.

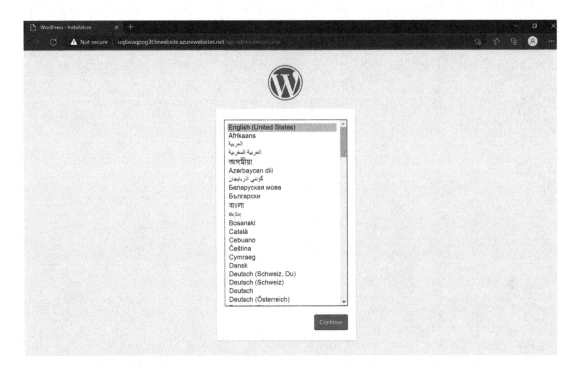

Figure 18-16. *WordPress site*

Ideally, with this, you now have a better understanding of GitHub actions and how you can leverage them to enable continuous integration for your future environments in Azure using ARM templates.

The complete code of this example can be found here:

```
https://github.com/daveRendon/github-actions
```

Summary

This chapter reviewed how you can enable automation through GitHub actions to deploy your ARM templates hosted in your GitHub repository to Azure.

We analyzed the components of GitHub actions and how you can start working on your actions.

Then we reviewed the process to deploy ARM templates to your environment using GitHub actions. So far, we have examined how you can extend functionalities beyond just the ARM templates and enable automation through different tooling such as Azure DevOps and GitHub actions.

The next chapter will discuss a more disruptive topic around ARM templates and review the new proposed native language for ARM templates: Bicep.

CHAPTER 19

Project Bicep

Chapter 18 reviewed how you can enable automation through GitHub actions to deploy your ARM templates hosted in your GitHub repository to Azure, and it covered the components of GitHub actions and how you can start working on your actions.

Then we reviewed the process to deploy ARM templates to your environment using GitHub actions.

This chapter will focus on the most recent initiative from Microsoft to leverage a declarative language for describing and deploying Azure resources: Bicep.

In this chapter, we will review the following topics:

- Why Bicep is relevant for you

- How Bicep works

- Converting ARM templates into Bicep files

- Using GitHub actions to deploy Bicep files

Learning ARM templates is not easy at all, and if you have made it to this chapter, I truly appreciate you taking the time to learn the fundamentals of ARM templates.

So far, we have seen all the benefits and goodness that we can get with ARM templates, including key benefits such as reuse, modularization, and versioning.

Working with ARM templates for larger environments means we must have the ability to modularize ARM templates. Modularization implies keeping control of versions, which often can lead to a time-consuming task.

Also, suppose you're not familiar with JSON notation. In that case, it might be a bit overwhelming for you to analyze ARM templates, and perhaps you might find some limitations describing your application in an ARM template.

These concerns made ARM templates a hard entry point for customers to engage with this technology.

But what if there was a better interface to ARM templates, like a more human-readable interface to describe and deploy Azure resources?

375

© David Rendón 2022
D. Rendón, *Building Applications with Azure Resource Manager (ARM)*,
https://doi.org/10.1007/978-1-4842-7747-8_19

That's where Project Bicep comes in: to help you and customers experiencing Azure to have a best-in-class deployment experience with infrastructure as code.

The Bicep language will simplify the way we describe infrastructure as code for Azure with an easy syntax, reduced JSON noise, and support for most of the existing Azure resources to ease people's pain when using ARM templates.

Bicep was born as an open source, domain-specific language (DSL) to simplify your declarative deployment experience in Azure. Bicep sits on top of ARM templates. It provides a transparent, abstract layer and makes it much easier to read and write infrastructure as code in Azure.

Think of the Bicep language as a transpiler; when you compile a Bicep file, it will translate the resources you describe in a Bicep file into an ARM template. ARM templates will be underneath the Bicep language.

ARM templates are JSON-based, which is not properly a programming language, while Bicep is a domain-specific language for Azure.

Why Bicep Is Relevant for You

There's a lot of innovation in the infrastructure-as-code space; you could look at Terraform and options like Farmer or Cloud Maker to generate your ARM templates.

One of the goals of Bicep is to reduce the current pain of working with ARM templates and provide a layer of abstraction on top of the existing infrastructure. This way, people who are new to Azure could have a frictionless way to learn a native language to deploy resources to Azure using infrastructure as code.

As a cloud engineer, you should understand the impact of Azure Bicep on your environments.

A huge benefit of using Bicep is that since it is built on top of the existing infrastructure, you can leverage all the benefits of the ARM platform; as mentioned earlier in this chapter, ARM templates will be underneath the Bicep language.

In Chapter 14, we reviewed some options to modularize ARM templates and share them with members of our organization; however, we reviewed some limitations regarding using an SAS token to access those ARM templates.

Bicep will help you improve modularization and simplify how you consume those modules. You will be able to consume them from an internal shared repository or an external source.

Think of Bicep as a declarative language for describing and deploying Azure resources; it compiles into ARM templates to provide a best-in-class deployment experience.

Now let's understand how Bicep works.

How Bicep Works

Bicep is defined as a domain-specific language (DSL) that will help you describe and deploy resources to Azure. Instead of authoring ARM templates, you will define your infrastructure as code in a Bicep file.

This Bicep file will transpile into ARM templates that will be deployed to Azure. Think of Bicep as a transparent, abstract layer that sits on top of ARM.

This means that most of the resource's types, API versions, and properties are valid in a Bicep file.

Figure 19-1 shows the workflow of the Bicep file to deploy resources to Azure.

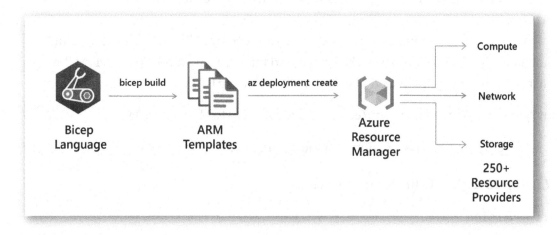

Figure 19-1. *Bicep workflow*

As shown in Figure 19-1, the Bicep language is a native DSL for Azure. When you author your Bicep file, you will describe all the resources part of your environment just as you will do in the ARM templates.

Bicep is built on a better interface that is more human-readable. When you author a Bicep file, you still declare all your resources, parameters, variables, and outputs; however, you will do it in a simpler way.

When you perform the build process of the Bicep files, ARM templates will be created and then sent to Azure Resource Manager, and resources will be deployed just as when you deploy ARM templates.

You can find the latest updates in the GitHub repository: `https://github.com/azure/bicep`.

Now that we have a better idea of how Bicep works, let's get our environment ready to work with Bicep files.

Preparing Your Environment to Work with Bicep Files

We have two prerequisites before we can start working with Bicep:

- Bicep CLI

- Visual Studio Code extension

The first step before we start working with Bicep is to ensure we have installed the Azure CLI.

We must have version 2.20 or later. Azure CLI is compatible with Windows, Linux, and macOS. We will work on a Windows-based machine; however, you can find the instructions for your preferred platform at the following URL:

`https://docs.microsoft.com/en-us/cli/azure/install-azure-cli`

To verify your current version, run the command in Listing 19-1.

Listing 19-1. Verify the Azure CLI Version

```
az --version
```

Once you complete the installation of Azure CLI, the second step is to install the Bicep CLI.

You can use the command in Listing 19-2 to install the Bicep CLI.

Listing 19-2. Install the Bicep CLI

```
az bicep install
```

You should see the output in Figure 19-2 after running the previous command.

```
Installing Bicep CLI v0.4.613...
Successfully installed Bicep CLI to "C:\Users\dave\.azure\bin\bicep.exe".
```

Figure 19-2. *Installing Bicep CLI*

To validate the installation, you can use the command in Listing 19-3.

Listing 19-3. Validate Installation of Bicep CLI

```
az bicep version
```

As of the time of writing, we are using version 0.4.613, as shown in Figure 19-3.

```
Bicep CLI version 0.4.613 (d826ce8411)
```

Figure 19-3. *Bicep CLI version 0.4.x*

The last step is to install the Visual Studio Code extension for Bicep, as shown in Figure 19-4. This extension can be downloaded from the following URL:

```
https://marketplace.visualstudio.com/items?itemName=ms-azuretools.vscode-bicep
```

Figure 19-4. *Visual Studio Bicep extension*

Once we have these three tools installed, then we need to configure our environment.

Configure Your Bicep Environment

Depending on the platform of your choice, you might need to configure additional settings. For our environment, we will use PowerShell and Azure CLI.

Azure CLI will install a separate version of the Bicep CLI that will not conflict with any other Bicep installs you may have. Azure CLI will not add Bicep to your environment PATH.

If you are familiar with PowerShell for automating the management of systems, build, test, and deploy solutions, there's a PowerShell module you can leverage for Bicep.

You have two options to install the Bicep PowerShell module: you can try the stable or the pre-release version. The module is available through the PowerShell Gallery:

```
https://www.powershellgallery.com/packages/Bicep/
```

Building Your First Bicep File

Bicep files will compile the ARM templates for our Azure Resource Manager deployment. Let's take a look at a quick example of how you can build Bicep files.

First, we will create an empty Bicep file and compile it to see the output from this process.

In Visual Studio Code, we will create a new file called `main.bicep`. This will be an empty file. You will also see the Bicep icon in Visual Studio Code if the configuration is correct.

Now in Visual Studio Code, open a terminal and run the command in Listing 19-4.

Listing 19-4. Build a Bicep File

```
az bicep build --file main.bicep
```

When you run the previous command, you will see that a new JSON file has been created with the same name of the file, in this case, `main.json`. This file contains the basic structure of an ARM template and a metadata section, as shown in Figure 19-5.

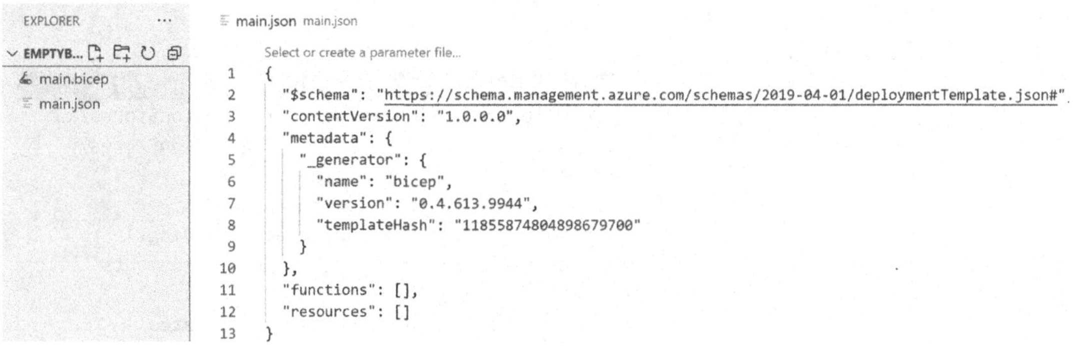

Figure 19-5. *ARM template*

As you can see in Figure 19-5, the Bicep file compiles into an actual ARM template. This is what will be deployed to Azure.

Now let's define some resources in the Bicep file. Going back to the file called `main.bicep`, let's add a resource.

Example: Creating an App Service Plan in Bicep

We will rename this file from `main.bicep` to `appServicePlan.bicep` and define an app service plan in this Bicep file.

So, how do we define resources in Bicep files? Similar to ARM templates, we will define the resource type and version we want to deploy, and then we will provide the properties of the resource in a friendlier way.

As you type, the Visual Studio Code extension will suggest the properties for this resource, as shown in Figure 19-6.

✎ appServicePlan.bicep 2 appServicePlan.bicep\ { } appServicePlan

```
1    resource appServicePlan 'app
```

⁏	'Microsoft.AppConfiguration/configurationStores'
⁏	'Microsoft.AppConfiguration/configurationStores/k…
⁏	'Microsoft.AppConfiguration/configurationStores/p…
⁏	'Microsoft.AppPlatform/Spring'
⁏	'Microsoft.AppPlatform/Spring/apps'
⁏	'Microsoft.AppPlatform/Spring/apps/bindings'
⁏	'Microsoft.AppPlatform/Spring/apps/deployments'
⁏	'Microsoft.AppPlatform/Spring/apps/domains'
⁏	'Microsoft.AppPlatform/Spring/certificates'
⁏	'Microsoft.AppPlatform/Spring/configServers'
⁏	'Microsoft.AppPlatform/Spring/monitoringSettings'
⁏	'Microsoft.NetApp/netAppAccounts'

Figure 19-6. *Bicep file*

Now we will define our app service plan. We have to provide the reserved word *resource* to define a new resource. Then we have to give the name of the resource and the type and API version. See Figure 19-7.

```
resource appServicePlan 'Microsoft.Web/serverfarms@2021-01-15' = {
  name: 'ifabrikAppPlan'
  location: 'eastus'
  kind: 'linux'
  sku: {
    name:'F1'
  }
  properties:{
    reserved: true
  }

}
```

Figure 19-7. *Bicep file that creates an app service plan*

Once we define the resource type and API version, we will define the resource's properties inside brackets, as shown in Figure 19-7. Note that we are hard-coding all the values like the name, location, kind, and SKU.

Now let's save and build this Bicep file to see the ARM template. With the command shown in Listing 19-5, we will build this Bicep file.

Listing 19-5. Build App Service Plan Bicep File

```
az bicep build --file .\appServicePlan.bicep
```

Note that the ARM template will be shown in your directory, and now we will split the view in Visual Studio Code to visualize both files: on the left side is the Bicep file, and on the right side is the ARM template. See Figure 19-8.

Figure 19-8. *Bicep file and ARM template file comparison*

As you can see, Bicep provides you with a cleaner interface and more straightforward syntax than ARM templates. ARM templates will still exist underneath Bicep.

To make this example a bit more dynamic, we will define some parameters in the Bicep file and pass them into the definition of the app service plan.

Example: Working with Parameters in Bicep Files

We will take the same Bicep file and modify it a bit. We will add the following parameters: appPlanName, location, and SKU.

We will use the structure shown in Listing 19-6 to define parameters with values.

Listing 19-6. Define Parameters with Values in the Bicep File

```
Param <property> <type> = <your-parameter-value>
```

Let's go to the Bicep file and add the parameters, as shown in Figure 19-9.

```
param appPlanPrefix string
param sku string = 'F1'
param location string = 'eastus'

resource appServicePlan 'Microsoft.Web/serverfarms@2021-01-15' = {
  //interpolate param
  name: '${appPlanPrefix}AppPlan'
  //pass on location param
  location: location
  kind: 'linux'
  sku: {
    //pass on sku param
    name: sku
  }
  properties:{
    reserved: true
  }
}

output appServicePlanId string = appServicePlan.id
```

Figure 19-9. *Bicep file with parameters*

Note that we have defined the three parameters before defining the resource. Instead of using a function like the concat() function on the name property, we interpolate the parameter.

Then we pass the parameters for the location and the SKU. Lastly, we include output for appServicePlanId.

A parameter can't have the same name as a variable, module, or resource. Don't overuse parameters. Parameters are often utilized when we need to pass on values that need to vary for different deployments.

For example, when you create a storage account, you need to provide the SKU and type; you could leverage parameters.

If you need to define a virtual network and subnets, you could leverage a parameter object for the virtual network and the subnet definition.

Try to provide descriptions for your parameters as much as you can. Your team and colleagues will appreciate it.

Note that we are not referencing all the parameters; when we work with modules in Bicep, the module exposes the parameters and outputs as contracts to other Bicep files.

If we build this Bicep file, we will see that it creates the ARM template, and it includes the definition of the parameters, as shown in Figure 19-10.

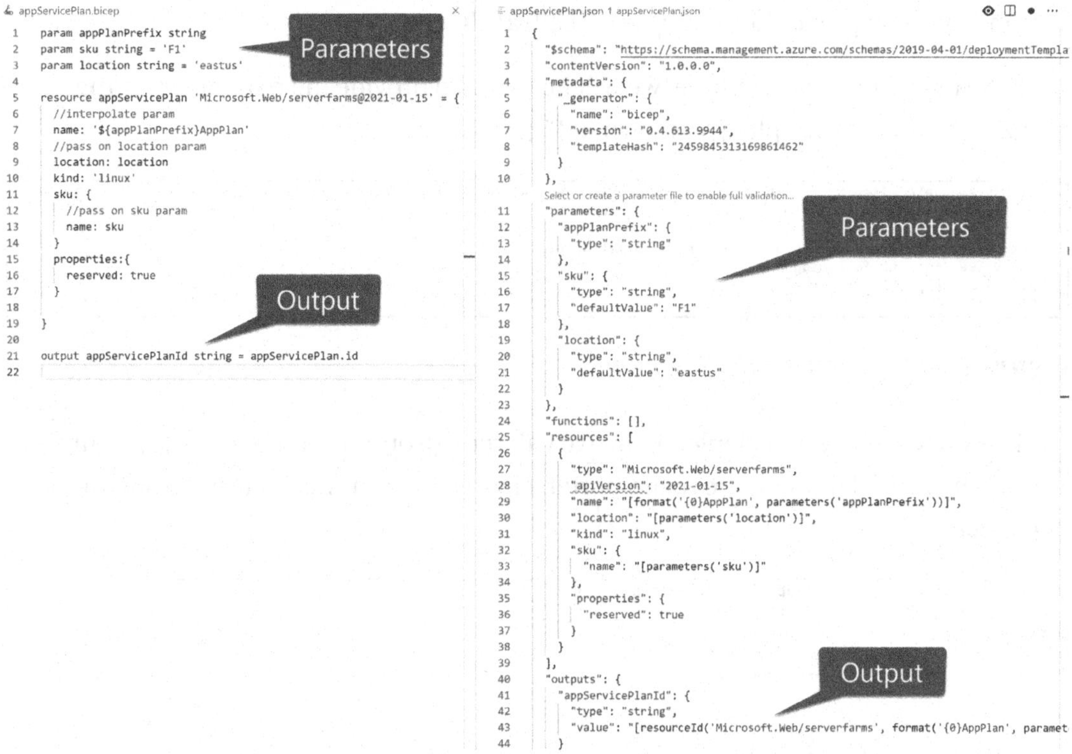

Figure 19-10. *Bicep file that creates an app service plan with parameters and output sections*

Now that we have defined our resource, let's deploy it to Azure.

Deploying Bicep Files

We deploy our Bicep files to Azure in a similar way as we deploy ARM templates. We will use PowerShell and log in to our Azure subscription and set the default subscription.

Then, we can target the deployment to a subscription or a resource group. The command shown in Listing 19-7 will deploy the Bicep file and target a resource group previously created.

Listing 19-7. Deploy Bicep File to a Resource Group

```
$date = Get-Date -Format "MM-dd-yyyy"
$deploymentName = "iFabrikDeployment"+"$date"
```

New-AzResourceGroupDeployment -**Name** $deploymentName -**ResourceGroupName** ifabrikApp -**TemplateFile** .\appServicePlan.**bicep**

Note that at deployment time, we will be asked to provide the parameter for the prefix of the app service plan, as shown in Figure 19-11.

```
PS C:\Users\dave\ArmTemplates\chapter-19\AppServicePlan> New-AzResourceGroupDeployment -Name $deploymentName -ResourceGr
oupName ifabrikApp -TemplateFile .\appServicePlan.bicep

cmdlet New-AzResourceGroupDeployment at command pipeline position 1
Supply values for the following parameters:
(Type !? for Help.)
appPlanPrefix: ifabrik
```

Figure 19-11. *Bicep file deployment*

Like an ARM template deployment, we will see the output from the deployment in the console and through the Azure portal. Figure 19-12 shows the result from this deployment.

```
DeploymentName      : iFabrikDeployment08-24-2021
ResourceGroupName   : ifabrikApp
ProvisioningState   : Succeeded
Timestamp           : 8/24/2021 3:27:18 PM
Mode                : Incremental
TemplateLink        :
Parameters          :
                      Name              Type                            Value
                      ===============   ===========================     ==========
                      appPlanPrefix     String                          ifabrik
                      sku               String                          F1
                      location          String                          eastus

Outputs             :
                      Name              Type                            Value
                      ================  ========================        ==========
                      appServicePlanId  String                          /subscriptions/
                          /resourceGroups/ifabrikApp/providers/Microsoft.Web/serverfarms/ifabrikAppPlan
```

Figure 19-12. *Bicep file deployment output*

Now that we have created the app service plan, let's create a new Bicep file to define an app service.

Example: Working with Modules in Bicep Files

In the following example, we will create a new Bicep file called appService.bicep that will contain the definition of an app service. Then, we will create another Bicep file called main.bicep that will consume two Bicep files: the appServicePlan.bicep and the appService.bicep.

Create App Service Bicep File

First, let's create our app service Bicep file. In Visual Studio Code, we will create a new file called appService.bicep and will contain the code shown in Figure 19-13.

```
 appService.bicep  appService.bicep\...
1    param appServicePrefix string
2    param location string = 'eastus'
3    param appServicePlanId string
4
5    resource appService 'Microsoft.Web/sites@2021-01-15' = {
6      name: '${appServicePrefix}site'
7      location: location
8      properties:{
9        siteConfig:{
10         linuxFxVersion: 'DOTNETCORE|3.0'
11       }
12       serverFarmId: appServicePlanId
13     }
14   }
15
16   output siteURL string = appService.properties.hostNames[0]
```

Figure 19-13. *App service Bicep file definition*

In the previous Bicep file, we defined three parameters: appServicePrefix, location, and appServicePlanId.

Then, in the definition of our app service, we are passing the previous parameters.

Lastly, we defined an output that contains the URL of the app service.

Now let's create a new Bicep file called main.bicep that will consume the appServicePlan.bicep and the appService.bicep as modules.

Create Main Bicep File

We will create a new Bicep file called main.bicep. This file will be our main file, and we will reference two Bicep files as modules.

Figure 19-14 shows the definition of the main.bicep file.

```
//parameters
param location string = 'eastus'
param ifabrik string = 'ifabrik'

//define target
targetScope = 'subscription'

//define new resoruce group
resource ifabrikRg 'Microsoft.Resources/resourceGroups@2021-04-01' = {
  name: '${ifabrik}Rg'
  location: location
}

//consume appServicePlan as module
module appServicePlan 'appServicePlan.bicep' = {
  name:'appServicePlan'
  scope: ifabrikRg
  params: {
    appPlanPrefix: ifabrik
  }
}

//consume appService as module
module appService 'appService.bicep' = {
  name: 'appService'
  scope: ifabrikRg
  params: {
    appServicePlanId: appServicePlan.outputs.appServicePlanId
    appServicePrefix: ifabrik
  }
}
```

Figure 19-14. *Main Bicep file definition*

In the previous code, we defined one parameter for the location and another as a string for the resource group name.

Then, we will target the deployment to a subscription level and define a new resource group in that subscription.

Lastly, we will consume the two previous Bicep files created: the appServicePlan and appService Bicep files that contain the definition of the app service plan and the app service.

Note that this is a similar approach to nested templates, and we will reference the parameters on each module.

The next step is to deploy this environment. We will deploy the main.bicep file and target to a subscription scope with the command shown in Listing 19-8.

Listing 19-8. Deploy Main Bicep File

```
New-AzDeployment -Name $deploymentName -TemplateFile .\main.bicep -Location
eastus
```

Note that we don't need to reference the two Bicep files consumed as modules, only the main Bicep file.

Figure 19-15 shows the output from this deployment.

```
Id                         : /subscriptions/                              /providers/Microsoft.Resources/deployments
                             /iFabrikDeployment08-24-2021
DeploymentName             : iFabrikDeployment08-24-2021
Location                   : eastus
ProvisioningState          : Succeeded
Timestamp                  : 8/24/2021 4:21:25 PM
Mode                       : Incremental
TemplateLink               :
Parameters                 :
                             Name            Type                         Value
                             ==============  =========================    ==========
                             location        String                       eastus
                             ifabrik         String                       ifabrik

Outputs                    :
DeploymentDebugLogLevel    :
```

Figure 19-15. *Deployment output, main Bicep file*

As a result, we have created a new resource group in our subscription and a Linux-based app service plan with an app service, as shown in Figure 19-16.

ifabrikRg ✗ ···
Resource group

+ Create ≡≡ Edit columns 🗑 Delete resource group ↻ Refresh ↓ Export to CSV ⊹ Open query | ⊘ Assign tags → Move ∨ 🗑 Delete

∨ Essentials

| Filter for any field... | Type == **all** ✕ | Location == **all** ✕ | ☆ Add filter |

Showing 1 to 2 of 2 records. ☐ Show hidden types ⓘ | No grouping |

☐ Name ↑↓	Type ↑↓	Location ↑↓
☐ 🏭 ifabrikAppPlan	App Service plan	East US
☐ 🌐 ifabriksite	App Service	East US

Figure 19-16. *Deployment output, main Bicep file, Azure portal*

So now that we have gone through the basics of Bicep, it is time to work with other features available in ARM templates such as loops.

We will see how loops work in Bicep, and before that, we will use an existing ARM template and translate it to a Bicep file.

Converting ARM Templates into Bicep Files

We have developed all our environments based on ARM templates; how does this impact those existing environments? Bicep will allow you to decompile your ARM templates into Bicep code. To convert ARM templates into Bicep code, we will use the command in Listing 19-9.

Listing 19-9. Decompile Bicep File with Azure CLI

```
az bicep decompile --file azuredeploy.json
```

By leveraging this feature, you will quickly translate your ARM template into a Bicep file. While this will help you get started, reviewing the Bicep file after decompiling to validate your files is highly recommended.

In the previous listing, we have utilized the decompile command with Azure CLI; in case you're not using Azure CLI, then you can use the command in Listing 19-10.

Listing 19-10. Decompile File Using Bicep CLI

```
bicep decompile --file main.json
```

Let's use the ARM template that creates a WordPress instance and decompile it. The code related to this ARM template can be found at the following URL:

https://github.com/daveRendon/iac/blob/main/chapter-19/wordpress/
azuredeploy.json

Download the previous ARM template and then run the command in Listing 19-11 to decompile it into a Bicep file.

Listing 19-11. Decompile File Using Azure CLI

```
az bicep decompile --file azuredeploy.json
```

You will see the warning in Figure 19-17 in the output.

```
WARNING: Decompilation is a best-effort process, as there is no guaranteed mapping from ARM JSON to Bicep.
You may need to fix warnings and errors in the generated bicep file(s), or decompilation may fail entirely if an accurat
e conversion is not possible.
If you would like to report any issues or inaccurate conversions, please see https://github.com/Azure/bicep/issues.
C:\Users\dave\ArmTemplates\chapter-19\wordpress\azuredeploy.bicep(23,5) : Warning BCP037: The property "name" is not all
owed on objects of type "SiteProperties". Permissible properties include "clientAffinityEnabled", "clientCertEnabled", "
clientCertExclusionPaths", "clientCertMode", "cloningInfo", "containerSize", "customDomainVerificationId", "dailyMemoryT
imeQuota", "enabled", "hostingEnvironmentProfile", "hostNamesDisabled", "hostNameSslStates", "httpsOnly", "hyperV", "isX
enon", "redundancyMode", "reserved", "scmSiteAlsoStopped". If this is an inaccuracy in the documentation, please report
it to the Bicep Team. [https://aka.ms/bicep-type-issues]
```

Figure 19-17. *Decompiling output*

You will see that a new Bicep file has been created, as shown in Figure 19-18.

```
param sku string = 'F1'
param repoUrl string = 'https://github.com/azureappserviceoss/wordpress-azure'
param branch string = 'master'
param location string = resourceGroup().location

var hostingPlanName_var = '${uniqueString(resourceGroup().id)}hostingplan'
var siteName_var = '${uniqueString(resourceGroup().id)}website'

resource hostingPlanName 'Microsoft.Web/serverfarms@2020-06-01' = {
  sku: {
    name: sku
    capacity: 1
  }
  name: hostingPlanName_var
  location: location
  properties: {}
}

resource siteName 'Microsoft.Web/sites@2020-06-01' = {
  name: siteName_var
  location: location
  properties: {
    name: siteName_var
    serverFarmId: hostingPlanName.id
    siteConfig: {
      localMySqlEnabled: true
      appSettings: [
        {
          name: 'WEBSITE_MYSQL_ENABLED'
          value: '1'
        }
        {
          name: 'WEBSITE_MYSQL_GENERAL_LOG'
          value: '0'
        }
        {
          name: 'WEBSITE_MYSQL_SLOW_QUERY_LOG'
          value: '0'
        }
        {
          name: 'WEBSITE_MYSQL_ARGUMENTS'
          value: '--max_allowed_packet=16M'
        }
      ]
    }
  }
}

resource siteName_web 'Microsoft.Web/sites/sourcecontrols@2020-06-01' = {
  parent: siteName
  name: 'web'
  properties: {
    repoUrl: repoUrl
    branch: branch
    isManualIntegration: true
  }
}

resource Microsoft_Web_sites_config_siteName_web 'Microsoft.Web/sites/config@2020-06-01' = {
  parent: siteName
  name: 'web'
  properties: {
    phpVersion: '7.0'
  }
}
```

Figure 19-18. *Bicep file*

Note that in the previous Bicep file, in the resource `siteName`, which is the app service, the property `name` is highlighted, as this property is not allowed on objects of type `SiteProperties`.

We will remove this property and then build this Bicep file with the command shown in Listing 19-12.

Listing 19-12. Build Bicep File

```
az bicep build --file .\azuredeploy.bicep
```

You will see the same warning as before, and we can compare the output from this build with the original ARM template. The new ARM template differs from the original ARM template in the definition of the variables. You will also see the metadata at the beginning of the ARM template, as shown in Figure 19-19.

```
{
    "$schema": "https://schema.management.azure.com/schemas/2019-04-01/deploymentTemplate.jso
    "contentVersion": "1.0.0.0",
    "metadata": {
        "_generator": {
            "name": "bicep",
            "version": "0.4.613.9944",
            "templateHash": "12868049720814293584"
        }
    },
    Select or create a parameter file...
    "parameters": {
        "sku": {
            "type": "string",
            "defaultValue": "F1"
        },
        "repoUrl": {
            "type": "string",
            "defaultValue": "https://github.com/azureappserviceoss/wordpress-azure"
        },
        "branch": {
            "type": "string",
            "defaultValue": "master"
        },
        "location": {
            "type": "string",
            "defaultValue": "[resourceGroup().location]"
        }
    },
    "functions": [],
    "variables": {
        "hostingPlanName_var": "[format('{0}hostingplan', uniqueString(resourceGroup().id))]",
        "siteName_var": "[format('{0}website', uniqueString(resourceGroup().id))]"
    },
```

Figure 19-19. *ARM template, build*

The `resources` section is consistent with the original ARM template, as shown in Figure 19-20.

```
"resources": [
  {
    "type": "Microsoft.Web/serverfarms",
    "apiVersion": "2020-06-01",
    "name": "[variables('hostingPlanName_var')]",
    "sku": {
      "name": "[parameters('sku')]",
      "capacity": 1
    },
    "location": "[parameters('location')]",
    "properties": {}
  },
  {
    "type": "Microsoft.Web/sites",
    "apiVersion": "2020-06-01",
    "name": "[variables('siteName_var')]",
    "location": "[parameters('location')]",
    "properties": {
      "serverFarmId": "[resourceId('Microsoft.Web/serverfarms', variables('hostingPlanName_var'))]",
      "siteConfig": {
        "localMySqlEnabled": true,
        "appSettings": [
          {
            "name": "WEBSITE_MYSQL_ENABLED",
            "value": "1"
          },
          {
            "name": "WEBSITE_MYSQL_GENERAL_LOG",
            "value": "0"
          },
          {
            "name": "WEBSITE_MYSQL_SLOW_QUERY_LOG",
            "value": "0"
          },
          {
            "name": "WEBSITE_MYSQL_ARGUMENTS",
            "value": "--max_allowed_packet=16M"
          }
        ]
      }
    },
    "dependsOn": [
      "[resourceId('Microsoft.Web/serverfarms', variables('hostingPlanName_var'))]"
    ]
  },
  {
    "type": "Microsoft.Web/sites/sourcecontrols",
    "apiVersion": "2020-06-01",
    "name": "[format('{0}/{1}', variables('siteName_var'), 'web')]",
    "properties": {
      "repoUrl": "[parameters('repoUrl')]",
      "branch": "[parameters('branch')]",
      "isManualIntegration": true
    },
    "dependsOn": [
      "[resourceId('Microsoft.Web/sites', variables('siteName_var'))]"
    ]
  },
  {
    "type": "Microsoft.Web/sites/config",
    "apiVersion": "2020-06-01",
    "name": "[format('{0}/{1}', variables('siteName_var'), 'web')]",
    "properties": {
      "phpVersion": "7.0"
    },
    "dependsOn": [
      "[resourceId('Microsoft.Web/sites', variables('siteName_var'))]"
    ]
  }
]
}
```

Figure 19-20. *ARM template, resources section*

Now we will deploy the Bicep file with the command in Listing 19-13.

Listing 19-13. Deploy Bicep File

```
$date = Get-Date -Format "MM-dd-yyyy"
$deploymentName = "iFabrikDeployment"+"$date"

New-AzResourceGroupDeployment -Name $deploymentName -ResourceGroupName
ifabrikApp -TemplateFile .\wordpress.bicep
```

Once you perform this deployment, you should be able to see the output in the console; see Figure 19-21.

```
DeploymentName         : iFabrikDeployment08-24-2021
ResourceGroupName      : ifabrikApp
ProvisioningState      : Succeeded
Timestamp              : 8/24/2021 5:50:51 PM
Mode                   : Incremental
TemplateLink           :
Parameters             :
                         Name            Type                        Value
                         =============== =========================== ==========
                         sku             String                      F1
                         repoUrl         String
                         https://github.com/azureappserviceoss/wordpress-azure
                         branch          String                      master
                         location        String                      eastus

Outputs                :
DeploymentDebugLogLevel :
```

Figure 19-21. Deployment output

Also, if you verify the deployment in the Azure portal, you should see the app service plan and the app service in the resource group. See Figure 19-22.

ifabrikApp ⚲ ⋯
Resource group

> + Create   ≡≡ Edit columns   🗑 Delete resource group   ⟳ Refresh   ↓ Export to CSV   ⚓ Open query | ⊘ Assign tags   → Move ∨   🗑 Delete

∨ Essentials

| Filter for any field... | Type == **all** ✕ | Location == **all** ✕ | ⁺⊽ Add filter |

Showing 1 to 2 of 2 records.   ☐ Show hidden types ⓘ

No grouping

☐ Name ↑↓	Type ↑↓	Location ↑↓
☐ 📊 uq6waqpog3t3ehostingplan	App Service plan	East US
☐ 🌐 uq6waqpog3t3ewebsite	App Service	East US

Figure 19-22. *Azure portal, resources*

Now that we have analyzed the options to convert ARM templates into Bicep files, let's review how you can work with loops in your Bicep files.

Using Loops in Bicep: Create Multiple Sites

Resource iteration is one of the best improvements in Bicep; while we are going to find the same functions for ARM templates as for Bicep, we will see that Bicep simplifies a lot of the syntax on functions.

In the following example, we will define a loop to create multiple sites.

Creating a Loop in Bicep

Loops can be defined within the definition of the resource. Before defining the properties object of the resource, we will create a loop, as shown in Listing 19-14.

Listing 19-14. Resource Iteration

```
[for i in range(0, Count): {<resource-properties> }]
```

The code in Figure 19-23 shows how you can create a loop to define the creation of multiple storage accounts in a Bicep file.

```
@maxValue(4)
param Count int = 3
param location string = resourceGroup().location

resource storageAccount 'Microsoft.Storage/storageAccounts@2021-02-01' = [for i in range(0, Count): {
  name: '${i}storage${uniqueString(resourceGroup().id)}'
  location: location
  sku: {
    name: 'Standard_LRS'
  }
  kind: 'Storage'
}]
```

Figure 19-23. *Bicep file, creating multiple storage accounts*

In the previous code, we defined a parameter called `Count` to keep track of the number of storage accounts to be created.

Then, we define the resource type and API version. Before determining the properties of the storage account, we will bind all the properties in a loop where the index `i` is utilized for the iteration.

Similar to ARM templates, you will be able to work in multiple ways with loops. You can define the resource iteration with arrays, conditions, and batches, and you can work with child resources.

Now let's look at another example to create an app service plan and multiple instances of app services.

Creating Multiple Sites

In the following example, we will create an app service plan and define a loop to create multiple instances of an app service.

Figure 19-24 shows the code of our Bicep file.

```
1    param sku string = 'B1'
2    param location string = resourceGroup().location
3    param siteNames array = [
4      'ifabriksite1'
5      'ifabriksite2'
6      'ifabriksite3'
7    ]
8
9    var hostingPlanName = '${uniqueString(resourceGroup().id)}appPlan'
10
11   resource appServicePlan 'Microsoft.Web/serverfarms@2020-06-01' = {
12     name: hostingPlanName
13     kind: 'linux'
14     location: location
15     sku: {
16       name: sku
17       capacity: 1
18     }
19     properties: {
20       reserved: true
21     }
22   }
23
24   resource site 'Microsoft.Web/sites@2020-06-01' = [for item in siteNames: {
25     name: '${item}'
26     location: location
27     properties: {
28       serverFarmId: appServicePlan.id
29
30       siteConfig: {
31         localMySqlEnabled: true
32         appSettings: [
33           {
34             name: 'WEBSITE_MYSQL_ENABLED'
35             value: '1'
36           }
37           {
38             name: 'WEBSITE_MYSQL_GENERAL_LOG'
39             value: '0'
40           }
41           {
42             name: 'WEBSITE_MYSQL_SLOW_QUERY_LOG'
43             value: '0'
44           }
45           {
46             name: 'WEBSITE_MYSQL_ARGUMENTS'
47             value: '--max_allowed_packet=16M'
48           }
49         ]
50       }
51     }
52   }]
53
54   output sites array = [for (name, i) in siteNames: {
55     name: site[i].name
56     resourceId: site[i].id
57   }]
```

Figure 19-24. *Creation of multiple sites in Bicep*

In the previous Bicep file, we defined a few parameters: one parameter for the SKU of the app service plan, a parameter for the location, and a parameter as an array for the sites.

Then, we defined a variable for the app service plan name. In the definition of this variable, we are using a function called `uniqueString()`.

We also defined a Linux-based app service plan, and then we defined a loop to create multiple instances of the resource `site`.

Note that for the loop, we defined the resource iteration before defining the actual properties of the resource.

Lastly, we defined an output to show the name of the sites and resource identifier.

We can deploy this Bicep file, and we can leverage the `whatIf` `-C` flag to confirm the deployment with the command shown in Listing 19-15.

Listing 19-15. Bicep Deployment

```
New-AzResourceGroupDeployment -Name $deploymentName -ResourceGroupName
ifabrikApp -TemplateFile .\create-multiple-sites.bicep -c
```

Figure 19-25 shows the output from the command in Listing 19-15.

```
Resource and property changes are indicated with this symbol:
  + Create

The deployment will update the following scope:

Scope: /subscriptions/d988cbee-043f-4c46-9a59-dedb2119e48c/resourceGroups/ifabrikApp

  + Microsoft.Web/serverfarms/uq6waqpog3t3eappPlan [2020-06-01]

      apiVersion:          "2020-06-01"
      id:
"/subscriptions/                              /resourceGroups/ifabrikApp/providers/Microsoft.Web/serverfarms/uq6waqpog3t3eappPlan"
      kind:                "linux"
      location:            "eastus"
      name:                "uq6waqpog3t3eappPlan"
      properties.reserved: true
      sku.capacity:        1
      sku.name:            "B1"
      type:                "Microsoft.Web/serverfarms"

  + Microsoft.Web/sites/ifabriksite1 [2020-06-01]

      apiVersion:          "2020-06-01"
      id:
"/subscriptions/                              /resourceGroups/ifabrikApp/providers/Microsoft.Web/sites/ifabriksite1"
      location:            "eastus"
      name:                "ifabriksite1"
      properties.serverFarmId:
"/subscriptions/                              /resourceGroups/ifabrikApp/providers/Microsoft.Web/serverfarms/uq6waqpog3t3eappPlan"
      properties.siteConfig:   "*******"
      type:                "Microsoft.Web/sites"

  + Microsoft.Web/sites/ifabriksite2 [2020-06-01]

      apiVersion:          "2020-06-01"
      id:
"/subscriptions/                              /resourceGroups/ifabrikApp/providers/Microsoft.Web/sites/ifabriksite2"
      location:            "eastus"
      name:                "ifabriksite2"
      properties.serverFarmId:
"/subscriptions/                              /resourceGroups/ifabrikApp/providers/Microsoft.Web/serverfarms/uq6waqpog3t3eappPlan"
      properties.siteConfig:   "*******"
      type:                "Microsoft.Web/sites"

  + Microsoft.Web/sites/ifabriksite3 [2020-06-01]

      apiVersion:          "2020-06-01"
      id:
"/subscriptions/                              /resourceGroups/ifabrikApp/providers/Microsoft.Web/sites/ifabriksite3"
      location:            "eastus"
      name:                "ifabriksite3"
      properties.serverFarmId:
"/subscriptions/                              /resourceGroups/ifabrikApp/providers/Microsoft.Web/serverfarms/uq6waqpog3t3eappPlan"
      properties.siteConfig:   "*******"
      type:                "Microsoft.Web/sites"

Resource changes: 4 to create.

Are you sure you want to execute the deployment?
[Y] Yes  [A] Yes to All  [N] No  [L] No to All  [S] Suspend  [?] Help (default is "Y"):
```

Figure 19-25. *Deployment preview*

Then we can proceed to deploy these resources. Figure 19-26 shows the output from this deployment.

```
DeploymentName          : iFabrikDeployment08-25-2021
ResourceGroupName       : ifabrikApp
ProvisioningState       : Succeeded
Timestamp               : 8/25/2021 12:50:17 PM
Mode                    : Incremental
TemplateLink            :
Parameters              :
                          Name                   Type                          Value
                          ===============        =========================     ==========
                          sku                    String                        B1
                          location               String                        eastus
                          siteNames              Array                         [
                            "ifabriksite1",
                            "ifabriksite2",
                            "ifabriksite3"
                          ]

Outputs                 :
                          Name                   Type                          Value
                          ===============        =========================     ==========
                          sites                  Array                         [
                            {
                              "name": "ifabriksite1",
                              "resourceId": "/subscriptions/                              /resourceGroups/ifabrikApp/providers/Micros
                          oft.Web/sites/ifabriksite1"
                            },
                            {
                              "name": "ifabriksite2",
                              "resourceId": "/subscriptions/                              /resourceGroups/ifabrikApp/providers/Micros
                          oft.Web/sites/ifabriksite2"
                            },
                            {
                              "name": "ifabriksite3",
                              "resourceId": "/subscriptions/                              /resourceGroups/ifabrikApp/providers/Micros
                          oft.Web/sites/ifabriksite3"
                            }
                          ]
DeploymentDebugLogLevel :
```

Figure 19-26. *Deployment output*

As you can see, Bicep simplifies the syntax of resources that will be part of our environment and significantly improves the way we define resources to be deployed.

While Bicep is still in its early days, it is worth it to start looking at Bicep as an alternative for ARM templates, although it sits on top of ARM.

The complete code of this example can be found here:

`https://github.com/daveRendon/iac/tree/main/chapter-19`

Summary

In this chapter, we reviewed the new domain-specific language (DSL) that will help you describe and deploy resources to Azure and showed how to define your infrastructure as code in a Bicep file.

We analyzed the syntax of Bicep files and how they transpile into ARM templates that will be deployed to Azure.

We also went through some examples of creating some resources in Bicep and showed how you can leverage parameters and functions.

Then, we analyzed how to consume Bicep files in a modularized approach.

Lastly, we reviewed how resource iteration worked in Bicep and showed a practical example of creating multiple sites.

Index

A

ARM extensions
    template viewer extension, 21–23
    tools extension, 20, 21
ARM templates
    azuredeploy.json, 36
    Azure portal, 46, 47
    benefits, 375
    core elements, 14–17
    debugging/validation
        deployment output, 293
        error codes, 291
        error output, 292
        inflight errors, 290
        preflight errors, 290
        resources, 290
        storage account, 291–293
        third-party solutions, 290
    deployment, 181
        output, 46
        PowerShell Command, 45
        process, 14
        resource group, 45
        workflow, 48, 49
    editor, 19
    file structure, 103, 104, 119, 120
    functions (*see* Functions, ARM
        template)
    infrastructure, 19
    Key Value secret, 274
    life cycle, 19

    modularization, 324
    PowerShell command, 181
    resources section
        apiVersion, 125
        deployment, 123
        format, 120
        items, 120
        network interface, 123, 124
        properties, 124
        resource properties, 123
        resource provider, 120
        resource type/the API version,
          120, 121
        snippets, 122
        storage account, 121, 122
    schema, 35
    secrets, 268
    security, 266, 267
    snippets, 36, 37
    storage (*see* Storage account)
    structure, 166, 167
    TTK (*see* Test toolkit (TTK))
    utilizing objects, 98–101
    variable, 180
    VSC, 35, 36
Artifact, 230, 231, 315, 341
Azure Active Directory (Azure AD), 77, 217
Azure CLI
    completed setup, 33, 34
    download, 32
    installation, 32, 33
    setup wizard, 32

403

© David Rendón 2022
D. Rendón, *Building Applications with Azure Resource Manager (ARM)*,
https://doi.org/10.1007/978-1-4842-7747-8

W, X, Y

Z

Printed in the United States
by Baker & Taylor Publisher Services